D1565681

POLITICAL CONDUCT

Mark Philp

Political Conduct

HARVARD UNIVERSITY PRESS

Cambridge, Massachusetts, and London, England

2007

ISBN-13: 978-0-674-02488-5
ISBN-10: 0-674-02488-5

The Cataloging-in-Publication Data are available from the Library of Congress.

Acknowledgments

This work grew out of a set of interests in political corruption that I developed during two terms as a Visiting Research Fellow, first in the Faculty of Arts and later in the Humanities Research Centre, at the Australian National University. My thanks to those institutions, to Iain Mc-Calman for arranging these opportunities, and to Heather McCalman, Jon Mee, and Martin Fitzpatrick for their respective contributions to the conditions required to realize them. The project in its present form took shape thanks to a British Academy/Leverhulme Senior Research Fellowship in the academic year 1999–2000. I am grateful to them for the opportunity, to my University and College for their willingness to support my application, and to the Department of Politics and International Relations for the later period of leave that has allowed me to complete the project. My thanks to those who discussed issues with me or commented on earlier components of the project: Liz Barrett, Rob Behrens, Chuck Beitz, Erica Benner, Dan Butt, David Charles, Selina Chen, Roger Crisp, Bruno Currie, Michael Freeden, Diego Gambetta, Hazel Genn, Philip Gerrans, Bob Goodin, Peter Hall, Gary Hart, Barry Hindess, David Hine, Duncan Iveson, Richard Jarvis, Des King, Chris Kraus, Gordon MacPherson, David Miller, Teresa Morgan, Joseph Nye, Alan Patten, Philip Pettit, Quentin Reed, Elvira-Maria Restrepo, Alan Ryan, Andrew Sabl, Vicki Spencer, Mark Stears, Helen Sutch, Dennis Thompson, Ernesto Garzon Valdez, Stuart White, Laurence Whitehead, Gavin Williams, and Ruth Zimmerling, and to various audiences in New Zealand, Australia, the United Kingdom, Hungary, Germany, and the United States. Special thanks are owed to Michael Aronson of the Press for his patience and interest; to Margaret Canovan, Matthew Clayton, Liz Frazer, and anonymous reviewers for the Press, each of whom commented on a full previous draft and especially to Adam Swift, who did so for two versions; and to Jerry Cohen, who responded to material from the project throughout its long gestation and who taught me (however imperfectly I practice the lesson) that while clarity is no guarantee of rightness, it is a precondition for it.

An earlier version of the middle section of Chapter 9 appeared in "Motivating Liberal Citizenship" in C. McKinnon and I. Hampsher-Monk, eds., *The Demands of Citizenship* (London: Continuum, 2000). The author is grateful to the publishers for permission to reprint and revise material from that essay.

This book took me longer to finish than I thought it would, largely because various university responsibilities preoccupied me. In that period I accumulated debts of a less intellectual, but nonetheless crucial kind to Elena Jurado and Dan Butt in Oriel and to Des King, Neil MacFarlane, and Bridget Taylor in the department. I dedicate this book to my family—Sarah, Joe, Ruth, and Hannah—with thanks for keeping me sane through these years, and for reminding me that the good life is exhausted by neither politics nor the life of the mind.

Contents

POLITICAL CONDUCT

Introduction

How should we understand and evaluate political conduct? The emphasis on *political* derives from the view that politics is a distinct sphere and type of activity that is not reducible to morality, while the emphasis on *conduct* indicates a contrast with the abstract political principles that are the subject matter of most contemporary political theory, such as justice, liberty, or equality. In this book I argue that the evaluation of political conduct is not simply an assessment of the extent to which it brings about certain antecedently specified goals, values, or principles, but must be grounded in an understanding of the character of politics and of the particular circumstances and range of possibilities within which political agents operate. *Politics* has many diverse meanings, and I make no claim to be exhaustive in my coverage; rather, I focus on politics as the struggle to secure and exercise political rule—the attempt to determine authoritatively who gets what, when, and how, to borrow Lasswell's phrase.[1] Political struggles occur over who is to exercise political power, its appropriate jurisdiction, how it is to be exercised, and over which values are to be pursued and the ways in which they are to be allocated.

One reason for starting with political conduct rather than with, for example, abstract principles of justice is that certain forms of political conduct, such as leadership, play a central role in determining the relevance and force of particular values and in securing their realization. Through political activity values are articulated and embraced, and they become powerful motivating forces in society at large. In that process these values are interpreted and given concrete and practical form in particular policies and objectives. The result is that political action and commitment and the dynamics of political struggle powerfully influence people's understanding and interpretation of what they value and must strive for, and what they

1

can accept as reasonable, fair, or just. Rather than politics acting as the instrument for realizing certain specified values, it plays a crucial role in the interpretation and projection of values and ideals. In that process people develop a sense of what certain values and ideals really mean for them and for the way they live. These values infuse their aspirations, becoming normative for them by informing their understanding of their most basic commitments and conditioning their interpretation of their responsibilities, ambitions, and interests. This process is not a frictionless transfer from value to action or outcome; it is a much more imperfect and human experience, and to portray politicians as simply endorsing values or goals and identifying the means to achieve them is to caricature the complex, costly, and often painful process by which people's hopes and ambitions are developed and come to influence others. Politics, as discussed in this volume, should be understood as a distinct process that plays a central role in the identification of such goals that simultaneously makes them concrete and normative for others.[2]

Similarly, in the evaluation of people's political conduct, the standards are not simply those we would apply to any ordinary moral agent. In his classic work on democratic theory, Giovanni Sartori draws a sharp (and somewhat caricatured) distinction between two views of the political process: one that sees political conduct as nothing more than the conduct we would expect of all moral agents, with no acknowledgment that there may be something distinctive about the demands of politics that distances it from morality, and another that sees politics as the untrammeled and amoral struggle of interests and egos, unconstrained by ethical principle. In rejecting both positions, Sartori insists both that political ideals and values have to be understood as being distinctively political, not simply moral, in nature and that politics cannot be understood in wholly non-normative, amoral terms: "consequently both political moralism and political cynicism are mistaken positions, the former because it stems from a premature merging of the political with the moral realm, and the latter because it is the result of an unjustified schism between them. Politics and ethics are neither identical nor separated from each other in watertight compartments."[3] Sartori's claim is one I endorse, but it is not one whose implications are easily spelled out. It requires an understanding of political rule that identifies the standards that are intrinsic and internal to it, together with some sense of the conditions under which those standards may come to have, or may lack, ethical weight.[4]

Rather than assessing political conduct directly in consequentialist terms, or against some external moral standard, I focus on the character, virtues, agency, and integrity of the actor as a player in the domain of politics.[5] Such judgments are not easily made: they must be acutely sensitive to the political and historical contexts in which people act. Those contexts have complex dynamics—what is politically possible can change rapidly—so that men and women find themselves having to make choices that they did not initially conceive and that they could not initially have imagined. Sometimes politics is a theater for tragedy; sometimes it is a setting for farce. As Marx recognized, those who struggle in politics can be driven by forces that they do not fully grasp: the traditions of dead generations weigh like a nightmare on the minds of the living, so that they both parody and live out their sense of the past, often blind to the significance of their actions.[6] Weber's conception of politics as the slow boring of hard boards may describe the work of the master craftsman when the structure is sound and the apparatus of rule is well established, but such conditions are not universal, and the rich sense of personal and professional integrity afforded the politician within such an order is not available to those desperately attempting to shore up beleaguered states or level the crumbling ruins of a tyranny.[7] For such tasks other skills are required and individual integrity may be shallower, more difficult to sustain, and often more difficult to recognize or admire because it may depart from a sense of well-considered and responsible action that a more secure political world can sustain. The standards of political conduct appropriate to a settled, consensually validated order simply cannot be normative for every political order irrespective of the conditions; to deny this is to take one's responsibilities as a political theorist less than seriously.

It is not my intention to dismiss the prevailing orthodoxies and approaches of political and moral philosophy, in large part because such work is appropriately concerned with questions of truth and value and has an important role to play in sharpening and articulating our sense of the values we might want to see realized and in acting as a critic of the claims that those in politics make. But this book differs from such work both in recognizing the impact that politics itself has on the development and realization of values and outcomes, and in focusing on how appropriate standards can be derived and applied to the conduct of those who act in politics. According to this account, the dynamics of political activity shape and complicate people's ambitions and the political principles they endorse. The virtues and character of political leaders, the impact of personal and political loyalties, the legacies of historical memories and resentments, and the way that certain forms of power distort political agency all have a major impact on the goods and values sought and realized in politics. The impact of these considerations can be profound—they go beyond a concern with which means best serve a given set of values and ends because they influence the way that such values and objectives are identified and pursued in politics, and they limit what we can reasonably expect of those acting in politics and thereby help determine whether and under what circumstances a posited principle or value becomes a feasible and desirable objective to pursue. If the political process and its struggles have a significant impact on the ends and values pursued in politics, we may come to see a higher than usual proportion of political philosophy as utopian—as something that, while perhaps instructive as a thought experiment, cannot reasonably be pursued.

In the course of this book I develop four main lines of argument. The first presents politics as itself powerfully influencing the norms and values that it is possible and appropriate to realize. The upshot of this argument is that the relationship between moral philosophy and politics is not deductive, and that many of the abstract values found in moral philosophy and much liberal political theory are profoundly inflected by their interpretation, implementation, and realization in political action. This view accords the political process a substantial degree of autonomy and an identity and character of its own. Politics, and political conduct in this view, needs to be understood largely, although not entirely, on its own terms, and those terms concern the political virtues and qualities of the actors involved. Accordingly, I begin with a discussion of the nature of politics, its distinctiveness as a set of practices and as a domain of activity, that continues throughout the book (most directly in chapters 2, 3, and 4, and, in relation to political service, contentious politics, and citizenship in chapters 7, 8, and 9, respectively).

The second, related set of claims is that politics is a much more internally complex, human, and grubby domain of activity than most recent political theory recognizes. It is a domain in which human passions, ambitions, loyalties, and treacheries have a major impact on who gets to exercise political power and on how it is exercised. Moreover, attempts to clean up politics are often based on the illusion that these elements can somehow be eliminated from the process. In making this argument, my goal is to encourage a suitably subtle appreciation of the character and demands of politics that recognizes that reform (itself a political process) is inherently limited in what it can achieve. This argument is central to the discussion in chapters 1, 4, 5, 6, 7, and 8 and informs the essentially skeptical conclusions about the possibilities for regulating political activity in Chapter 10.

The third line of argument is that there are, nonetheless, standards for political conduct, albeit their specific demands are heavily contextual in character. The appropriate coinage for the evaluation of political conduct is that of character, virtues, and abilities rather than deontological constraints or consequentialist considerations. Integrity is, to varying degrees, possible within politics and we can distinguish between politicians who act well and those who do not using an assessment that draws on the norms and institutional setting in which they act and on issues of character and judgment. Such evaluations must also acknowledge the distinctive demands that different positions in a political system will make on their occupants. Specifically, I address the expectations it is reasonable to have with respect to the conduct of political leaders, to those who serve them, and to citizens within democratic orders. Recent literature has extolled the virtues of citizenship and the kinds of demands we must make of citizens to achieve stable, self-governing, liberal democratic orders. This book is concerned with politics more widely, with liberal democratic orders being exclusively addressed mainly in the final three chapters (as well as parts of chapters 4, 5, and 7). This is partly because such polities are only a small portion of the states that have existed in the last three thousand years but it is also because, rather than defining the central elements of politics by reference to liberal democratic orders, I see these as offering only one set of instantiations of these elements. To that extent, although it is important to acknowledge the valuable and often pathbreaking work of a number of recent scholars who have similarly focused on issues of political conduct, this book works beyond the traditional boundaries (but not to the exclusion) of liberal democratic thought.[8]

Finally, the arguments advanced here recognize that certain types of institutional systems can dovetail with their society and culture to realize to a high degree the values that liberal (or other) political theories so prize (see chapters 9 and 10). Nonetheless, the institutionalization of political rule and its regulation with procedures, rules, and norms to produce a stable and moderate regime is a fragile achievement—one that is, historically, the exception rather than the rule—and even where it exists there remain tensions among the dynamic, innovative, and open-ended character of political rule, the attempt to regulate such forces in a well-ordered state, and the potential for political agency and decision making to generate new constituencies of opposition and contention.

Two further points should be made concerning sources and method. The first is that, as a contribution to political theory, this work is informed by the reflection on politics and its demands that runs throughout the history of political thought. Many in this tradition have things of importance to say about the character and the problems of political action. Their role in this text is as fellow commentators on politics in general and as examples of worlds of meaning that, while they are often very different from those faced by contemporary political theorists, provide us with insights into political conduct that help us to recognize that features of older political conflicts and attempts to rule can contribute substantially to understanding our own institutions and activity.

The methodological point is that, in identifying politics as a distinctive sphere of activity, it is necessary to understand both what makes it intelligible and meaningful to those who participate in it, and what makes it intelligible more generally as a sphere of activity within societies. In some cases this involves interpreting historical events and actions in an attempt to capture the meanings that informed people's choices and actions and to understand better what they valued, what they regarded as normative for them and for others, and how far they acted consistently and coherently within that set of meanings. In other cases, tackling more abstract questions, my concern is to try to understand, for example, the character of loyalty as a category of meaning that involves both a certain type of psychological state and a certain impulse for action, and to consider the conditions under which it may develop, flourish, or take one form rather than another. The interaction between particular examples on the one hand, and the more general categories of authority, leadership, loyalty, service, citizenship, and so forth, on the other, allows us to recognize that particular instances of action also involve more general and abstract features of meaningful behavior that permit a degree of comparative study and assessment.

I have stated these arguments baldly, but the full character and weight of these claims must be developed in detail and through an appreciation of particular contexts. To identify both definitional and ethical criteria for political conduct involves establishing certain general features of political rule and agency and teasing out standards of conduct from those features. It requires another step to contextualize these standards to show that they could be recognized by those acting in politics, and a further step to acknowledge that there is an inherent degree of variability both in the standards and in the degree and depth of integrity that politics can achieve or permit. Furthermore there is the final issue of how those standards relate to other, more general normative principles, standards, or claims. Yet there are other activities where a similar interaction exists between the character of an activity, agent motivation, and intent, and some deeper standpoint that can contribute to the validation of those standards and the conduct they demand, or can question it, as in many games. The analogy is worth pursuing, even if the disparities finally provide a sharp lesson in the complexities of political conduct.

> Being in politics is like being a football coach.
> You have to be smart enough to understand the game,
> and dumb enough to think it's important.
> —*Eugene McCarthy, 1968*[9]

McCarthy's quip suggests that politics is a rule-governed activity with meaning and purpose, and with players, strategies, and moves through which this purpose is realized. But his analogy also alerts us to some very basic questions about the activity: Is good politics, or football, solely about winning particular exchanges or games? Is playing well to be understood entirely consequentially, in terms of the outcome of a particular game, or do we have a more profound sense of the point of the activity that recognizes the value of the game itself and the greatness of a performance independently of the result—as when we distinguish between playing well and winning? Moreover, in politics there is a basic distinction between activities concerned with gaining or retaining political power and office, and activities undertaken in the exercise of political office. Some institutional arrangements ensure the two are very closely linked (as in the U.S. House of Representatives), some keep them apart (as in stable, hereditary monarchies), and in many there is a changing interplay—a revolutionary autocracy may increasingly concern itself with ensuring the conditions for its continuance rather than with pursuing the ideals for which it seized power. But gaining office is not in itself the "end" or *telos* of politics—office demands rule. When we have played the game sufficiently well to gain office, what constitutes ruling well?

The analogy between politics and games also holds up on the issue of the underdetermination of the activity by formal rules. Just as there is a distinction between merely sticking to the rules and playing well in sports, so too in politics do rules often fall far short of providing a comprehensive account of what we can expect or hope from those in power. Managers and spectators may judge players to be unfit, unfocused, or incompetent, but the rulebooks rarely provide the basis for such assessments. There are rules that govern access to public office and set out official responsibilities, but often the rules primarily focus on the types of misconduct that the political system is most concerned with preventing or feels most confident about identifying, or that members of the current political elite believe most threatens their power. Rulebooks may list what can and cannot be done, but they are harder pressed to state the point of the activity, and it is this implicit standard that the interpretation and understanding of the rules must take as their reference point. To attempt to specify this point as the achievement of excellence or as playing or ruling well would be tautological: What counts as excellence depends on what the point is, as does what counts as ruling well.

Rules, even in the form of constitutions, statutes, regulations, codes, principles, norms, and practices, must be interpreted to be applied to particular cases and, when interpreting and applying them, politicians, judges, and commentators need a deeper sense of how they hang together to provide structure and coherence to the activity. Moreover, most political rulebooks (in the broadest sense) are made, interpreted, and amended by politicians; if these processes are subordinate to partisan influences, we may end up with a systematically distorted political order. How can we know if the game we are observing is being played well if it is played in conformity to rules that are themselves the result of corrupt forces? How do we understand an activity that we have seen undertaken only by cheats and incompetents? Unless we have some sense of the point of politics, and of what practices, motives, and ambitions on the part of its various participants are compatible with that point or would allow that point to be more fully realized, we will lack criteria for identifying good or poor performances or for recognizing when those participating in the game begin to turn it to ends that go fundamentally against that point, thereby corrupting it.

The sources for understanding the point and character of politics involve three basic elements. We can ask of a game: (1) What is its basic structure and character—What makes it this game rather than another? (2) What is it to play it well? and (3) What makes it worth playing, and what other ends does it serve? The first two questions invite reference to the "rules" of the political game within which men and women act and that distinguish political activity from other activities within that society. However, we need a broad understanding of these rules, going beyond those formally enshrined in constitutions, legal codes, codes of practice, and conditions of office to include more tentative judgments about competence, integrity, and so on, and to question whether the formally defined boundaries of a practice capture the full range of appropriate activity. (Is the interaction of players and spectators a component of the game? Are dimensions of the personal also significantly political?) The second question presses these shared characteristics further to ask what this activity demands of its participants in accordance with its internal criteria of success. This question generates hypothetical imperatives for those acting in politics that derive from an understanding of the point of the activity; that is, "if you are going to get involved in politics, to succeed (in terms of the activity) one must x, y, or z."

The third element addresses the point or purpose of the activity and reflects on its value, potentially comparing it to other activities. In many games, what makes the game worth playing is the sense of mastery and the associated pleasure. But in politics, "worth playing" involves more than a judgment about the pleasures it accords to those who participate. It involves judgments about the necessity for political activity in society, about the substantive ends that the activity pursues, and about the proper scope of that activity with respect to other activities. What gives politics its value as an activity is in part the tensions, conflicts, and aspirations to which it responds, and in part the goods it realizes—where these are not limited to an individual agent's purposes but include those intrinsic to the activity within which those purposes are intelligible. The ambitions of those in politics can be grandiose, mundane, or frankly sordid, but we should not confuse these personal goals with what creates the need for this kind of activity within a society: in broad terms, the need to impose order and discipline and to coordinate and conciliate people's conflicting interests and activities. Political rule becomes urgent when conflict, disorder, and violence impose substantial harms on a society, and where other nonpolitical coordination and conciliation mechanisms (familial, associative, contractual) are on some dimension or other less effective than politics. Once established, political authority may extend to other tasks, albeit not always appropriately. Invading familial or domestic domains, enforcing contentious religious observance, or imposing a controversial conception of the good on a people may extend political rule into domains best left alone (because some areas of personal relations are so important and so fragile that any attempt to intervene in them authoritatively through the political system will cause unacceptable or radical harm; or, more conditionally, because the benefits of intervening are in a particular case outweighed by the costs of doing so). Politics is one system of allocation and rule. In most modern states it claims a degree of sovereignty over other systems—communal, market, familial—but it is a matter of judgment as to when, over what domain, and to what degree that sovereignty is appropriately exercised.

The analogy between politics and games is always going to be stretched, but there are three respects in which it collapses more or less dramatically.

First, politics is itself implicated in the ongoing struggle to establish the point and the rules of its own activity. We can usually distinguish between what it is to play a game and what it is to disagree about its purpose or point; in politics that distinction collapses extremely quickly. Political thought and practice are centrally concerned with interpreting the end of the activity in such a way as to make that interpretation normative for others and sovereign over the political system more widely, so that the point of the activity is something that the activity is itself attempting to define. This means that what counts as conflict, what is seen as necessary to order it, what activities are accepted as legitimate in the struggle to determine who (and whose interpretation) shall rule, and on what goods and values the political system should ground its claim to legitimacy, are all potentially open to contest. What gives some coherence to this arena is the attempt by those involved to gain and exercise power and authority through at least some appeal to legitimacy, which involves securing endorsement for one's interpretation of the ends of one's office, but how far down legitimacy can or must go depends heavily on context and on the type of rule exercised.

A second difference is that a central component of politics is rule setting, not just rule following. Some aspects of politics, like electoral competition for office in modern democratic states, are highly structured and rule bound.[10] Once attained, however, political office involves creating and interpreting rules in the light of a particular conception of the point of the activity and making and implementing decisions and rules that govern the behavior of others and set standards and norms for their conduct. Winners in sports are not, for the most part, given the power to amend the rules of the game they have just played or the opportunity to change fundamentally the distribution of economic and cultural resources on which other players can draw. In contrast, political will can sometimes radically change a society, transforming its self-understanding and its related understanding of political legitimacy and of what is politically possible—transforming the criteria of assessment from above, rather than simply meeting standards imposed from below.

The third disanalogy is simple: politics is not a game. What makes it worth "playing," in competition with other practices, is that it fundamentally frames the activities of its community, projects certain ends for that community, and affects the conditions of life of those within (and often of those outside) its borders. It has an ethical significance that the term *game* obscures. Politics profoundly affects the liberty, security, and quality of life of millions of people. In nation-states and in the domain of international affairs, it provides the structures within which most people live their lives, and political decision-making rules on some of the most basic normative questions in fixing the role the state plays in society and the ends it pursues. Because the choices that politicians face are often of deep ethical significance, the terminology of "games" and "skills" needs to be set aside in favor of a language of political virtue.

This is not to say that every politician, political commentator, or participant has a clear grasp of the character of his or her activity, or that each recognizes its ethical significance. Understanding the character of one's activity is neither a necessary nor a sufficient condition for being a great player—although recognizing that one's conduct does have ethical significance is probably, in the case of politics, a necessary condition. Even so, great players (by definition) are rare in any game, and they are also rare in politics. Average players are (again, by definition) the norm, but while games can thrive with these and many polities can tolerate them, there are also instances in which being average in politics can have disastrous results. Were politics simply a case of complying with rules and norms, a generation of mediocre technocrats would produce a dull polity but not a damaged one. But the sovereign, rule-setting, political culture–defining character of politics does call for men and women who have an appreciation of the importance of their activity and a sense of the ends that their activity must seek to promote, with respect both to the citizens of the state and to the state's relationship to other states. In the spirit of Weber, politics demands of its participants a type of integrity and a sense of responsibility. If these are absent, political rule threatens to go rogue.

Decision making is further complicated because politicians act in a world that is always incompletely under their control, and because their own political vision and how they act can change the horizons of political possibility (not always intentionally) for both themselves and others. Political decision making remains stuck in the distinctively human dimension of interpersonal action: it requires the coordination of wills, interests, and political aspirations and imaginations. The ability to stand back from politics and to manipulate the elements of the political scene impartially to effect a particular decision is inherently limited. Political agency works with people—with their virtues and vices, their contacts, alliances, and loyalties, and their fears and anxieties—and their own actions are rarely free from the influence of that complex of attitudes, emotions, and interests. People respond to flattery and bribery, to promises and threats, but they also respond to conviction, vision, flair, and charisma, and to the invoking of more abstract ideas and claims of duty and obligation. These characteristics are not simply components in an arsenal from which politicians must choose; at least some are hardwired into many of the men and women who seek power and authority and who thereby seek to rule others.[11]

Even if politicians are able to retain their humanity, it can be a mixed blessing. History is replete with examples of those whose human qualities were exemplified by their frailty rather than by their responsiveness to the needs and concerns of others. How those who rule us conduct themselves has more than ordinary significance because of the power they exercise, and yet that experience of power—the difficulty in gaining it and the need for a streak of ruthlessness both toward those who resist and toward those within one's own camp who might otherwise usurp one's position and its attendant prospects—can make it difficult to retain the self-control and sense of proportion required to act responsibly. Some are tempted to act in ways they should not; but the more serious problem is that how one should act is often unclear, and the more fragmented and disordered the world within which one acts, the more difficult it is to chart a path. Indeed, as the "decisionists" of the late nineteenth century recognized, it is not that there is always a right decision that those in office must make (even if they cannot always see it), but that they have to take decisions that they believe they can make right by their commitment to seeing them through. Our evaluation has to consider what else they might have done, why they followed the course they did, how far they were able to bring about their objectives, and what value those had. The complexities of such an inquiry should not be underestimated, but making the attempt can give us a clearer

sense both of the difficulties of assessing political conduct and of the importance of such an assessment.

Like McCarthy's politician, I am dumb enough to think that politics is important—the reader must judge from the chapters that follow whether I
understand the game. I have tried to identify the character of political rule
and to consider the motives of those who rule and those who serve or
follow. The result is not a set of rules we should expect politicians to follow
so much as an account in broad terms of the demands that different political roles make of their practitioners and the difficulties they face in
meeting these demands. Attempting something more detailed would require us to go much deeper into particular contexts, and the room for doing
this is limited.

The potential for dramatic instability in politics, which much contemporary political theory ignores, leads me in Chapter 1 to examine the collapse
of the Roman republic under Julius Caesar, with Machiavelli's consequent
dismissal of Caesar as lacking the necessary qualities of character for rule. In
Chapter 2 I go on to explore Machiavelli's wider position and argue that we
have to understand Machiavelli as suggesting, rightly, that the assessment
of political conduct involves something like a version of virtue ethics. Both
Caesar and Machiavelli have been accused of being unprincipled, but in
each case there is much to be said for recognizing their concern with the political virtues. The "unprincipled" reading has little to recommend it; the
two cases demonstrate the interdependence between context and agency
that enables a better appreciation of the nature and limits of integrity where
politics is deeply disordered. Machiavelli's account of the virtues and what
they demand, however, is not automatically appropriate to different circumstances. We have to read his account in relation both to the particular
circumstances in which he wrote and to a deeper sense of the character of
political rule, which I address in Chapter 3. We also need a fuller understanding of the character of political leadership—the way that central
players interpret, exemplify, and extend the game (Chapter 4). In the fifth
and final chapter of Part 1 I address the issue of whether those who exercise
power in politics are necessarily corrupted by the task. I show that there are
major obstacles to acting well for those who attempt to exercise political
leadership and that modern liberal democratic states certainly are not free
from these, but I take this to be more a ground for reflection on the place

accorded politics and politicians in modern states than an encouragement of cynicism toward those who attempt to exercise political leadership.

In Part 2 I focus on more subordinate actors, discussing the problems inherent in loyalty in politics (Chapter 6) and then turning to the complex issue of how we should conceive of public servants and the character of public service (Chapter 7). In both cases, the types of fealty and obligation that seem essential to relationships of service are not easily reconciled with the more procedural and impartial demands modern states make of those who work in the public domain. This raises further questions about the compatibility of political commitments and loyalties with the basic system of rules, expectations, and values that frame most Western liberal democracies.

In Part 3, I offer an account of social protest and contentious politics in modern democratic states (Chapter 8) and argue that a central feature of politics, in addition to ordering conflict, is (through that very activity) to generate the potential for new sources of conflict. Chapter 9 follows this discussion by considering arguments within the liberal democratic tradition for the types of virtues that liberal democratic polities require of their citizens if they are to achieve stable and widespread legitimacy and compliance. While we can sketch a picture of the kind of relationship we want between citizens and a democratic polity, in practice such a picture rests very heavily on a range of background material, social, and cultural preconditions that are not easily realized. As a result, while the ambition for liberal democratic states is seemingly clear, the reality is that they are, for the most part, less resilient and more fragile than is generally acknowledged, making politics at once more urgent and demanding. In Chapter 10 I examine the potential for institutional design in setting boundaries for political action. For all the attractions of institutional design as a way of settling conflicts and issues within a state, a major obstacle to success is simply that the process of design is one that is as subject to the vagaries of politics as are other political agendas.

Again, I do not claim to be comprehensive in my discussion of political regimes, historical epochs, or even types of political malfeasance. The raw material is copious! I argue that there are certain persistent features of politics that set standards for conduct that are often ignored in the approaches that currently dominate political theory and political science and that set limits on the extent to which general moral principles can be used to evaluate political practice. As will be evident, I have learned a great deal from Anglo-American political philosophy, but that discipline is often silent or naive about the impact that political agency and struggle have on the realization of political values and in its construction of the domain of politics. Republican theories have influenced my understanding of the character of political agency, but I remain unconvinced of its continuing relevance for our understanding of citizenship in modern democratic states. Similarly, more structuralist accounts of politics have helped me frame some of the issues with which I deal without leaving me satisfied that they can answer the questions I believe should be asked. The result is an attempt to think through what politics demands of its participants that argues that these demands must be recognizable as reasons for action by those must who act in situations, the precise details of which can dramatically affect what can or cannot be achieved.

Many who have inquired about this project over its long gestation responded to the phrase *political conduct* with something like a snort and a comment as to how venal, grasping, or otherwise craven politicians are. When pressed, all acknowledged that their comments implied some set of standards to which they believed politicians should conform, but their pessimism about the realization of these standards did not diminish the belief in their importance. Indeed, the more strongly they criticized politicians, the more important these standards inevitably became. My aim is to try to help us clarify what sort of standards might be appropriate and how they might be grounded, while also acknowledging that they must be standards that can be met in practice. This means that in some contexts we have to scale down what we think can be demanded; in others, where political rule is on the verge of collapse, it may be difficult to see how even the most minimum of standards of conduct could be met. In most cases a complex balancing is required between arguments for what standards of political rule are appropriate and what motivational resources exist to sustain or develop this rule in a stable form. The outcome of such an exercise is not reducible to a set of general principles, but offers an appreciation of the demands of politics that recognizes both general features of the activity and the impact that particular contexts have on how these are realized in practice. I will have succeeded with my skeptical friends if I persuade them that, before they rush to judge the conduct and chosen ends of those in politics, they owe an attempt to understand the distinctive character of that activity in its context.

PART I

Rulers

CHAPTER 1

Rendering unto Caesar

The idea that politics has some of the characteristics of a rule-based, complex game with certain broad goals and objectives that provide a framework for its actors and has a deeper normative significance is an attractive one. The shortcomings of this comparison, to which I drew attention in the Introduction, do not overthrow the picture entirely but they do point to some of the complexities that the analogy obscures. Those complexities are multiplied in fragile political orders, which must depend to a much greater degree on the agency and virtues of those who contend for and exercise power than on the rules and procedures that frame more stable orders. This does not mean that stability and rule-based government are always to be preferred in political systems, but it is easier to grasp a culture's political norms and purposes when they are enshrined in institutions and codified in laws, and where these institutions frame that society's political activity. It is more difficult to gain a firm critical perspective in cases where the instability or fragility of the political order either exaggerates or diminishes the significance of individual actions, rendering their results more extreme or less predictable. Instability can enhance agency, but it can also render utterly contingent and unpredictable the connection between action and outcome.

In *The Prince* Machiavelli addresses precisely these conditions; that is, circumstances in which new princes, by their will and virtue, produce order out of chaos. In his *Discourses*, he tackles cases in which the political order has become corrupt and requires systematic reformation. In both cases he sees an increase in political instability as providing an occasion for heightened human agency, and some of his most damning criticism is leveled at those who, when faced with such challenges, choose not the reform of the state but its continuing despoliation.

Truly, if a prince seeks earthly glory, he should have the desire to possess a corrupt city, not to ruin it completely, as Caesar did, but to reorganize it, as Romulus did, for the heavens cannot bestow upon men a greater opportunity for glory, nor can men wish for a greater one. . . . Nor should anyone be deceived by Caesar's glory, hearing him celebrated with the greatest praise by ancient writers, because those who praise him are seduced by his good fortune and terrified by the duration of the empire which was ruled under his name and did not permit writers to speak freely about him. But anyone who wishes to know what writers, when free, would say about him should see what they say about Catiline. Caesar is all the more detestable, just like the man who is to be blamed more for committing an evil deed than for wishing to do so.[1]

Machiavelli sees Caesar as failing to restore Rome's liberties and intentionally completing its corruption (as Catiline aspired but failed to do). The charge is damning, yet the expectation that Rome's liberty be restored is not obviously reasonable. As we will see here and in subsequent chapters, the assessment of political conduct presumes a degree of agency on the part of individuals, but context can have a profound effect on the depth and extent of agency open to those in politics and, while Machiavelli freely acknowledges the force of *necessità* as a constraint on princes, he appears to make no such allowance in Caesar's case. He assumes that the restoration of the republic was an option, and that it was one that Caesar rejected despite having the extraordinary abilities needed for such a task. Machiavelli condemns Caesar for the collapse of the republic on three counts: that he had the opportunity to restore it; that he had the necessary (if extraordinary) skills and abilities to do so; and that his failure was a function of his corrupt character and intent. As we shall see, it is not easy to sustain the first or last of these claims. In contrast to Machiavelli's rather sweeping assessment, there are grounds both for recognizing Caesar's manifold political virtues and for seeing the republic as no longer able to contain the aspirations and abilities it had itself engendered. If such an account is defensible the argument for opportunity falters, as does the attribution of corrupt intent, but it leaves uncertain the interpretation of Caesar's abilities, since the language of virtue might be inappropriate for the description of characteristics that brought about the republic's fall. While it may seem odd to begin a book on political conduct with an example in which agency is conquered by circumstance, the case I want to make is that the complex and intricate political order of the late republic generated aspirations, abilities, and expectations among its ruling elite that the order could not itself continue to contain or meet, ultimately leading to its demise. Contra Machiavelli, political virtue is not always enough. (My argument in this and the next chapter is that it is, nonetheless, political virtue.)

Although there is substantial support for Machiavelli's suggestion that Rome was corrupt, there is considerable dispute over the point at which the republic slid into irreversible decline. Scholars have variously identified the rule of the Gracchi brothers, Sulla and Marius, Pompey and Caesar, and Augustus and Mark Antony as key turning points. It is certainly incontestable that the Roman political order and constitution were under increasing strain after 130 BC and that the struggle for ascendancy between the traditional nobility and office holders (the *optimates*) and those defending the interests of the Roman citzenry (the *populares*) became more violent and more destructive. Power came to reside increasingly with those who commanded armies and who rewarded their soldiers with the spoils of war and by distribution of land when they returned home. While it is possible to see these events as evidence of a long-term process of structural decay against which political will was wholly ineffective, whatever the deeper tensions, the republic eventually fell through the particular actions of individual men and women. Indeed, according to Gruen's account, it is in the specific details of the period prior to Caesar's move into Italy that one can recognize that things might have gone otherwise, and that the forces that broke the alliance with Pompey and led to the civil war were contingent and political in character.[2]

While it is true that the extensive violence and unrest suggest considerable instability, the period also sees the passage of major pieces of legislation and a basic continuity in the character of the order. Additionally, the republic faced substantial difficulties in dealing with those whose military success ensured them a standing and a loyal following of troops but who could not find recognition in the political process. This situation led to increasing conflict as political leaders assumed military commands and subsequently turned these to political ends. When Sulla assumed the dictatorship he used it mercilessly against his enemies, but he also left it to resume life as a private citizen after he had, in his view, secured the Republic. Similarly, many who fought the republic did so to reestablish what they saw as central to its existence—although success sometimes bred excess, as with Marius in 87 BC. For the most part, the evidence is of a struggle for dominance between contending forces within an order, rather than attempts wholly to transform that order—with notable exceptions, such as Spartacus's slave revolt and the (very different) Catiline conspiracy.[3]

Brutal and merciless as many of the campaigns were, they were fought in the name of the republic, not to over-throw it. One outcome of this, however, was that it became increasingly difficult for responsible political leadership to emerge because the political order had diminishing control both over the actions and dispositions of its military commanders and over those who, like Clodius, championed the popular cause in pursuit of their own ends. In turn, this further weakened any efforts to go beyond the immediate interests of the parties concerned to a genuine sense of an order shared by all. Cato the Younger ensured immortality in the republican canon with a series of rearguard stands defending the order, but his unwillingness to compromise only heightened the tension between the nostalgic picture of the republic that his oratory sketched and the conflict-ridden, pressing social reality which it denied.[4] Lesser men, like Cicero,[5] caught between these contrasting images of their world, found it increasingly difficult to reconcile the need for pragmatism and compromise with the rhetoric of republican sacrifice and glory that their literary and historical education, and their ambition, had impressed upon them. In this fragile political system, its collective resources increasingly partitioned between rival leaders who nonetheless still recognized the tradition of Roman glory and *imperium* as normative for them and as giving their lives a unique meaning through the potential for fame and honor, it was ignominious and cowardly not to act and increasingly difficult to know how to do so. The order was one that people sensed as threatened, but that none thought lost. Indeed, the populace seemed largely unaware that they increasingly lacked the collective ethos and sense of unity they had once possessed. But is Machiavelli right to claim that it was Caesar who destroyed the order, and that he intended to do so? What was the right way, in these conditions, to conduct oneself politically? Was there a way in which someone with Caesar's abilities could have acted that would have secured the republic, rather than bringing it closer to its collapse?

One line of argument, which draws heavily on classical sources, suggests that Caesar had always had monarchical leanings, finding evidence for this in his activities prior to 59 BC.[6] Yet the evidence from the earlier period is difficult to weigh. Too often knowing what comes after provides an interpretive gloss to the past. Caesar's early confrontation with Sulla, his refusal to divorce his wife at the height of Sulla's campaign of proscription, his dramatic encounter with pirates, and his foray against Mithridates in Asia in 74 BC suggest a mixture of arrogance, audacity, and an acute sense of his own status and standing, but hardly more than that. As a young man in Rome he had a reputation for extravagance and debt but his natural ability as an orator was also acknowledged, and he won acclaim for his performances in the trials of Dolabella and Publius Antonius. He also had a basic ability to make himself liked, partly by seeming to give people what they wanted and partly by the easy and friendly way he had of mixing with them. His extravagance gave a certain splendor to his life, albeit coupled with a political edge, as when he provocatively brought Marius's image and reputation back into public life at the funeral he arranged for his aunt Julia, Marius's widow.

Clearly, Caesar was ambitious—but that was something Rome demanded of its social and political elite. Indeed, the psychology of republican Rome revolved around issues of standing and respect to which ambition was integral.[7] What distinguished Caesar was neither his ambition nor his concern with his standing but his considerable abilities and the shrewdness with which he built his political support. His lavish spending on the rebuilding of the Appian Way during his term as curator, and his provision of gladiatorial contests, theatrical performances, and public banquets as *aedile* were designed to secure popular support, and he rose swiftly in political circles. He became *questor* and a member of the Senate in 69 BC, *aedile* in 65 BC, and, after spending heavily in the election, *pontifex maximus*, the highest religious honor in the state, in 63 BC. He was *praetor* in 62 BC and he used his subsequent *pro-praetorship* of Further Spain to restore his finances. When Pompey returned to Rome following his wars against the pirates and Mithridates, Caesar became his enthusiastic supporter. He brought Pompey into an alliance with Crassus that he cemented with marriages, and he secured their backing for his election as consul for 59 BC.

In all this activity the dominant theme is Caesar's ambition as a young and able member of the patrician nobility who recognized the importance of cultivating popular support and who was cavalier with the rules concerning bribery in elections, as were many of his contemporaries. He sought high office as a fitting tribute to his abilities but his ambition was set in the context of the republic—it involved no design against it.[8] As consul he gave further evidence of his willingness to follow through what he saw as a mandate and his agreements with Pompey and Crassus without troubling himself too much about the niceties of the established norms and practices of the republic. His first objective was to provide land for Pompey's veterans through a new agrarian law. The measure he drew up was carefully formulated and the Senate could find little fault, save that they knew it would enhance Caesar's personal following and power. In consequence, by an obstructive filibuster, Cato talked out the proposal, insisting that there should be no change in the status quo. Caesar had him arrested but backed down when he saw he was losing popular support and he took the legislation to the popular assembly. Support was given freely there but Bibulus, Caesar's co-consul and supporter of the *optimates,* sought to prevent further meetings by declaring the days on which the *comitia* met to be public holidays. Caesar had the Forum occupied overnight and Bibulus was attacked when he tried to close proceedings. The law was passed, including a clause requiring all senators to swear by a given date to uphold it. Cato and others resisted complying until the last moment, but the measure drove Bibulus to stay at home for the remainder of his term of office and led many leading *optimates* to retire from active political life.

While the methods used by Caesar were controversial and almost certainly unconstitutional, he managed to secure some of the moral high ground.[9] His legislation covered a series of important issues to the republic that required resolution, and his solutions were often extremely adept. Nonetheless, driven largely by acute mistrust and some jealousy, the Senate and its majority resisted him at every step. That, in turn, forced Caesar to act in ways that further exacerbated their hostility and their sense that the constitution was being grossly infringed. As a result, he stood every chance of being held to account by the Senate and the courts for his conduct in office at the end of his term.[10] Moreover, prior to his taking office, in a measure specifically directed against him, the Senate required the consuls (Caesar and Bibulus) of 59 BC to undertake "two offensively insignificant administrative tasks" (policing the forests and roads of Italy) for their subsequent proconsulship.[11] Of the triumvirate only Caesar was liable to prosecution for his actions, but Crassus and Pompey had every interest in supporting the laws he had passed; to do that they had to continue to defend him. Accordingly, exploiting concern over unrest in Gaul and the death of one of the proconsuls selected to attend to it, the popular assembly agreed to pass *lex Vatinia,* which gave Caesar command of Cisalpine Gaul and Illyricum together with the legions necessary to control these areas for a period of five years (renewed for a further term by Crassus and Pompey in 55 BC). Moreover, at

Pompey's instigation, the Senate agreed to add Transalpine Gaul and a further legion to Caesar's command, although this additional command required annual renewal. Despite the fact that Caesar and his allies were subjected to a constant stream of humiliating personal and political attacks by Bibulus and others and were losing popularity, he passed further laws of real significance—such as *lex Iulia de repetundis*, which sought to control corruption and maladministration in the Empire.[12] At the end of his term Caesar left Rome, staying close to the city only long enough to make sure that the Senate would not declare his acts as consul invalid. Instead, they offered to re-pass his legislation by constitutional methods, but Caesar rejected the offer (because doing so would imply he had acted badly in the first place—an imputation incompatible with his honor and standing in the republic) thereby further alienating the Senate.[13] His military success in Gaul led to an extension of his command and, over eight years, brought the unification of the whole of Gaul (plus two invasions of England), which ensured him a standing at least equal to that of Pompey (Crassus died in 53 BC) and earned him the abiding loyalty of his troops.[14]

As Caesar's campaigns and command drew to a close, he sought reelection as a consul but without sacrificing his *imperium* (without which he would have been an open target for prosecution by his enemies for his actions as consul). To begin with, he saw a stubborn minority in the Senate wishing to resist all his efforts, despite the passing of a decree permitting his candidacy *in absentia* by the ten tribunes under the guidance of Pompey as sole consul in 52 BC.[15] Next came a series of campaigns by C. Marcellus, Metellus Scipio, and others to undermine the coalition with Pompey by attacking Caesar's position. These attacks came increasingly from the very *nobilitas* whom Pompey had sought to incorporate in an alliance against the more stubborn aristocratic element of the Senate around Cato.[16] Extremists on both sides further undermined all trust between Pompey and Caesar; the breaking point came when Curio secured Senate support for the proposal that both Pompey and Caesar resign their commands and discharge their armies—a proposal that struck hard at Pompey, whose command had been conferred until 47 BC. The Senate's decision was dismissed as advisory by Metellus (consul and Pompey's new father-in-law), who then entrusted Pompey with the defence of Rome, giving him command of all forces within Italy. The Senate minority persuaded the majority that the situation justified demanding that Caesar relinquish his forces and that the Senate withdraw permission for him to stand as consul *in absentia*. The attempt by

Caesar's tribunes to veto the decision was itself overturned by the passing of a *senatus consultum ultimum*—which was tantamount to a declaration of war. In a matter of weeks, power passed directly to the most intransigent of Caesar's enemies who sought formally to deprive him of his standing, his immunity, and his armies.

The civil war was started formally by Caesar crossing the Rubicon, but his reasons for doing so deserve careful scrutiny. In *Discourses* Machiavelli implies that Caesar acted to destroy the Roman republic; in his "Tercets on Ingratitude" he offers a more nuanced account which shows some sympathy for Caesar's position: "Often a citizen becomes a tyrant and goes beyond the bounds of his country's law in order not to suffer Ingratitude's injury. This made Caesar snatch the throne; and what Ingratitude did not bestow, rightful anger and rightful resentment gave him."[17] Caesar's account, understandably, is more detailed:

> For himself, he said, his standing had always been his first consideration, more important than his life. He felt hurt because a favour granted by the Roman people had been insultingly wrenched from him by his enemies; he was being dragged back to Rome with six months of his governorship stolen from him, even though the Roman people had sanctioned his candidature in absence at the next elections. This loss of office, however, he had accepted with equanimity in the public interest, yet . . . men were being conscripted all over Italy, the two legions which had been taken from him on the pretext of the Parthian war were being sent there, and the community was under arms. What was the purpose of all this, if not to destroy him? None the less, he was ready to descend to any depths and put up with anything for the sake of the republic.[18]

Of course, it is possible to doubt the sincerity of Caesar's account—and to assume that his primary concern, following the death of Crassus, was to end Pompey's dominance of Rome (exemplified in Pompey's unprecedented assumption of office as sole consul in 52 BC) and to establish his own personal ascendancy over Rome and its empire. On that assumption, the civil war flows from a desire for tyrannical or despotic control and disdain for the forms and institutions of the republic; however, such an interpretation makes no sense of his conciliatory gestures. It also renders the account he gives in *The Civil War* utterly disingenuous,[19] an account that is clearly intended to persuade his audience of the justice of his cause.[20] Certainly he cannot have hoped to ensure the suppression of every contending account. Moreover, his troops would have been less likely to remain loyal had they believed he was conniving to establish a tyranny.[21] To this extent, there must be an element of sincerity in his account—which reflects his sense that others might read it and find justification for the steps he took. Whether he in fact took the steps for the reasons he gives is another matter, and one which is impossible to determine, yet his reasons for action and his rationalization of them align better the more we accept that his attempt to persuade was sincere.

One way to find Caesar's account utterly unpersuasive is to interpret his claim that his "standing had always been his first consideration" as indicating a motivational ground indistinguishable from self-interest. That reading is implausible, however, not least in the light of Cicero's *Partitiones Oratoriae*: "There are two kinds of man: one uncultured and rustic who always puts his own advantage before what is right, the other cultivated and refined who puts his standing *(dignitas)* above all else."[22]

Caesar's *dignitas* is not his pride or merely a grasping sense of what he deserves. Rather, it speaks to his standing within an order—simultaneously constitutional, social, and political—that gave rise to legitimate expectations on his part and that shaped his expectations of how others should treat him and of how he should respond to them.[23] To violate those expectations would be to attack the order in which that standing has meaning and significance. *Dignitas* should be understood not as a matter of personal integrity and a devotion to duty, but as political prestige, influence, and worthiness within the regime.[24] Of course, Caesar and his contemporaries were sometimes touchy, overbearing and arrogant, quick to take offence, and suspicious of the motives of those with whom they clashed. Moreover, the complex, overlapping patterns of rank and order were not interpreted by all in the same way. Some members of the old *nobiles*, perhaps including Caesar, might have had a more fiercely personal sense of their *dignitas* and a less scrupulous attitude toward the legal and constitutional forms of the republic. Even so, there is no necessary implication that they thought themselves sovereign over those forms. It is entirely plausible to think that they could evision the danger of rigorous compliance with procedure when those forms were being systematically distorted and ignored by demagoguery, political violence, and the ruthless use of the mob to serve the ends of individuals. Successive leaders in the hundred years before Caesar gained power had ignored political procedures in the name of saving the republic and their *dignitas* (albeit not always with justification), and in doing so tied their *dignitas* to the spirit rather than the letter of the republic. Indeed, Cicero, in *Pro Sestio,* announced the true end of all good and honorable men as "peace with dignity," but went on to say: "For just as it ill befits men to be so carried away by the dignity of a public career that they are indifferent in peace, so too it is unfitting for them to welcome a peace which is inconsistent with dignity."[25] Moreover, *Pro Sestio* continues by differentiating those with "an exalted spirit, great ability, and great resolution" who are prepared to take the difficult and stormy path which their *dignitas* and the welfare of the state demands, from those whose recklessness and abandon incites them against the state.[26] This being the case, Caesar might well have seen himself as following Cicero's injunction by refusing a peace inconsistent with his own dignity and, in his eyes, the dignity of the republic.

At certain points, as in 49 BC, Cicero saw Caesar's actions as unequivocally failing both peace and dignity: "Wretched madman never to have seen the shadow even of right! Yet all this, he says, is done to support his dignity. Can there be dignity without honesty: and is it honest to retain an army without sanction, to seize the cities of your country that you may strike the better at her heart, to contrive the abolition of her debts, the restoration of exiles, and scores of other crimes?"[27] As it turned out, Caesar did not deserve this hysteria. In keeping with his sense of the connection between *dignitas* and order, the civil war was fought in a distinctive spirit. Although he was often more ruthless and skilled as a military leader than his opponents, he was also consistently more generous and lenient in his treatment of those who fought against him. The Gauls, Britons, and Germanic tribes had not, for the most part, been as fortunate, but time and again in the civil war Caesar showed an unusual degree of consideration and respect for those who fought for Pompey. That he did so from the outset calmed the panic that the start of the war and memories of the days of Cinna, Marius, and Sulla had provoked. His policy was directed by a concern to win over all citizens of good will. So, while still a war, his campaign was conducted with a view to conciliation and in the spirit of *clementia*—albeit this increasingly took on connotations of a god-like benevolence that would envelope all those he subdued (which further outraged his enemies).[28] In the end it was clemency plus subordination; which is why Cato preferred suicide and why Caesar was angered by his choice: "Cato, I must grudge you your death, as you grudged me the opportunity of giving you your life."[29]

Although Caesar's concern with his *dignitas* was genuine and was linked to a sense of the standing of the individual within the broader sociopolitical order, acknowledging this leaves open the issue of the point at which that *dignitas* had been adequately established. Caesar believed that civil war was justified because he was threatened with political subordination, prosecution, and almost certain exile and exclusion from future office despite his many astonishing achievements on behalf of Rome. The Senate's attitude betrayed a spirit of faction and cabal that threatened the very security of the republic. This legitimates his bitter comment on his victory on the plain of Pharsalia: "They made this happen; they drove me to it. If I had dismissed my army, I, Gaius Caesar, after all my victories, would have been condemned in their law courts."[30] The machinations of Metellus Scipio, Lentulus, and others had intentionally fueled mistrust between Caesar and Pompey and pushed both men into a position where they could avert war only by backing down and accepting conditions that each would have found humiliating (a consideration that was certainly as important as any risk to their person). Neither was prepared to do that, but that can hardly have been a surprise. The possibility of reconciliation that remained throughout the months prior to the Rubicon rested on the possibility of mutual confidence between Caesar and Pompey; and this was progressively destroyed by those hostile to Caesar and by the anomalous positions that each now held within the republic. The republic had elevated Pompey to a unique position contrary to its own traditions, and while Caesar was unwilling to tolerate subordination to Pompey (not least because he no longer trusted him), Pompey was unwilling to tolerate equality with Caesar.[31] In judging Caesar's actions one is struck by the fact that the very virtues and qualities prized by the republic that allowed his rise to prominence eventually brought him into armed conflict with it, in large part because of the complex politics of the republican nobility and the growing problems in reconciling popular forces to the conservative lead of the Senate. Yet if this tense dynamic associated with standing and the threat of humiliation legitimates Caesar's refusal to surrender his army and his pre-emptive invasion of Italy, it does not add up to a practical political program to pursue once the war was settled—something Caesar accused his enemies of lacking—and it leaves unresolved the question of what his standing would now be.[32]

Caesar's brief period of rule was remarkably free from the arbitrary exercise of power—at least in comparison with the proscriptions undertaken by

Marius's collaborators or Sulla, or subsequently by Octavian Augustus. Indeed, just as the civil war was dominated by his clemency, so too was his legislation designed to enhance the stability of the state and the empire. It did not systematically harm or benefit any particular class or group within the state, and his attitude toward the empire was substantially more generous than his predecessors. To reduce the disparity and conflict between rich and poor, poorer members of the populace were to be provided with citizen colonies overseas, the middle class was to be expanded by extending citizenship to doctors and teachers who settled in Rome and to rich provincials, and the ostentation of the wealthy was to be curbed by sumptuary laws. He increased the size of the Senate (to 900), adding his own followers who were often of obscure and provincial background, so that members of the old *optimate* order were increasingly outnumbered by new men. He also expanded the number of offices to create the basis for a large imperial civil service. His concerns seem directed mainly at establishing Rome as the central power in, and the Romans as the upper classes of, a huge empire, rather than with concentrating on reordering the republic itself—as if he recognized the incompatibility between the two objectives. Some of his plans were monumental: a canal was to be built across the isthmus of Corinth, Ostia harbor was to be extended, the Fucine lake was to be drained, a new road was to be built across the Apennines, the Tiber was to be moved to the west to free up land on the Vatican plain, a library collecting all Greek and Roman literature was commissioned, as was a unification of civil law. And, in keeping with his clemency, political opponents were allowed to return and statues of Sulla and Pompey were restored.[33]

He undertook this program by using authority derived from an accumulation of offices. He was appointed Dictator in Rome in 49 BC and again in 48 BC, and in 46 BC he was reappointed for ten years and then transformed into *dictator perpetuus* in 44 BC. He also secured a consulate in 48, 46, 45, and 44 BC, the *praefectura morum* in 46 BC, and the *tribunicia sacrosanctitas* in 44 BC.[34] The position he occupied was an amalgamation of traditional offices and innovations of uncertain significance (the Dictatorship had originally been intended for brief periods of emergency, although Sulla had held it for several years), which testify to the *sui generis* nature of his standing in the state. That standing resulted in an increasingly difficult relationship with the Senate. Although Caesar began by consulting senior Senators, and occasionally referred matters to the Senate, the Senate's positive role in lawmaking soon diminished; much of the legislation was passed by decree and in outline with the detail being filled in later.[35] Although he did not de-liberately destroy the Senate, its formal role was increasingly eclipsed. So too was its informal role as a source of advice and support from the political elite. With many of the *optimate* class bitterly opposed to Caesar, he fell back on men whose interests were more inimical to the state—such as Mark Antony, whose personal conduct while *magister eqitum* was scandalous and whose conduct in office was brutal. As the Senate was increasingly by-passed, elections to key public offices became increasingly redundant, with Caesar making appointments rather than tolerating the contingencies of public opinion. In both respects there was some legitimacy to be drawn from his Dictatorship, but he continued to act in this role even when the danger to the state (not unconnected with his own actions) had clearly passed.

Those whose virtues enable them to rise to power are not automatically equipped to meet the demands that exercising that power involves. While Caesar had been conscious of his own *dignitas* in starting the civil war, he became increasingly careless with that of leading *optimates* and treated them with a discernable lack of tact.[36] This derived in part from the extraordinary position he occupied, which allowed his plans for administration and em-pire to be implemented largely by *dictat.* The way he gained his office freed him from the need for conciliation, negotiation, and debate, and turned projects that might have taken the republic a lifetime to agree on into the tasks of days. He became an autocrat rather than a legislator because he sought to exercise his will instead of looking to establish (or reinvigorate) institutions and practices that could become self-sustaining. He coupled this with a failure to curb his acerbic tongue. His every comment was relayed throughout Rome, persuading those whom he offended that he had tyran-nical intentions and enabling rumor to give the impression of a groundswell of opinion against him. By 45 BC he seemed to chafe against his formal, quasi-constitutional standing, reacting with impatience to criticism or con-straint and thus increasing the sense that he was becoming tyrannical even among those who, like Cicero and Brutus, had earlier defended him. At the peak of his success he suddenly seemed to be failing, losing touch with those upon whom his continued rule depended. It is difficult to know what to make of suggestions that Caesar aspired to become king, nor how far such talk originated from his camp, from his enemies, or from a confused attempt on the part of popular forces to find an appropriate way of hon-oring him. Although much confusion surrounds the affair, his reaction to

the placing of a *diadem* (the Hellenistic symbol of kingship) on his statue—
he jailed the tribunes who ordered its removal—implies that he sought the
recognition. For his contemporaries, Caesar's attack on the tribunes was an
attack on the very office that he claimed he had crossed the Rubicon to defend.[37] He clearly recognized the Roman people's resistance to the idea of a
king, but the increasing impact of Hellenism on Roman culture and among
the outreaches of the empire made the idea of a monarchy much more acceptable outside Italy. Torn between his belief that he was owed a standing
that acknowledged his unique position and his recognition that Romans
found the idea of monarchy abhorrent, he sought to distance himself from
the proposals and in the process managed to appear lacking in gratitude,
more autocratic, and more vain. Caught between these pressures he sought
some way of reinforcing his distinctive standing (by deification) while
finding attractive the prospect of a return to war against Dacia and Parthia.
In war he had a defined position and purpose and a secure standing among
those whom he led and those he conquered, whereas in Rome his standing
had become the sport of rumor, malicious gossip, and the froth of public
opinion, whose consequences were potentially lethal.

This sense of a disjunction between Caesar's initial intent and the final
outcome of his actions does not make it easy to settle the issue of his broader
responsibility for the fall of the republic. It also complicates the counterfactual question of whether Caesar (or any other leader) could have reformed
the republic—which Machiavelli implies was possible.[38] Yet there is ample
room for doubt that the republic could have been restored; it faced too many
internal tensions and conflicts that would have been difficult to conciliate in
a stable form. Moreover, the Roman Empire demanded a degree of central-
ization of administration and military organization that was incompatible
with the dispersed authority of the republic's institutions. Even if those
needs could have been met within the republican form, it is a separate question as to whether Caesar would have restored it—not just whether he
would have seen this as a desirable and feasible goal, but whether such an
attempt would have been recognized and trusted by those who most desired
it.[39] In winning the civil war Caesar emerged with no equal, and finding no
equal he may well have become contemptuous of many of those around
him; although, even without such contempt, the inequality alone was
reason enough for deep resentment among the *optimates*.[40] Had he sought
the reconstruction of the republic, he would have done so autocratically, as
their superior, alienating the *optimates* and the new men around him by his

presumption. Once peace was established, the leading citizens of both the old and new orders began to question the need for the position that Caesar occupied. Unlike Sulla's systematic elimination of his opponents, Caesar's clemency left in place many of the statesmen of the republic who had initially resisted him. From his perspective, Caesar's continued rule was essential; he could not surrender power and retire from public life as Sulla had done because he had, without design, instituted an order in which his own continuing dominance was indispensable. Those who opposed him failed to see the necessity of reordering the republic, the difficulty of doing so, or the high risk of a complete breakdown. They did not acknowledge how fundamentally divided it was, how easy it was to destabilize, how complex a task it was to impose upon it a lasting order, and how much central control and authority was needed for the task. As it turned out, it took Augustus's monarchy and the systematic elimination of a large part of the political elite to impose order on the state after Caesar's assassination.[41]

What an individual demands from his or her political order must be proportionate to that order, as must be the means used to pursue those demands. The revolutionary can see little or nothing to demand from the order against which he or she rebels, and overthrows it in the name of something better. For those actions to have integrity, the order to which the rebel aspires must be proportionate to his or her ability and circumstances. But there is widespread agreement that Caesar was not a revolutionary.[42] One way of looking at the events of 49 BC is as a proportionate action on Caesar's part: necessary to protect himself and to secure his dues and flowing from the complex order of the late Roman republic. Caesar's conduct in the civil war confirms that sense of proportion.[43] Indeed, much of his behavior referenced the institutions of the republic. His insistence on being awarded triumphal processions for his victories abroad in the civil war (something normally restricted to wars against a foreign enemy) indicates that he sought the highest marks of status available within the republic, even if, in demanding them, he was overriding his own sense (evident after Pharsalia) that these conflicts were at best a tragic necessity. In this, as in many other respects, Caesar's sense of what he was due did not lead him to seek the overthrow of the republic so much as bring about its collapse by demanding of it something that it could no longer deliver.

The assessment of Caesar's political conduct is not easy. There are many aspects of his life that modern readers would regard as repugnant—the huge human cost incurred by the Gallic wars and civil wars, the violence he orchestrated against his fellow citizens and senators, or the wanton destruction of human life he encouraged in the games and gladiatorial contests. However, in the main, these are features of ancient Roman life, not peculiar to Caesar, and part of an order that framed his choices and actions. Accordingly, when we assess his political conduct we do so for the most part without reference to such matters. Clearly, choice and interpretation were involved in many situations he faced—for example, Cato (and others) accused Caesar of having acted beyond any reasonable mandate in his activities in Gaul,[44] but there is little to suggest that he was wholly maverick. He interpreted his objectives in ways that both conformed to expectations and sometimes exceeded them. He kept firmly to certain central Roman values and took an utterly pragmatic approach to institutional and constitutional niceties; he did so partly from personal ambition and partly in the name of more exalted ideals and ambitions for an empire united under Rome. These ends were not disjoint: his personal ambition, and his conduct in pursuit of it, were authentically true to Roman mores and were integrally tied to his sense that the potential for universal dominion would bring Rome its greatest glory. The tragedy is that in the fragile last years of the republic, his demand for the recognition that his services to the republic should have commanded drove him to a position that set him at loggerheads with the *optimates* in Rome who sought to humble him. The ensuing civil war further emphasized his superiority. Caesar could no longer be contained within the republic; and it, in turn, could not survive his death.

That said, Caesar's sense of his public duty was dramatically affected by the weakness of the political order in which he acted. Instability debilitates the force of public norms while simultaneously making demands on people to act in ways that encapsulate and support the spirit of public office, even if they do so at the cost of breaking rules. States whose political systems are fragmented or disordered need leaders with a grasp of the dynamics of the disorder that threatens their state, with the vision to see how it might be reordered, and with the will and courage to risk supererogatory action to achieve order—such men and women are rare. This is precisely the situation Rome faced after 60 BC, and it was precisely this type of heroism that Machiavelli castigates Caesar for falling short of. But Machiavelli's judgment is harsh; it identifies Caesar's failure in terms of his intent and the consequences of that intent yet it is difficult to show that Caesar aimed to overthrow the republic, or that he intended what he brought about. On the contrary, it seems more accurate to think of Caesar as locked in a set of expectations and mores that had dominated the republic for centuries, and—in keeping with Roman *optimate* traditions—as deeply psychologically centered on his standing and public face. His ambition and his immense abilities led him to seek the highest offices and standing that the state could confer, but at a time when the political order was already fragile, and when it could not, as a result, securely deliver the *dignitas* to which his achievements entitled him. In claiming his entitlement he further weakened the very order within which his position had meaning and value. To think of him, as republicans have done, as a tyrant destroying a prized order is unwarranted. To think of him in moral terms as a failure because of the consequences of his conduct, or because of his obsession with his dignity, is to miss the complex relationships between Roman mores and individual psychology, between his intent and its consequences, and between the intricacies of the social and political order and the dynamics of the context within which he acted.[45] His death at the hands of so many suggests shortcomings as a political leader, but it is not clear that he failed to see its imminence. It is possible that he surrendered to it (rather than to the wholesale repression necessary to avert it) because he could see no way to unite the forces in the capital to establish a stable, imperial Rome. That said, he is an unlikely candidate for a republican hero—he did not plot the republic's destruction but he did not recognize the threat he posed to it nor did he see the importance of reestablishing it, since his concerns were more focused on the imperial order. His elevation lost him his approachability and charm, and strained the loyalty of those about him as he became distant to their concerns. A justified pride in his achievements probably did turn to arrogance. Even had Caesar seen the institutional challenge, it is doubtful he could have met it—partly because of who he was, but also because of the overwhelming difficulty, perhaps impossibility, of doing so.

Judging the conduct of men and women in politics is not easy. In times of massive social, political, and economic change and disruption it is still harder, not least because we have an intuitive sense of how things might go right that tends to overwhelm our recognition of the huge obstacles to their doing so. Often the greatest challenges are those that arise because the men and women who find themselves having to design and construct the new order are themselves the products of the old. While Hegel derives a sense of completion by seeing Caesar as doing "what was necessary to overthrow the decaying freedom of Rome," albeit meeting his own end in the struggle,

those with a less sure sense of historical development might more realisti-
cally think of him as driven by his intense identification with the republic to
live out the increasingly self-defeating character of its ethical and political
order.[46] This is not a causal fatalism so much as a proposal for recognizing
the intelligibility of his conduct and the fragility of its context.

Machiavelli's disappointment in Caesar's path to civil war, and in the fall
of the republic, should not, however, obscure the fact that in many respects
Caesar had the qualities and abilities that Machiavelli wanted from his
"prince"—expecting that such characteristics would issue in dramatic, innovative, and constructive political agency that would rejuvenate states and
would warrant the term *virtue*. In Chapter 2 I begin the discussion of that
picture of agency and go on to press the question of what makes it appropriate for certain political abilities and capacities to be thought of as virtues.
While the story I have told renders Caesar's conduct intelligible and recognizes that he had considerable abilities, Machiavelli and many others would
still resist seeing these qualities as virtues.

CHAPTER 2

Machiavelli and Political Virtue

Machiavelli's criticism of Caesar is directed at his political conduct; he finds Caesar wanting because he acted in ways that a virtuous politician would not have acted, not because he lacked ability but because he put those abilities to the service of his own personal ends, and did so because his character was weak or corrupt.[1] Although Machiavelli has been both denounced and hailed as a supreme realist and consequentialist with respect to politics, his assessment of Caesar suggests that he works with something like a theory of the virtues—with a distinction between ability and virtue that allows him to recognize the former but not the latter in Caesar. There is some appeal in understanding Machiavelli's position in this way, and I develop this interpretation in this chapter to raise some wider issues about the application of virtue ethics to the domain of politics so that we are in a better position to appreciate some of the complexities associated with judgments about political conduct.

Machiavelli holds, in broad terms, the core commitments that this book defends: that the political process fundamentally affects the kinds of norms and values that can be realized within a state; that politics is an internally complex and grubby domain of human activity that engages a range of passions and ambitions; that there are, nonetheless, certain standards of conduct for those acting in politics; and that institutions can be created that structure and support political orders, although these are always potentially fragile. Perhaps most surprising for those with only a passing acquaintance with Machiavelli, is his insistence that there are standards of conduct for those in politics and that Caesar is to be condemned for failing to meet them. It may seem inconsistent for someone renowned for his brutal guidance to new princes, suggesting that they must learn how not to be virtuous and instead must take whatever steps they believe necessary to maintain

their states, to argue that politics makes certain ethical demands on its practitioners derived from the proper ends of political rule. Yet Machiavelli certainly believes that Caesar failed the republic and did so because he failed to
grasp the point and purpose of the political rule he exercised, thereby betraying his lack of virtue.

Machiavelli's work is widely acknowledged within the canon of Western
political thought, with modern republicanism embracing his enthusiasm for
republics and for a *vivere civile e politico*.[2] His sense that political orders are the
product of will and a degree of ruthless pragmatism in contexts of flux and
disorder and his view that as much attention has to be paid to the founding
and reestablishing of states as to the conditions of "normal politics" has
evinced much less interest. Although it is partly his pessimism about human
nature and his practical experience of its shortcomings that leads him to
focus on the fragility of political orders, in so doing he raises enduring questions about the kinds of political ends it is reasonable to expect men and
women to pursue, and about the qualities and motivation they must bring
to such a pursuit.

The central role Machiavelli accords the prince is a function of his commitment to something like a severe entropy principle: Left to their own de-
vices things go to pieces since human life tends to flux and disorder. The
ability to impose form upon this recalcitrant matter and to give it shape,
order and meaning is, although highly valued, extremely rare. Machiavelli
takes Aristotle's comment that man outside the polis must be either a god or
a beast and emphasizes the view that in almost every case they turn out to
be the latter; further, beasts collectively lack the political virtue and intelligence to bring a political and social order into being. What is required is an
exceptional man who, by his *virtú*, can impose his will on a fragmented,
formless, and fissile collection of people and by doing so unite and rule
them. Once the state is stable, institutions are formed, the people become
accustomed to the demands of political rule, and they begin to develop a
collective *virtú*; at that point it may be possible for a state to move from prin-
cipality to republic. Indeed, those princes with greatest *virtú* act as legislators; that is, they create states with institutions that form the basis for a free
republic, sustained by extensive citizen virtue.

For Machiavelli, then, politics might be said to have two different modes.
In its extraordinary mode it concerns individuals acting in situations of
chaos or disorder whose *virtú* enables them to impose their will upon
others, forming them into a social and political unit within which an ordi-

nary or *normal* politics—involving participation in the direction of the affairs of the state—might subsequently develop. Even in normal politics, some occasional extraordinary activity will be demanded so as to reestablish the republic on first principles. What is required in both cases are leaders capable of recognizing what must be done to succeed and with the capacity and commitment too see their actions through to their ultimate end.

Although Machiavelli is famously attributed the view that the ends justify any means, the ends a prince properly pursues are quite firmly delimited, as are the means it is legitimate to use. Agathocles the Sicilian and Oliverotto of Fermo fall foul both with respect to the means they used and the acceptability of their ends. They used countless treacherous and cruel deeds to attain power in their respective states (Syracuse and Fermo), which led Machiavelli to exclaim:

> Yet it cannot be called *virtú* to kill one's fellow-citizens, to betray one's friends, to be treacherous, merciless and irreligious; power may be gained by acting in such ways, but not glory. . . . If one bears in mind the ability displayed by Agathocles in confronting and surviving dangers . . . there is no reason to judge him inferior to even the ablest general. Nevertheless, his appallingly cruel and inhumane conduct, and countless wicked deeds, preclude his being numbered among the finest men.[3]

They also fall foul of the ends criteria. It is not wrong, in Machiavelli's book, to seek power. The ambitions of both men are understandable. Agathocles held power as *Praetor* (military commander) of Syracuse and Oliverotto looked up on Fermo as his due patrimony, but neither was satisfied. Both wanted unbridled power for its own sake. This objective is incompatible with princely *virtú*. One may seek power, but one must do so continently and for a further end. It is in his deeper understanding of the point of political power that Machiavelli provides the grounds for a sense of political virtue, which is neither moralism nor wholly an account of the skills needed in the struggle for dominance.

One initially plausible ambition for the proper end of princely power is simply to secure and preserve one's state. Yet this is something that Agathocles achieved, although Oliverotto did not. It also raises the questions of what further end is served by that achievement and what is supposed to motivate the prince to pursue those ends. Neither egoism nor vanity is an adequate motive, since for Machiavelli (with Weber) the actions of such a man become hollow and meaningless and such a leader will not survive long in a new state.[4] The most plausible motive for Machiavelli's prince is the pursuit of glory, yet to the modern reader this is difficult to distinguish from egoism. Moreover, it suggests a potential tension between what the proper ends of the prince should be and what it is that the prince wants out of his pursuit. These two elements are closely connected in Machiavelli's concept of *glory*.[5]

Machiavelli's glory is a complex phenomenon: one wins glory by deeds and achievements; in particular, a new prince wins it by the virtuosity he displays in forging a set of norms and institutions for his state—norms that help both to define and serve the interests of the citizens of the state. Indeed, to win glory is partly to win the respect and deference of one's citizens and contemporaries, although it is also to win renown among subsequent generations through history. In the long run the prince is dead, but glory is the plaudit of history; the authoritative criterion for *virtú* is that one's deeds and reputation withstand historical scrutiny. Although the judgment of contemporaries is often less demanding than that of future reviewers, it is a necessary precondition for glory because without winning their respect (at least in the form of fear and deference) one cannot consolidate one's state and it will not survive one's death. This means that the prince has both to impress most of his own people most of the time as well as the most informed and discerning critics through time.[6]

The action of the prince, legislator, or leader cannot, then, be wholly self-interested. The prince has to act in a disordered world to project and instantiate a set of political and social norms and institutions that will provide stability within the state and safeguard the security of its subjects. He is assessed with respect to how far he successfully innovates and establishes norms and institutions that realize the common good. If he does succeed, his state will be secure and he will win honor and glory for his name—glory and the ends of politics appear inseparable.

To win glory one must have *virtú*—perhaps the most troublesome term in Machiavelli's lexicon. Whether and how far *virtú* involves the classical virtues depends on what the prince must do to secure his state. He will need to exemplify the classical virtues as and when he can, but he should do so only if they will serve his ends. Were the world a different place, were men less corrupt, these virtues might be central to good ruling but, given the way the world is, a prince who is bound by them will lose his state at the expense of his subjects and will be justly despised.

Machiavelli appears to distance himself from classical Greek and Roman conceptions of the virtues in three ways. As classically understood, to have a virtue is to have a disposition of character that is exemplified in the way a person acts but is not itself something about which the agent deliberates. A courageous person acts courageously, but does not deliberate as to whether he or she should be courageous; nor is honesty something chosen after deliberation.[7] These, and most other virtues, are dispositions of character—a settled way of being in and responding to the world. Some believe that Machiavelli is arguing (consistently with Aristotle's recognition of different spheres for different virtues) that the prince has to know when and where to practice particular virtues, but most read him (rightly, I believe) as suggesting that the prince must be able to some degree to manipulate his own character and to counterfeit aspects of his character to mimic the virtues, and thus exhibit behavior consistent with the virtue in question rather than virtuous behavior itself.

The second break with the classical picture of the virtues is that whereas classical sources generally argue that the virtues are consistent with each other and are linked and ordered in a good life to achieve *eudaimonia,* Machiavelli inserts a wedge—the concept of *virtú,*—between agency and the virtues that undercuts such claims. For example, if honesty is deployed instrumentally, then it is not inherent in the agent's character and so cannot form an integral part of his character and mind, on which the concept of *eudaimonia* is predicated. That said, Machiavelli does recognize limits to which character can be treated instrumentally:

> That man most luckily forms his plan, among all the persons in Fortune's palace, who chooses a wheel befitting her wish . . . yet while you are whirled about by the rim of a wheel that for a moment is lucky and good, she is wont to reverse its course mid circle.
>
> And since you cannot change your character nor give up the disposition that Heaven endows you with, in the midst of your journey she abandons you.
>
> Therefore, if this he understood and fixed in his mind, a man who could leap from wheel to wheel would always be happy and fortunate, but because this is denied by the occult force that rules us, our condition changes with her course.[8]

Virtú, then, remains partly linked to character but, in the third break with classical models, it picks out very different virtues than those classically celebrated. Flexibility, shrewdness, decisiveness, resolution, and cunning (among others) form an integral part of the prince's character and are seen as qualities that are not themselves the subject of choice: one does not decide to act cunningly—such hubris courts disaster—one either is cunning or is not. In this sense these virtues are not simply skills or abilities we can choose to exercise, they are a fundamental part of a person's make-up. They are dispositions and attributes that some men and women have and others do not, but that no one has to an infinite degree. As such they are a matter of character, whereas for Machiavelli the classical virtues are either not, or should not be. The prince who is classically virtuous will fall prey to the world, whereas Machiavelli's suggestion is that one who has *virtú* may succeed in imposing order on the world through his will. That will is not contentless: it has a character (*virtú*) that is responsive to the demands of politics and attempts to impose form on the recalcitrant human matter in his state.

There is, then, a very close connection for the prince between glory, *virtú,* and the securing of one's state. The new prince who lacks *virtú* and tries but fails to establish a state will leave no monument and, accordingly, will secure no glory. The lack of success and glory betrays the shortfall of *virtú.* For Machiavelli, *virtú* is not merely the means a ruler requires to achieve his own ends, it is what he must have if he is to identify, pursue, and secure those ends. The prince demonstrates his *virtú* by understanding the challenges that face him in the establishment of a state, by appreciating what is needed to achieve that end, and by recognizing what it is possible to achieve under the specific conditions he faces. The task is exceptionally difficult because, acting in a radically disordered world, the prince is more than ordinarily exposed to the play of *fortuna.* Here too lies a test of *virtú*: leaders of great *virtú* will tame *fortuna.* The glory to be won is great, not least because success is so elusive.

If the prince is driven by vanity, cruelty, or arrogance he is unlikely to succeed. While Machiavelli seems to imply that this *outcome* is the reason that we would not describe such a person as virtuous, the example of Agathocles suggests Machiavelli's commitment to a much more reasonable claim—that a person who is driven in this way lacks *virtú.*[9] The prince certainly seeks power but, like Weber, Machiavelli demands from him a sense of proportion and responsibility.[10] The prince may want glory but he must be aware that enduring glory attaches only to real *virtú,* and real *virtú* requires a range of skills and traits—such as flexibility in conduct, determination, strength, spiritedness, and prowess—and the application of those in the creation of a well-wrought state.[11] In this sense Machiavelli is at one with the classical virtues; that is, one is not flexible (or courageous or shrewd) just for the sake of being flexible. Certain types of situations (as well as certain types of reasons and ranges of facts)[12] evoke specific responses, and the prince's *virtú* is evidenced in his responses to these situations. That he responds in such a way enables others to recognize that a matter of character is involved, and by concurring that this was the right response we acknowledge the action as virtuous. Being flexible for the sake of glory would shortcut the chain: We respond to a situation with flexibility because that is the right way to respond to that situation (it is the right way because it is the way someone with *virtú* who grasps the importance of and seeks to build a well-ordered state has to behave, and someone who achieves an ordered state through their own agency and character is acknowledged as a man of *virtú*).

This appears to resolve the issue of the prince's motivation—eliminating the view that the prince acts directly to secure glory. To act simply because others will offer praise lacks virtue since, while it may still take courage, the act is not a response to the reasons or facts that should prompt such behavior, and this dramatically diminishes or crowds out any sense that they are acting virtuously.[13] This does not mean that the prince has no interest in glory—Machiavelli is clear that he does—but we cannot reduce his motivation, and thereby his *virtú,* to the direct pursuit of glory.[14] Nonetheless, as in Caesar's case, for one's conduct to be demeaned and disrespected would give rise to justifiable resentment and enmity. Princes act convinced that what they do is the right and appropriate thing, and that others should (or in the future will) recognize that this is so. In this sense they are not immune to the assessment of their conduct.

It is now possible to clarify Machiavelli's account of the proper end for the prince: he (or very occasionally she) must seek to establish a state that will endure.[15] To act as a roving bandit is not prudent nor is it politically or ethically intelligible.[16] A prince who acts intelligibly will seek to create and sustain a state in response to the challenges issued by the disorder he faces with a will to impose order and to rule. In so far as he responds to that challenge well (both appropriately and successfully) he will be accorded glory, which is a fitting tribute to his *virtú*. The ordering of the state, and the securing of its stability, are achievements to which the virtuous prince attaches intrinsic, not merely instrumental, weight. The obstacles to this achievement are the weaknesses of men and women; the ease with which they are corrupted or perverted; and the violence and disorder that follow from their unchecked passions, ambition, and envy. Moreover, the situations princes face will reveal every flaw and exacerbate every weakness in their characters—but this merely underlines Machiavelli's sense that what matters is this character, and that it is this character that is rightly celebrated in a prince's reputation and glory.

Even though Machiavelli's claims for the prince's *virtú* have something in common with more traditional claims for the virtues (as reasons for action and a source of motivation), it remains the case that the examples of *virtú* that he cites depart dramatically from more classical claims for honesty, justice, benevolence, or generosity. For many, Machiavelli's lack of interest in *eudaimonia* as the end of a life of virtue and the fact that the qualities he seeks seem simply too instrumental in form demonstrate that he lacks a recognizable theory of the virtues.

Certainly, Machiavelli expressly repudiates some features of classical virtue ethics. Most significantly, he makes no attempt to offer a theory of virtue per se as a contribution to an understanding of the good or the good life.[17] Accordingly, his account of princely motivation does not appeal to an understanding of the *moral* virtues, and it expressly repudiates the relevance of such an understanding for the prince and for our appreciation of how he must act. Nonetheless, Machiavelli advances a position that has a basic structural equivalence to virtue ethics, but he expressly relates the concept of *virtú* to the domain of politics, treating politics and its associated elements and practices as the appropriate frame of reference for the evaluation of conduct. What we have then is not a general theory of the virtues derived directly from an account of human well-being, but a political theory in which a specific range of virtues or qualities of character are necessary for the establishment and maintenance of political rule. This rule is necessary to secure what is distinctively human and fine in life, yet *virtú* is defined, not directly by these goods, but by the distinctive qualities needed to establish the order within which these goods can be attained.

Does this help us to understand how Machiavelli's motivational account works? As we have seen, the prince's actions must be directed by a desire to form and order his state, which prompts the question of why princes are so motivated. One could suggest that princes are men of ability with a distinctive will to power that they exercise in the struggle to establish their state. This theory sits uncomfortably with Machiavelli's own love of politics, but a more basic objection is that it appeals to a motivation that is wholly external to politics itself. A more promising route is to see the prince's motivation as intrinsic to politics: in a world of constant individual, group, and interstate competition that threatens us with chaos, men and women with certain abilities and capacities are able to recognize the challenges that politics poses and to respond appropriately. Like the classical virtues, the range of reasons relevant to each virtue will differ—a poor man elicits compassion and charity; a generous act elicits our gratitude; the exposure of others to danger elicits courage; and so on. Machiavelli felt that these general relations between a situation and our appreciation of the right spirit in which to respond were not well-known in politics; indeed, were systematically misrepresented in the "Mirror for Princes" genre and in the classical texts to which he implicitly refers.[18] What he offered instead was a series of discussions of different (historical) contexts and of appropriate and inappropriate responses to them. He often describes the actions these situations should (and occasionally do) call forth rather than identifying the particular quality or character trait it should elicit, and thus demonstrates how the politically alert man or woman responds to such challenges. If we understand the significance and urgency of politics, we will also understand that *virtú* is exemplified in being alert and responsive to the imperatives of political life, in identifying with its ends, and in recognizing that there is something fine and noble in establishing a state and ordering a community. Just as we need some of the virtues to recognize the ethical virtues of others—unless we have a sense of generosity ourselves we will not comprehend what others are doing when they act generously—so too we need some sense of the political and its dynamics and practices to appreciate the *virtú* of others in that domain, and to appreciate what drives them. It seems undeniable that Machiavelli himself had that sense, and that he wrote in part to emphasize it and to elicit its recognition in others.

In his *Short History of Ethics*, Alasdair MacIntyre points to the fact that Machiavelli, in contrast to Plato and Aristotle and other predecessors, treated the natural condition of the state as one of turmoil.[19] Starting from that position one must recognize that to achieve anything of value there needs to be a degree of order, a basic level of security for those involved, and an institutional framework within which more complex and subtle relationships and practices can develop. In this sense a whole range of human values, from freedom through to "the good life," are seen as the products of political orders and as conditional on its existence. For someone who sees the world in this way, politics and *virtú* have causal, and thus normative, priority over other virtues and values. This does not mean that politics and *virtú* are incompatible with other values, in many respects working for the establishment of the political order is a case of working to secure the conditions for other values, but (being conditional on politics) those other values cannot act as categorical constraints on politics, and the gentler virtues cannot be too deeply rooted in the characters of those who act in politics. Machiavelli essentially offers an account of how and why politics and morality are in significant ways disjoint. One difficulty facing those who think in this way lies in identifying the appropriate lexicon with which to describe and assess the conduct of those in public office. The use of the term *virtú* by Machiavelli, and the entirely appropriate reluctance on the part of some translators to give it another form, speaks directly to this difficulty. Nonetheless, in the assessment of political leaders and princes, despite MacIntyre's suggestion that Machiavelli judges actions solely in terms of consequences, it is clear that the prince's character and agency matter.[20] We may find the outcome of the prince's rule commendable, but that commendation is for the prince and his *virtú*. Moreover, *virtú* is surely the right coinage for the evaluation of political conduct: consequences may matter greatly, but it is by attaching consequences to agency that we turn brute causal facts into matters of praise or blame. That which no one could prevent or bring about is a matter of regret only in a very abstract way.[21] The political elements that we are most fundamentally concerned with are what people recognize as required; what they try to bring about; what they actually achieve; what qualities and resources they bring to the task; how well-formed their conception of that task is, and with what motives, qualities, and commitment they pursue it. To the extent that we are concerned with these aspects of political conduct, we are concerned with attributes of character, thought, analysis, and agency—qualities of character and agency that warrant the term *virtues*. At the same time, that these qualities may include cunning and flexibility, and may require cheating and lying, simply reproduces the tension between *virtú* and virtue that Machiavelli willfully introduced, raising starkly the question of how far and in what ways a theory of political *virtú* can cohabit with a theory of the virtues in general.

To broach that question we need to look more closely at what it is that makes something a virtue and ask how far political virtues can draw on the same sources of support or foundations as the more commonly discussed moral virtues.

A natural starting point for the examination of virtue is Aristotle's *Ethics*. Rather than presenting his account of the virtues, my aim is to focus on his discussion of what it is that distinguishes a virtue from a skill, and whether the kinds of things that Machiavelli talks about in terms of *virtú* should be understood as wholly a matter of skill or political craft *(technē)*. Is *virtú*, like *technē*, simply a set of abilities that people may or may not have that enables them to achieve certain ends when applied well and result in failure when applied badly? If so, they seem to have little ethical weight, since the ethical assessment would attach not to the abilities but to the decisions made to exercise them on a particular occasion and to their outcomes. If they are to be recognized as virtues, in what sense are they virtues, and how do such political virtues mesh with, if at all, the more normal range of moral virtues invoked within ethical theory? Many are prepared to follow Aristotle in thinking that there is an essential consistency to the virtues such that if we are lacking in one area it has consequences for our conduct in other areas, and in thinking that the coherence and objectivity of the virtues links the virtuous life to the good life *(eudaimonia)*. However, the view that political *virtú* may be in tension with moral virtue directly challenges that thesis.

Aristotle is clear that there is a distinction to be drawn between activities associated with a craft and those associated with a virtue, even if there are controversies about some of the more sophisticated dimensions of the distinction. Behavior that involves craft skills or virtuous action expresses knowledge rather than being accidental or serendipitous; however, Aristotle goes on to say that "the products of a craft determine by their own character whether they have been produced well; and so it suffices that they are in the right state when they have been produced."[22] For actions expressing virtue, both the action *and* the agent must be in the right state. A craftsman may be grumpy, debauched, or ill-willed and still produce a product that meets the highest standard of his craft, but a virtuous act must be undertaken with the right commitments: the agent "must know that he is doing virtuous actions; he must decide on them for themselves; and he must do them from a firm and unchanging state."[23] In a craft, Aristotle explains, knowing how to do something counts for everything, whereas in virtue that element counts for much less than the other two conditions; that is, the person is consciously committed to the rightness or goodness of acting in a certain way, and the commitment is a firm and unchanging one. The commitment to the act—knowing that one is doing virtuous actions and deciding on them for themselves—is a complex one. It sounds over intellectual, as if we have reflected in depth about what it is for something to be virtuous and are doing the virtuous act because it is the virtuous thing to do.[24] In fact, the core idea is that the virtuous person is someone whose character is such that he or she does the virtuous thing in a situation, and does it because it appears to be the fitting thing to do (and thus what one ought to do). As suggested earlier, when we act courageously we do not choose courage as the preferred course of action because it is virtuous to be brave; rather, our reaction to a situation is one that exemplifies our courage, about which we may be more or less articulate. We can make sense of the concern that the action is for its own sake by emphasizing that it is not chosen for some other reason but is done as the appropriate thing to do in that context (hence the need for others to have at least some of the virtue themselves in order to appreciate the aptness and value of the act). In other words, when people act virtuously they do what they think is fitting—where what is fitting is not deduced from abstract principles but is a matter of reacting to the particular features of the situation and responding emotionally, intellectually, and practically to those facts in ways that give them due weight. Of course, there may be a chain of actions (for example, I sell x to buy y to make z that I sell so as to be able to repay A to whom I owe money), but what makes the sequence just is if, and in so far as, I do so because I am committed to repaying my debt as the right and proper (not simply the prudent) thing to do.[25]

In Aristotle's writings the virtuous man acts in ways that are in themselves noble or fine.[26] It is not just that we value the outcome of an action, it is also that the action itself has a quality, is itself fine or noble, that is the more lasting and highest valuation of the act. The difficulty for Machiavelli's account now seems clear, since many of the things that he commits princes to are not easily so described. Eliminating one's enemy is not, for the most part, a fine and noble thing in itself, nor are lying and cheating. However, it matters greatly what description an act falls under. It may be noble to commit oneself, responsibly and conscientiously, to building a state even if the actions falling under that description include lying, cheating, and involve a certain brutality. Seen in this way, we might take Aristotle's suggestion that the agent is concerned not just with honor but with the excellence to which honor is justly paid, as itself furnishing the parallel to the idea that the exercise of a virtue is, in itself, fine and noble. When we classify the prince's acts, not in terms of lying and cheating, but in terms of actions that exemplify the excellences of character and judgment to which honor is justly paid by those who understand the demands of politics, we can see them as, to some degree, intrinsically fine or noble.[27]

Aristotle's final clause about the commitment being a firm and un-changing one rules out those who may do the right thing, and may do it for the right reasons, but who have no firm grip on their emotions and rea-soning—and so may do something very different on the next occasion. This clearly detracts from their virtue, whereas a craftsman who is distracted from his craft on an occasion is not thought any less skilled for that. *Akrasia* (weakness of the will) affects our judgment of a person's virtue; whereas we judge the skilled man in terms of the products he makes.

In judging how much Machiavelli's *virtù* is really just a collection of skills or technical abilities, rather than virtues, we must recognize that, in making a judgment about a politician, we want to move past his particular actions to assess his character. We want to know not just what he did and with what consequence, but in what spirit and with what end. Consider, for ex-ample, a political leader who inaugurates a redistributive system of taxa-tion, not because he is committed to the justice of the scheme (because I want to leave more familiar moral virtues to one side), but because he sees it as a way of strengthening the middle class at the expense of the rich, which he sees as a necessary prerequisite for diminishing class tensions within society, thus facilitating orderly political rule. If we share his analysis of the situation we are likely to praise his shrewdness. Moreover, our sense of his shrewdness might be increasingly compounded by the other measures he takes, or may be undermined by the extent to which he adopts contra-dictory and incoherent policies. Knowing how to act, being committed to the spirit of the act, and showing a firm commitment to acting in this way are all characteristics we might find in a politician and that provide the basis for a judgment of character and thus of virtue. Nonetheless, we are not making any claim about the person's general moral virtues. In Machiavelli's view, the politician may not display many of the traditional moral virtues simply because the thing to which he is most fundamentally committed, re-sponding to the exigencies associated with the establishment and consolida-tion of political rule, does not allow him the luxury of such virtues as benevolence, gratitude, and friendship. Indeed, Machiavelli's case is cer-tainly that the ruler cannot have these as inflexible attributes of his char-acter, since to be firm in one's commitment to them would be to leave one-self dangerously exposed.

In Aristotle's account, someone who knows what to do, is committed to acting in this way for its own sake, and shows a firm and unwavering com-mitment to acting in this way demonstrates a deeply rooted quality of character. But what makes that quality a virtue? According to Aristotle it is because it has this structure, because implicit in this structure is a role for reasoning in choosing an act for its own sake that connects with the disposition on the part of the agent to act in a certain (virtuous) way, and because the act itself is fine or noble.[28] The role of practical reasoning is central to ensuring that the various dispositions of the agent hang together in a way that makes for a harmonious whole, rather than in an internally contradictory way, and it is also underpinned by an objective account of the human good. The problem for *virtú* is twofold: it is unclear how *virtú* connects to the good of the agent; and it demands conduct that clashes directly with many traditional virtues that are directly linked to the agent's good. Neither problem, however, is unique to Machiavelli. The recognition, for example, that the virtues enjoined by Homer, Aristotle, Benjamin Franklin, and Jane Austen are often widely at variance with each other raises prospects of a plurality of conceptions of virtue and of the agent's good and of a clash between claims as to which virtues are to be held as fundamental.

In his discussion of the virtues, which acknowledges the substantial differences in the way the virtues are conceived in these different traditions, Alasdair MacIntyre argues that to make claims about the virtues intelligible, we need to recognize the practices within which a virtue operates, to grasp the narrative order of a single human life, and to identify the moral traditions within which these two components must be embedded.[29] MacIntyre's account is well-known and I make no attempt here to convey it fully, but certain features are helpful in grasping the distinctiveness of the political virtues and the way we assess those who act in politics (although doing so goes against MacIntyre's account). The first element of value is the idea of a *practice*—an activity that involves standards of excellence as well as the achievement of goods, but where at least some of the goods achieved are internal to the practice. The idea of goods internal to practices is that it is only by engaging in a practice and absorbing its rules and standards that one comes to appreciate fully the nature of the activity and the values or qualities that it realizes for those engaged in it—independently from the external goods it realizes. For MacIntyre, virtues are "the human qualities the possession and exercise of which enable us to achieve those goods which are internal to practices."[30] Those practices may also secure external goods such as wealth and power, but we exhibit the virtues in valuing the practice for the internal goods it brings, and we reveal our vices in so far as we allow our participation in the practice to be suborned by our desire for external goods.

Weber's recognition of the sense of "holding in one's hands a nerve fibre of historically important events," and the sense of one's standing with others, both count as such internal goods.[31]

The practice, which is MacIntyre's first step, helps meet the concern about Machiavelli's *virtú* failing to connect with a theory of the good, and it also shows why *virtú* can be seen as more than a skill, but it leaves open the prospect of multiple, competing practices (and thus a fragmentation of the virtues) that lack an overview or sense of the *telos* of a whole human life that would allow us to compare and evaluate different practices and make judgments about what life (involving what practices) it is best to live. MacIntyre's resistance to that fragmentation leads him to take the further steps of invoking the concept of the unity of an individual life, so that the virtues cut across the spheres in which people act and the roles they fill to provide a coherent sense of the person, not simply as an agent with certain skills, but as someone whose individual commitments become intelligible when set against the narrative of his or her life, and where that life, in turn, is grounded through the traditions of the society that the individual inhabits. In this way, the virtues that arise in practices become generalized into features—not just of their participation in an activity but of them as people— and their commitments as people gain intelligibility when set against the traditions of the societies whose roles, institutions, and practices they inhabit.[32]

While there does seem a basic coherence brought to the virtues by practical reasoning in respect to such traditions, where they exist, an equally powerful case can be made (was made, I am arguing, by Machiavelli) for the view that the political virtues hang together in the same sort of way, but without such traditions. Politicians with these virtues are alert to what it is possible and necessary to do, what costs must be borne, what is expedient, what is essential, and what is irrelevant to the creation and maintenance of political rule. There may be other ways of life with their virtues, as Berlin suggested, but for Machiavelli the *virtú* of the prince is dedicated to rule, and within the frame of that set of practices the demands of practical reason cohere independently of other moral virtues.[33]

To see politics as an activity that is in part constitutive of the social order, and constitutive also to some degree of the traditions and narratives within which people understand their lives, is to see it as partly outside that order. The creative agency of the prince is incompletely framed by existing norms and practices, to the extent that, while many of those who have some sense of the demands of political rule will be able to understand the prince's achievements (or failures), they may only do so after the fact. We may share a sense of the just thing to do, or of what gratitude demands, but Machiavelli's insight is that, in many instances, what the prince does is to make an outcome simultaneously imaginable and possible—to make it desirable by making it actual. In appreciating the personal qualities that enable him to do that, we recognize in him a range of political virtues. *Normal* politics suggests something closer to MacIntyre's sense of a practice framed by tradition, but that view might also be resisted. The practices of modern democratic politics are often complex and demanding: to secure office, to turn power into authority, to achieve specific political goals, and to sustain one's tenure against rivalries, opposition, and public opinion all take a range of skills. These skills are not simply a matter of technical know-how, they also involve a secure grasp of the way the order and the deeper demands of politics work; a capacity to absorb, weigh, and respond to information; and the ability to *inhabit* the system—to find it intelligible and challenging, to recognize the values it is capable of achieving, and to rise to those demands. Thus far this sits comfortably enough with MacIntyre, but the more we emphasize that politics is fundamentally concerned with competing interests and competing values and normative commitments, the less available it seems is a narrative and tradition capable of sewing together such practices into a whole. Indeed, it is MacIntyre's more polemical thesis that modernity has lost the integrity of traditions and narratives that allow a coherent language of the virtues to be spoken, and Machiavelli's point that these are conditions that routinely face politicians. Even normal politics is a practice that, through the actions and commitments of its participants, makes objectives and goals normative for people, to give them a sense of what might be shared. In doing so, politicians play a creative role in people's lives that can lead us to judge them as having demonstrated precisely the strength of commitment and character that is central to our recognition of their political virtue.

MacIntyre's concept of a *practice* offers us a way of thinking about Machiavelli's concept of political activity and agency. To fully engage in a practice one has to absorb the rules and standards of the practice, come to identify with the ends served by it, and come to grasp through experience the intrinsic goods secured by it. Machiavelli is far from suggesting that there are no standards in politics; rather, his point is that these standards are not in the form of strict rules—for example, to tell the truth, abide by the law, be just in all one's dealings, and so on. The standards relate to the demands and responses that are embedded in the practice of politics, and we need to be thoroughly steeped in the practice of politics to recognize these demands, to see their point, to become adept at knowing how and when to respond to them, to develop a sense of how to act and to what ends, and to appreciate the intrinsic satisfactions associated with the practice of politics and the shaping of the world in which we live. Machiavelli did not himself tie such conceptual matters down very firmly, but there is no doubt he wrote fully aware that politics was the very ether of his own life—hence his desolation at his exclusion from Florentine politics by the Medici, and his willingness to court favor by every possible means so as to pave the way for his return.

This account of the practice of politics has parallels with the distinction that Bernard Williams draws between thin and thick ethical concepts. A *thick* ethical concept is one in which, at a general level, issues of truth and relevance cannot be separated "since you cannot make the judgements without having the concept, and you have the concept only if you do count such considerations as relevant in deliberation."[34] Machiavelli's concepts of *virtú, gloria, fortuna, occasione,* or *necessità* provide examples of this, as does his use of the term *corruption.* The same blending of descriptive and prescriptive elements comes with a range of other Machiavellian concepts: cunning, courage, determination, flexibility, and so on. To underline a point made earlier, we have to have a sense of that world and its challenges to grasp the full meaning and the practical implications of these concepts. Unlike MacIntyre, however, we do not need to see this as a practice, consolidated by tradition. It is, in part, the very fragmentation of the world that makes the challenges of politics so urgent, even as it robs it of a framework that might restore a completely integrated moral world to us.

I have framed this discussion of politics and the virtues around Machiavelli, largely because his position is one that offers many insights into how we might understand the relationships among politics, conduct, and the virtues—in ways that resist direct consequentialism. Nonetheless, Machiavelli's is a particular account, drawing extensively on classical sources and the experience of contemporary Italian city-states, and it is very much a creature of that context.[35] As such, his account of politics and *virtú* is a local account, rather than one applicable in detail to every political order; indeed, for all his knowledge of classical literature, his grasp on the rather different structures, mores, and imperatives of the politics of the Roman republic failed (I would suggest) to help him see the extent to which Caesar's conduct was a response to the different but still powerful set of demands and imperatives of the late republic. It is tragic that Caesar could not escape these demands and that in meeting them he helped bring about the demise of the republic, but it seems difficult to justify failing to acknowledge his deeply rooted Roman political virtues—even if we recognize that these ceased to aid him once he had broken the mold and assumed personal rule.

How far can we meaningfully generalize about politics beyond the immediate confines of each particular context—either Machiavelli's or Rome's—each with its various thick ethical concepts? In the next chapter I address this concern by identifying a number of broad features of political rule, although the instantiation of these general features always has a distinctive local character. I also examine the issue of how far it is possible to move from the discussion of agency embedded in practices to a more general evaluation of particular political orders. In Chapter 4 I will return to the practicalities of political virtue in more detail.

CHAPTER 3

The Character of Political Rule

To help ground claims about the virtues of those in politics, and to justify the claim that we are dealing with something deeper than a set of technical or craft skills on the part of politicians, we need a better sense of the character of political rule and political conduct and we need to identify what is distinctive to political activity and what demands it makes on its practitioners. We also need a grasp of when and under what conditions politics and its virtues exhaust their ethical content. Of course, there will be considerable contextual variation, but the intelligibility of claims for political virtue across contexts is sustainable only with something like this underpinning. In this chapter I argue that politics involves, in part, the attempt to exercise authority, and that it does so as a way of resolving or limiting conflict in one or more of four dimensions. I argue that these two elements give political conduct a consistency of depth across different practices and contexts that justify the use of the term *virtue*.

When most modern political scientists and constitutional theorists think about political rule it is predominantly as a mode of authority, and they do so primarily in terms of the regular exercise of formal and legal-rational authority over men and women who would not otherwise have clear incentives to act as they are commanded. These two components seem fundamentally right—that political rule involves at least some claim to authority, and that part of what makes rule political is that it is exercised over others who are not inevitably compliant. In contrast, brute force determines outcomes but it does so coercively, not authoritatively. It is integral to political rule to invoke at least some claim to authority and thereby to legitimacy and a corresponding right to rule. Those who rule politically expect compliance from those they rule not simply because they are able to make compliance the prudent course of action (although they may also use incentives and sanctions to ensure compliance), but because they claim a right to rule, which implies some recognition of this on the part of citizens. The core aspiration of political authority, and the condition of its intelligibility as a distinct set of claims, is a relationship of command and compliance where compliance is elicited not by threats, persuasion, or incentives, but by the subject or citizen acknowledging that those who rule have a right to do so.[1] Reasons for conforming may abound, but we respond to someone's authority when we acknowledge that he or she has a right to our compliance. Some forms of traditional, charismatic, or familial forms of authority may rest on habit, custom, or essentially implied claims, but authority becomes expressly political in character when it invokes a more or less explicit claim that the right to rule rests on some specific or principled ground (for example, it may appeal directly or indirectly for its authorization to our consent, or make claims of justice, fairness, public utility, welfare, or the common good as its justification). These principles may themselves be clothed in other garb such as nationalist sentiment, historical tradition, and common culture, but such particularist claims will not be entirely free from more abstract principles.

The view that political relations are authority relations that involve (even if they are not exhausted by) a claim of the right to rule—grounded in a general, public-regarding justification—is closely related to the distinction, at least as old as Plato and Aristotle, between personal and political forms of rule. The rule of a despot or tyrant is personal: he treats his state as his personal property for disposal as he sees fit, and his capricious will is the only form of rule. The limits set by the theoretical construction of personal rule led to the development of a contrasting set of norms for and claims about the distinctive character of political rule. This understanding took a more prominent and public form when the distinction between the king *qua* person and the crown as the sovereign institution developed in the public language of rule.[2] In practical terms, personal rule weakened as rulers found some benefits to the institutionalization and delegation of certain functions, a process often hastened as royal power became subject to countervailing forces within the state that had to be conciliated by acknowledging limits on the extent of the ruler's authority.

Political rulers may crave unlimited power, but in seeking to legitimate their commands and make them authoritative rulers become in part hostage to the norms and principles to which they appeal (and to the expectations generated among those whom they rule). Legitimacy ceases to attach wholly to the person of the prince and becomes associated with the offices and the institutions of the state—with the office being referenced to broader normative claims (such as the public good) even if its occupancy is settled in more communal fashion (for example, by hereditary right or tradition). In this way, to claim the right to command increasingly invokes an authority that attaches to an office that the agent fills. This "routinization" sharpens the potential disjunction between the interests of the individual who holds office and the responsibilities associated with that office by recognizing formal rules and norms for politics that can act as a critical standard against which to assess the conduct of those who rule.

The referencing of rule to certain public and institutional norms has given political discourse a distinctive character. Once the office is distinguished from the holder, and the authority is identified with the former, the legitimation and justification of political rule comes to be couched in terms of the distinctive rights and responsibilities of the political body in relation to its subjects or citizens. With this development, political activity becomes structured by the need to secure and exercise authority in ways that command consensual compliance (although how widely authority is sought and can be legitimated will vary considerably from context to context), and by the formal and informal rules and norms governing political office and its accompanying powers. These considerations set out, in broad and abstract terms, the character of the political game and the rules that attach to playing it—both with reference to the struggles to secure political power and with respect to the exercise of political rule. In advanced Western constitutional orders, a great deal of political activity is highly structured and very much the creature of procedure, principle, and a shared framework of norms for the exercise of public office.

Few political orders and their accompanying principles and norms, however, are unconditionally authoritative in their territory. Depending on how inclusive the political system is, there may be groups whose domination and/or exclusion leaves the legitimacy of the order still partial, although it may not be especially fragile as a result, and any system may face attempts to impose a fundamental reconfiguration of the political order and a reconstruction of its patterns of authority and legitimacy. The very process of exercising authority, and the skills of those who exercise it, may enhance, perfect, or damage the legitimacy of their claims. Any given set of political norms and principles have a conditional character because political orders are the complex products of will and circumstance, crosscut with claims and counterclaims to authority and legitimacy, thereby ensuring that the full character of political rule cannot be exhaustively enumerated by reference to a particular set of "rules of the game." Furthermore, political systems vary considerably (across regimes and within regimes over time) in the extent to which such principles have become routinized and widespread, rather than simply being projected in the exercise of power in an attempt to make them normative for others. Clearly the process by which principles and norms are produced and interpreted is a complex dynamic in which political rule and the innovative agency of those acting in politics can play a major role, not just in new states but, potentially, in any state given certain conditions.

What complicates the task of understanding authority in politics is this combination of formal components, in which bureaucratic offices exercise sharply defined responsibilities and powers, and more potentially disruptive dimensions in which authority is not a given of office but an element forged in the political process. Thus, Machiavelli's prince wins glory by securing his state by transforming the naked exercise of power into an institutionalized order that is able to command authority over its subjects and secure legitimacy only *ex post*. With Weber, the state begins simply as a body of armed men. We should not be tempted to think that Machiavelli offers us a distinction between a kind of "revolutionary" politics, on the one hand, and "normal" politics on the other[3] (for example, between a dramatic and creative form of agency that revolutionizes or overturns an order and outlines the structure and lines of a new order, and the detailed and regulated flow of political business within an order whose form is essentially fixed and in which innovative agency is largely excluded and routinized). Were this so, it would be only at the founding of states that political agency and leadership would play an independent role in determining the kinds of norms and values that can be realized. Once founded, political orders could efficiently pursue sets of ends, call for particular virtues from its practitioners, and provide an ordered domain within which these values could be systematically realized. In fact, Machiavelli's *Discourses* certainly does not encourage such a view: political life is always potentially fragile, even if the new prince is uniquely exposed to *fortuna* and if his political order is largely a function of his own agency. Even if Machiavelli cannot be so categorized, it is clear that many modern political scientists do think of the political system as being precisely a systematic organization of rules, norms, and principles for political decision making that is relatively free from the vagaries of individual agency or innovation.

When David Easton described politics as "the authoritative allocation of values for a society," he characterized politics as revolving essentially around the policy-making process.[4] The reference to the allocation being authoritative is surely right but it opens up his formula to a broader set of concerns about the dynamics underlying command and compliance. Easton was reticent, for the most part, about the nature of authority—emphasizing the dimension of compliance—yet attempts to forge and secure, consolidate, deepen, and exercise authority constitute at least as significant a part of the political process as the particular values and objectives pursued by those in authority. Moreover, there is a systematic dimension of political rule that pushes the limits of regulated authority and plays a positive, creative, and projective role with respect to the establishment, exercise, and legitimation of that rule. Authority is central to political rule, and central to its development of a broader legitimacy and stability, but it is also intricately linked to political agency. While it regulates that agency, it is also in turn shaped and structured by it. Indeed, at times, it may be wholly a creation of such agency. What we should learn from Machiavelli is not that there are two dramatically different types of political order, one concerned with innovative action aimed at establishing a regime and the other concerned with the routines of rule-governed decision making within an essentially consensual order, but that in any and every political system, political agency and innovation remain components, and they remain so especially with respect to creating and consolidating (or, indeed, challenging) the authority and legitimacy of the political order and of those who rule in it.

Many contemporary liberal political theorists have attempted to identify the fundamental principles upon which a just and free society should be founded, but rather little thinking has focused on how to realize those principles in real world states. In contrast, a theory of political agency and rule recognizes that such principles must be activated in politics through the will and agency of men and women in processes that draw on both rational and nonrational, principled and nonprincipled elements, and that these play a partly constitutive role in the forging of the political ideals and values by which they justify their claim to authority. The exercise of political rule involves precisely the attempt to create possibilities and realize them—to render the dead weights of history, inertia, and structure subject to political will. What is politically possible is neither pre-given (wholly framed by formal principles and procedures and conditioned by causal constraints) nor entirely open; it is something that political agency helps determine by uniting under its authority elements that would otherwise be in conflict and by overcoming divisions to achieve a common order, by engendering a collective will, or by securing agreement on practices and principles by which to regulate their conflicts and their common affairs. One major factor in determining what is politically possible is what those ruling can legitimate and render authoritative. The less demanding their aims, the less widely they need be legitimated to be implemented; the fewer and more similar the competing agendas, the easier the task, and vice versa. Demanding agendas are a function jointly of context and ambition, where success involves the ability to resolve those conflicts and divisions that stand in the way of securing those objectives authoritatively.

Through their political conduct men and women play the role of an independent causal variable in the explanation of political events. As such political agency implies a degree of autonomy—the actor is not simply a victim of forces and pressures around him and beyond his control, nor simply a transparent vehicle for the expression of antecedent norms and principles. Agency can be compromised by others' control of incentives and constraints, to the point that policy is effectively directed by agents other than those formally responsible. It can be subverted if the actions of others foreclose all but one option for the actor or if the decisions of the actor are not implemented or are otherwise derailed so as to remain ineffective. While political agency can be enhanced by appeals to principles and norms that secure it legitimation, the enhancement of authority does not move hand in hand with subordination to principles and procedures, since these can diminish and narrow the legitimacy of those who rule and can sometimes immobilize them. Political systems can become rule-bound, overregulated, and destructively inefficient. There is no natural and obvious balance between innovation and agency and the factors that routinize and regulate that agency. Because of this there is in political rule an almost inevitable pressure to push its current limits; that is, to use principles and procedures opportunistically, and to look for ways to elude the limits so as to free up new areas of activity that one might seek to legitimate in new ways. Hence Machiavelli's sense that claims to authority are often projective in character—they are bids against the pressures and constraints of the system that, if successful, allow the agent to overcome these obstacles and to determine

the actions of others by securing endorsement *ex post*. Authority enables political agency, but political agency also creates and sustains authority since it
is in part forged through the projection of claims and principles that those
who rule are able to make normative for their subjects or citizens. Moreover, the term *forged* captures precisely the sense that the innovative ruler
falsifies in claiming an authority he does not have, and yet (if successful),
makes that falsification true by securing legitimacy for his conduct.

Gaining political power and ruling are related but distinct activities. As we
have seen, those who gain political power against huge odds, such as
Caesar, are not necessarily well equipped to exercise it. The innovative style
and virtuosity of the prince may not be well suited to the more prosaic tasks
associated with rule—hence the tendency of the great legislators to do their
work and move on.[5] In more institutionalized systems, the principles by
which political office is allocated need to remain congruent with the way
that political rule is conducted and legitimated. Two central concerns for
popular forms of government are how far the contest for office weakens the
authority of that office, and whether the office is exercised in order to hold
on to power rather than to address the responsibilities of rule. In these and
a number of other ways the authority of institutions can be weakened or
misused, but the attempt to create and exercise political power remains the
basis of all political rule that meets a minimum standard of competence.

If one element of political rule concerns the attempt to exercise authority,
another arises because authority is exercised over men and women who are
not naturally inclined to act as it commands in its absence. Anarchist
utopias aside, political authority has a point because (and insofar as) there
would be disorder, conflict, or chaos without it, and because it can realize
goods that are unrealizable without coordinated action. Moreover, the
ubiquity of conflict (and the potential for it) and the need for coordination
justifies the continuing role for political agency, even within apparently
well-ordered societies. Of course, it is a common assumption within liberal
political thought that the function of the political order is to resolve conflict.
Rawls's *Political Liberalism*, for example, offers us a way of thinking about the
political order as a system that provides for a basic structure in society that
can be endorsed by all its members, despite the fact that they are divided in
their conceptions of the good and their chosen plans of life. Rawls starts by
stipulating that his society will be extremely homogenous and that any pluralism is "reasonable," and, I would suggest, by underestimating the poten-

tial lines of conflict that may affect societies.[6] Nonetheless, Rawls shares with a long liberal tradition the aspiration that politics will serve to order all such conflict authoritatively; that is, in a way that commands the willed compliance of those it rules. The issue is how much we can generalize about the sources or forms of conflict that face political orders so as to develop a sense of how far and under what conditions such an aspiration might be plausible, or to appreciate the extent to which brute power remains an irreducible element in political rule.

In the history of political thought it is possible to identify at least four broad dimensions of conflict that require political rule for their resolution and that have profoundly influenced Western understanding of the nature and ends of politics over the last several hundred years.[7] Each dimension uses politics as a solution to conflict and social disorder, but characterizes the threat, and thus the solution, in different ways. These conflicts comprise the variety of conditions that political rule must address. Although each position emphasizes a particular form of conflict, real world states face a number of these conflicts concurrently and it is often not possible simultaneously to order or resolve each authoritatively. Some of those conflicts issue in the use of force, and in some cases such conflicts extend to a resort to war. In other cases a political order may be able to legitimate its authority over only a very small proportion of their population; in a deeply divided state the balance between authoritative political rule and the exercise of power and coercion to maintain the subordination or acquiescence of sectors of the population may be heavily weighted toward the latter. The point of trying to rule politically is to use authority, not domination, to negotiate, conciliate, and further the interests of those within the state, rather than to seek to impose one set of interests over all others. That said, not every conflict can be resolved, nor every difference settled; domination is a recurrent element in most political systems, and while some cases are evidence of political failure, it also can be evidence of the intractability of the problems faced. And, as Caesar may finally have realized, systems of rule may collapse when they are no longer able to conciliate the conflicts and demands that their own success fosters. Political stability and order are not once-and-for-all achievements.

While the emphasis in this account is on the role of the state as the key political actor, it is possible to recognize politics at a suprastate level—where international politics is not analyzed reductively in terms of the joint or coordinated actions of individual states. Globalization has been much touted as evidence of a new era for national and international communities, but whether or not one is skeptical about the global character of politics, it is possible to see in this context a rather traditional set of concerns—with the management of conflict, the ordering of relations between global forces, the effect of trans-state activities on the lives and welfare of members of one's own nation-state, and the creation of a degree of collective action and coordination. There may be more governance than government, more conciliation and networking than authoritative imposition of rules and regulations, but the attempt authoritatively to allocate values continues. The same must also be said for substate entities. There is organizational politics, and community politics, and the personal also can be political. Conflict, and the negotiation and ordering of competing claims, occurs at numerous levels below the state, as well as above it. In referring to such domains as *politics* we implicitly present them as areas in which it is appropriate to establish authoritative and legitimated means for the recognition of claims, the regulation of conflicting interests, and the achievement of collective goods. In the establishment of those means, agency and innovation can play as constructive a role as in other domains of politics. Nonetheless, in what follows, I focus largely on conflicts that are ordered politically at the level of the state.

The four dimensions of conflict can be distinguished as follows. In the first, conflict is an inevitable consequence of the heterogeneous character of the social order, giving rise to class antagonisms, or to factions and groups competing for ascendancy. Such conflict results in disorder, exploitation, and domination (rule without willed compliance). Political rule uses institutions, rules, and procedures to acknowledge in part the interests of the various groups while subordinating their pursuit to regulation by a common authority. The stability of such an order rests on the ability of those in political office to get those subordinated to acknowledge the legitimacy of the rulers or rules that constrain the pursuit of their interests. The more the political order must rely on coercion to constrain groups, the less complete its political authority is and, in the long run, the more fragile it is. In some systems it is possible to secure such legitimacy only among a small subset of groups or interests in the state, with others being coerced. The concern with social conflict and the need to balance the various groups and classes within a common authoritative order is at least as old as the middle books of Aristotle's *Politics,* and plays a central role in Polybius and Machiavelli and in subsequent traditions of mixed government.

A second dimension of conflict is to be found in the struggle between individuals for ascendancy; the motivation for this may be variously understood, as in the equivocation in Thomas Hobbes between the motives of
competition, diffidence, and glory.[8] In this scenario the aim of politics is to
find solutions that substitute the sovereignty of the state with its creation
and protection of individual rights and liberties for the war of all against all.
In contrast to the class antagonism view, this account recognizes a basic instability in the relationship between individuals who require authoritative
ordering, to avoid outright conflict, and coordination, to secure certain basic
values or goods. In this case, political rule may attempt to secure legitimacy
by using the political order and the power to impose sanctions to create a set
of basic constraints on people's pursuit of their competing interests that
guarantees each a partial optimization of their interests; or, it may recognize
that the creation of a sovereign state is itself sufficient to ensure that people
will trust the state to defend their security rather than acting preemptively
and competitively with respect to one another. Either account can look to
Hobbes for support.[9]

In the third case the existence of institutions claiming public authority is
a source of conflict between those who rule and those who are ruled. Political authority, then, also involves organizing the public powers to avoid
conflict between those entrusted with public power and those subject to it.
The potential for those in public office to use their power, designed to resolve other conflicts, to advance their own interests and ends gives rise to a
set of concerns about how best to structure government and sustain its accountability so as to avoid it going rogue. Although these considerations
play a slight role in studies of mixed government, they play a more substantial role in theories of the separation of powers and checks and balances,
and in theories of political representation and accountability (in which the
aim is to ensure that power is exercised in ways that respect the constitutional constraints within which it was generated). Although Montesquieu is
generally recognized as having advanced the theory of the separation of
powers, it is much more in evidence in the Federalist Papers and subsequent constitutional theory.

The fourth type of fundamental conflict is that between units of sovereignty. From this perspective, politics is centrally concerned with the maintenance of sovereignty within a territory and/or over a nation-state, and the
practice of politics is irretrievably connected to negotiating and sustaining
that sovereignty in the face of competition from other groups or states. War

is always potentially a component of political rule. This derivation of politics is clearly presented in the work of late nineteenth-and early twentieth-century "decisionists"—most notably Carl Schmitt, for whom "The high points of politics are simultaneously the moments in which the enemy is, in concrete clarity, recognised as the enemy."[10] However, we may also argue that, perhaps especially for states in the developed West, there are aspects of international politics that go well beyond the assertion and defense of sovereignty and that raise issues about global justice and the responsibilities of states to their poorer neighbors. As global inequalities and differentials (some of which arise from the ecological damage inflicted by advanced economies) become an increasing source of conflict within the international community, they will have a growing impact on the exercise and defense of national sovereignty and on the further development of an international institutional order. Schmitt's account emphasizes the state against other states, whereas in the modern world it is clear that there are advantages to the development of an international economic, legal, and, in part, political order, but nations face major challenges in developing this in ways that do not preserve or create inequalities that will prove systematically destabilizing to both the order and to the individual states that play a leading part in it.

In each of these four perspectives, political rule is centrally concerned with the creation of order and the subordination of conflict. Most modern states face elements of each type of conflict and their political systems are effective only insofar as they successfully regulate these conflicts to produce conditions for the acceptance of their claims to authority. Indeed, failure to control and regulate these conflicts inevitably comprises political authority. We can see this still more clearly if we construct a matrix (Table 1) using four distinct areas where conflict can subvert political rule—in the access to or allocation of office; in the formation of policy; in the implementation of decisions; and in direct challenges to the authority of the state—and the four potential types of agent who may provoke conflict—individuals; groups, classes, or factions; members of the political order and the bureaucracy and administration; and competing powers or states. There are other possibilities than those indicated, such as the involvement of foreign powers in dynastic struggles to influence succession to the throne in medieval and early modern Europe or the kind of faction-based struggles around elected office and Tribunate and Senatorial decisionmaking in the late Roman Republic, for which the term *electoral malpractice* seems rather inadequate. The

Table 1. Dimensions of Conflict and the Subversion of Political Rule

		Area of subversion			
		Access to office	Controlling policy	Blocking implementation	Denial of legitimacy/ resistance
Agents in conflict	Individuals	Bribery, campaign funding, buying votes, nepotism	Inducements and threats directed at office-holders	Noncompliance/ free-riding	Lawlessness
	Factions/classes	Electoral malpractice, gang warfare, intimidation	Patronage/class rule	Noncooperation/ class war	Terrorism/revolutionary movements
	Bureaucrats/ élite	Raising thresholds of entry, exploiting access to public opinion	Oligarchy	Elision of formal controls	Coups
	Foreign powers	Funding of status quo or of subversives	Exploiting dependency or venality/ transnational state capture	Support for noncompliant groups	War

point of the matrix is to suggest the dimensions of conflict that require resolution if the political order is to rule authoritatively, rather than collapsing into the exercise of power on behalf of one individual, group, or class over all others. If political rule essentially concerns the creation and exercise of authority, then that authority is both rendered necessary by these forms of conflict and must offer a way of resolving such conflict that stands some chance of securing legitimation from those it regulates.

A further feature of political rule needs emphasis. The creation of a political system changes the context of action for members of a society. The establishment of a state, even the establishment of a body of armed men who seek to impose their will on others, dramatically affects the salience of existing conflicts and may generate new conflicts. Those who rule attempt to create order for a community through the establishment of institutions and by legislation and administration, but the very existence of such power will generate attempts to influence it by those subordinate to it and who hope to gain from doing so. The relationship between conflict and the political system is not, then, a case of a relationship between two independent factors—a problem and a solution. Rather, the components are interdependent, locked together within the particular history of the state in relation to its people, with the tasks that face a political order often being a legacy of its own past actions. That this is so inevitably complicates the nature of politics, the demands on political agency, and the task of evaluating political conduct. Men and women act against the background of a history in which the interaction between conflict and order generates distinctive problems and solutions that can be understood only historically and cannot be sidestepped.

The four dimensions of conflict provide us with something like a threshold for understanding politics. A theory that does not acknowledge the lines of conflict between social groups, the need for coordination, the threat from individual self-government, the potential abuse of power by the state, and that has no conception of the potential subversion of sovereignty from within or without will have no sense of the need for political rule and will have no standard by which to assess its exercise. When we recognize one or more of these fundamental forms of social conflict, we can see the motive for and challenge of political action, and the drive to establish an order that contains or resolves such conflicts. We can see why it is this "game" that needs to be played, and we get a sense of its point or purpose— that it attempts to end disorder and domination, to permit collective action, and to resolve conflict in a way that is not simply a case of one side winning. Moreover, we get a sense of why abilities in this area have normative weight and why political conduct needs to be understood in terms of virtues that track certain values rather than simply technical abilities that can be put to any end. There are more ambitious accounts of what politics might offer[11] (and some more negative ones),[12] and part of the complexity of the political struggle is that what is desirable and possible are themselves the subject of controversy and political agency, but even this rather minimal account recognizes that the qualities discussed above are properly understood as virtues.

Politics, then, is concerned with the ordering of conflict—albeit perspectives differ over what balance of *Recht* and *Macht* are required to achieve this. Even where, as with Schmitt, *Macht* is predominant, its purpose is to define an arena that is subsequently relatively free of the need for it.[13] The timeframe may be long-term and may involve actions that seem to run against this end (for example, revolutionaries who seek to accentuate class conflict as a necessary step in establishing an order that resolves all conflict) or that actually do so (for example, the means comes to eclipse the end by celebrating the struggle to the exclusion of the goals it was meant to serve). That political action may be derailed is inevitable, but the standard of assessment remains integral to the ends of political agency that I have indicated. Some liberal theories associate the conciliation of conflict and the delivery of security to citizens as the only appropriate ethical goal of politics; although this view can be attractive, we must not confuse the recognition that it is the nature of politics to be concerned with the establishment of authority under circumstances of conflict with the claim that the activity has ethical weight only as far as it constrains conflict optimally in terms of individual liberty.[14]

That conflict management and resolution are part of a much more complex story about the value and depth of politics is affirmed by the fact that there is a very basic issue about the relative urgency of these different conflicts and their amenability to control. Samuel Pepys's use of his office to indulge his nasty proclivities with the wives of those seeking employment may be of marginal significance where the central task of politics is to weld together the different interests and classes within a polity deeply divided between court and country, in which the civil service is an adjunct to a patronage machine designed to meet these purposes, and where the overriding concern is to finance the military activities of the crown in the international arena. In contrast, where the fundamental political problem involves arranging the exercise of legitimate authority without domination, or where domination is seen as the major source of harm in interpersonal relations, Pepys's activities would be condemned as a deeply corrupt extension of political power into the private sphere—corrupt because it is self-serving and arbitrary. Modern claims that the personal is political arise, in many cases, from the recognition that apparently consensual relations often conceal domination, exploitation, or otherwise demeaning relations sustained by the insidious and illicit exercise of power by one group over others. In these situations, activities that might otherwise be considered outside the political process can fundamentally challenge its legitimacy.

Furthermore, because the pressing need for political rule can be understood in quite different ways in any particular context, basic disagreements about the priorities faced and the actions that can be legitimated are endemic. For example, a state that takes Draconian action against an internal faction in defense of its sovereignty is open to challenge from interpretations driven by a distrust of power. While Machiavelli can celebrate Cesare Borgia's skill in dealing with Ramiro de Orca,[15] or Schmitt *might* have thought that it was necessary for Hitler to eliminate Ernst Rohm,[16] liberals concerned with the way that political power quickly becomes arbitrary and self-serving could see both as self-serving actions, designed to protect the ruler, not the office, and thereby as threatening to corrupt the character of true political authority. In clashes between such systematic interpretative commitments we face both the practical question of which imperatives must be settled to ensure the stability of the order, and the broader question of the desirability of the order that is stabilized. It is crucial to keep separate the question of whether an action stabilizes a system from the question of whether that system, however stable, has any merit. Moreover, even if it has merit there remains the issue of whether the outcome could have been effected more efficiently, or in forms and ways that are preferable on other grounds.

The underlying purpose of political action and struggle is its attempt authoritatively to manage and order conflict (or to introduce a system in which conflict is eliminated or moderated). Recognizing this acknowledges the depth and value of the fundamental purposes of politics and thereby warrants recognition of its best practitioners' virtues, but it does not directly resolve the issue of whether and to what extent any particular instance of such activity has ethical value.

There is no doubt that Machiavelli's sense of the fragility of political order and the need for exemplary and innovative political action offers some disturbing precedents. The rhetorically seductive celebration of the brutal mechanics involved in securing one's state tends rather to eclipse Machiavelli's own deeper sense of the nature and ultimate point of such activity—to impose order upon conflict and chaos and to lay the foundations for a *vivere civile e politico*. In subsequent generations, a few politicians, political philosophers, and apologists have been tempted down the road of such realism, usually coupling their theories with an indifference to the virtues that Machiavelli thought were necessary for those attempting to create and hold political office and to the ends that he sought ultimately to promote. If there are circumstances in which hard political decisions need to be made and heavy costs inflicted, we are better equipped to make such decisions if we recognize that the character of political activity and the values it pursues are just as often subverted as they are served when such decisions are made.

The wide range of practices that fall under the general description of politics include many that have the potential for excess. Insofar as the struggle to attain office becomes all absorbing—to the exclusion of concerns with retaining it or putting it to good use in the pursuit of certain ends—then the activity is clearly of diminished value and demonstrates a shortfall in vision and sense of proportion, but this does not warrant denying it the description *political*. Someone who has acted in this way, failing in some central way with respect to political virtue or *virtú*, would have a flawed character and this flow would be identified as arising from a failure, or set of failures on the agent's part, to respond to the demands of the political world in a way that sustained a recognition of the many dimensions of the activity and an awareness of the deeper aim and point of the activity. Yet their behavior still may be recognizably political. This tension between the descriptive and the normative is in large part a function of the recognition that while *politics* and *the political* are thick ethical concepts—involving both descriptive and evaluative judgments—the descriptive and the evaluative can part company. The political provides us with a context in which the commitments and activities of those who attempt to rule gain an intelligibility and can be associated with judgments of character through an assessment of how they see and respond to the demands of politics in a particular context. At the same time, there are cases in which political forms, institutions, and arenas of activity are exploited in ways that mimic or partially sustain the form of politics while becoming increasingly divorced from the commitments, reasoning, and ends that would render them intelligible and admirable as political activity. As such, they increasingly lose their ethical substance; they cannot be understood as expressions of political virtue; and the political form, if it is retained, is increasingly hollow.

Political rule attempts authoritatively to create order. It characteristically uses mobilization, organization, law, regulation, negotiated compromises, and systems of signalling, together with a certain degree of personal authority, claims to legitimacy, and, more often than not, some force or coercion. We can recognize politics in all these various forms, and we can recognize more and less intelligible forms of political action, just as we can recognize variations of a game or practice. Whether in any particular case the actions of those involved are judged to demonstrate political virtue will depend on a complex assessment of how far they respond to the demands of the situation in ways that sustain a recognition of the ethical substance of the practice and its ends.[17]

It is not difficult to see how something like Schmitt's concept of politics could be combined with virulent antisemitism to legitimate Hitler and Himmler's identification of a "Jewish Problem," and their search for a "solution" to it. What they eventually did (and much they did on the way) was grotesque and inhuman, but it is difficult to deny that it was undertaken in part through politics. It was political because they sought to adopt and extend existing forms of political authority, they relied on an array of traditional political institutions and mechanisms to achieve their ends, and they acted authoritatively. But even if the construction of the problem and the search for a solution was political in this sense, it was driven by a reading of the situation of the German state and its people in which blind prejudice, mythological fantasies, and paranoid fears, coupled with a fundamental disregard for any basic sense of humanity, led to an increasingly distorted set of political ambitions and an increasingly coercive political regime. The order retained (for a while, but with increasing tensions) a political form, but it was less and less concerned with securing its authority as opposed to establishing its domination. Recognizing that the order had a political form does not require that we think that those acting within that form were acting intelligibly in the light of the demands of the practice and the context, let alone acting in any exemplary or virtuous way. Even if a Schmittian perspective was a plausible reading of the condition of inter-war Germany and identified the single most pressing challenge facing the political system, it does not follow that the actions of those leading the state were thereby warranted. Other concerns about conflict and its ordering—a liberal concern about the misuse of public powers, or a republican concern about the dangers of faction and conflict between different elements of the social order, or a Hobbesian concern about life in conditions of fragmentation—suggest questions about the way in which the Nazi state functioned that challenge any claim that it was engaged in a process of responsible political rule. The secrecy with which the more abhorrent policies were carried out (the hospital experiments; the euthanasia program; the practices in the concentration camps and the conditions inflicted on forced migrant workers; the shooting of Russian Commissars; and, above all, the extermination of Jews, Poles, Romanies, and other groups) demonstrates that the state simply could not legitimate its activities, and would have forfeited its claim to a right to rule had its activities been made public.[18] Indeed, it is doubtful that it could have retained the allegiance of many of those who were central to the successful running of the state. What Himmler's address to the Gauleiter conference in Posen on 6 October 1943 shows is that Germany was being run by a cabal within the state—an inner state that had no publicly legitimated or legitimatable right to rule, that had succeeded through the use of terror in breaking all chains of responsibility to the broader political community. Moreover, those within that cabal (and those whom Himmler, with Hitler's agreement, sought to incorporate through that speech) had, as Hitler put it in 1943, burned their bridges.[19] Their conduct in office was such that they could not turn back, and their activities subsequently can be recognized as driven by the recognition that they could protect themselves only by adopting still more obscene and brutal measures. Their conduct becomes increasingly corrupt and repugnant as they tried to protect themselves by shoring up their power, covering their tracks, and attempting to limit their responsibility by implicating others. Many of those who worked in the state, without being privy to the more abhorrent aspects of Nazi policy, must have found themselves faced with questions about what was really happening and had to decide whether they should try to answer those questions. A great many, doubtless encouraged by the official doctrine of minding one's own business, likely found themselves compartmentalizing their activities to avoid these questions. In doing so, their judgments about their responsibilities as public officials and citizens became increasingly subverted, either from fear that forced them to deny any broader sense of public responsibility or by allowing themselves to indulge their prejudices and passions by sacrificing all critical assessment of the ends of their office. Either way, the allocation of values in the state became less and less transparent and authoritative, and more imposed by coercion and manipulation. Although some form of political rule was preserved in a few areas of the Nazi state, it was being rendered increasingly irrelevant to the real activities of those directing the state and those administering its activities in detail. As such it serves as an example of the progressive corruption and breakdown of the entire political order, and in doing so we can also see that instincts and capacities for brutality, backstabbing, and maneuvering were being exercised, not to the ends of political order and the legitimation of political authority, but to satisfy savage emotions, fears, and fantasies, and to meet the desire for power and its trappings irrespective of the character of the ends their actions ultimately served. If this started as a set of practices with political form, it quickly became deadly, coercive, and brutal, and increasingly lost intelligibility as a political order. Many who came to realize this did so only too late. If it is possible to attribute political virtues to a few in the beginning, by the end there is no such case to be made.

The example of the Nazi state is not unique. People have manipulated political orders to eliminate various peoples throughout history. It would be somewhat reassuring if the worst excesses in human conduct could be blamed on the collapse of political order, but that view is not tenable. The powers associated with political rule have been used systematically to eliminate class, ethnic, and other social groups both in the distant past and very much in the present.[20] As things move in this direction, however, it becomes increasingly incoherent to describe the relationship between the political order and its victims as political in character; rather, the order retains its internal political character by effectively denying that those it attacks have standing within its political community. This capacity to exclude people from the political order and thereby inflict costs that cannot be justified within the community is not new (quite the opposite, consider the Ancient Greek institution of slavery), and it underlies the common sense that political orders must be judged by some higher standard than those internal to the practice. While the potential for that moment of judgment must surely be preserved, the difficulty it faces is that, in the search for order and the establishment and exercise of political authority, the fixing of the boundaries of the state (with its identification of those included and those excluded from the state) is a legitimate issue and a legitimate object for political activity. To that extent boundary issues cannot be set by some standard external to politics but are central to the practice of political rule.

Political rule is a conditional good that can be put to good purposes or bad, but making such judgments is not simply a case of standing outside politics and adumbrating the standards we expect politics to meet. What is politically possible is a major constraint on what can be expected and thus on our assessment of people's political conduct. In the end those judgments must come down to appraisals of character, ambition, and motive, framed by an appreciation of the nature of the political system and the challenges that face those who seek to rule it. These judgments of political conduct will often have to concede much that a more universalist picture would be reluctant to concede; such as acknowledging that for generations war was considered a glorious activity, or an acceptable and justifiable instrument of policy in relations between states, or recognizing the extent to which the social and cultural system of a polity makes the integration or protection of foreigners unthinkable. We may judge such systems to a greater or lesser extent, unfortunate or abhorrent, but our judgments of the political conduct of those within such states cannot expect them to start from our own more "enlightened" judgments. How much ethical ballast there is for us outside the political order is equally contestable, but the core of my argument is that, in making judgments about political conduct, we have to start from the political context, the challenges that any competent political actor should recognize in that context, the obstacles and aspirations that set the agenda for the agent, and the abilities and commitments that he or she brings to the task. Our assessment must be directed to the virtues of agents in response to the demands of politics. We may not want to rest there, but to get to wherever else we want to go we have to ensure that our judgments could have been intelligible at some basic level to someone caught up in the particular political context we are examining. This is not an easy criterion to specify in detail, or to operationalize in practice. We know that when the political arena becomes corrupt many of the players become increasingly concerned with protecting their interests and maximizing their spoils, and in doing so develop an ethos that is resistant to acknowledging other, ethical, constraints on their conduct, but it is not difficult to deny them the distinction of the virtues. Political systems can also spiral into chaos and disorder, and under such conditions the task of making the ends of politics attractive to those picking over the carcass of the political system is likely to be a thankless one, yet it is difficult to claim that those ends would be literally unintelligible in all but the most parlous of states. Where things are that bad, those involved deserve our compassion, hard as it might be to give. There is no denying that politics can go badly wrong and identifying the point and norms of the local political game and trying to bridge between this and the more abstract and general criteria that I have identified as components of political rule is immensely complicated in such cases. Because this is so, few are willing to allow that such an approach provides the final word in the evaluation of political conduct, even if it is acknowledged as a starting point. Nonetheless, the difficulty in invoking other, external, standards is that these must themselves be grounded in some way and must enter the political arena, either international or domestic, and must function as a way of challenging the legitimacy of the actions of those in politics. That is, these standards must become elements in the political process at both national and international levels. Values may have origins outside politics, but in sofar as they are to make a difference to what people do in politics and to become a component in the assessment of their political virtue, it will only be by becoming integrated in people's conception of the nature and ends of politics, which is itself a partly political process. The nature of political rule certainly involves the depth of purpose that warrants our using the language of the virtues to describe the conduct of those who take that calling fully seriously—because of the ends that are served, because of the demands it makes on the characters of those involved, and because it is not clear that there is any firmer ethical ground on which to stand.

CHAPTER 4

Resolved to Rule

In friendship false, implacable in hate;
Resolved to ruin or to rule the state.

—*John Dryden,* Absalom and Achitophel, *lines 173–174*

Machiavelli's prince provides leadership. He instances a dramatic form of free agency that shapes and structures the world of which he is a part, rising above it to re-order it. In Machiavelli's account, there is little margin of error for the prince in both his ability to avoid disaster (a function of luck or *fortuna,* neither of which can be relied upon) and the virtuosity with which he handles the various conflicts (arising from ambitious individuals vying for dominance, conflicts between rich and poor, and from the predatory behavior of other states) that threaten to fragment his fragile state. He faces fewer problems with his administration because there is little of it, and it is crosscut with both class divisions and the ambitions of individual *grandi;* but, if he cannot get them to love him, he can always rely on fear. Beset by these conflicts, a prince must either shape his world or be crushed by it, he must work "directly, daily, personally, to produce and re-produce conditions of domination that are even then never entirely trustworthy."[1]

This type of political agency is anathema to much liberal political theory; it is unacknowledged by those who have sought to reinvigorate the classical republican tradition and demonstrate its relevance to modern democratic states;[2] and there is no theoretical space for it in more structuralist accounts of politics, despite the fact that Marxist regimes seem to have relied rather heavily upon it in practice. Even if Machiavelli's depiction of the extreme character of the prince's agency may be less relevant in the twenty-first century than it was in fourteenth-century Italy, it is undeniable that leadership remains a central feature of politics.[3] After a century in which specific individuals have consistently been identified with some of the most horrific and brutal behavior toward their people—not least (and certainly not exclusively) Adolf Hitler, Joseph Stalin, Idi Amin, and Pol Pot—and, by contrast, with those who contributed more positive experiences (even if these are often more contested)—such as that played by Mahatma Gandhi in Indian independence, by Nelson Mandela in South Africa's transition from apartheid, by Charles de Gaulle in the construction of a stable French republic, by Franklin D. Roosevelt in the restoration of confidence among the American people during the Great Depression, or by Winston Churchill in sustaining British morale in the Second World War—it would be perverse to deny the role of leadership. Of course, it is possible to debate how much difference particular individuals made to specific outcomes, how far they fully intended the consequences of their actions, and how far they could have acted otherwise, but it is implausible to think that answering such questions would wholly eliminate their individual role. We may come to a more sympathetic understanding of the extraordinary pressures and constraints under which individuals have acted, and their own limited grasp of the options open to them, as we did in the case of Caesar, but in none of the cases cited above is it likely that we could eliminate their agency and intent or seriously doubt that they had some responsibility for the results they produced.

We may define a *leader* as someone who sets the pattern of action for others and a *political leader* as one who does so by claiming a right to rule or by acting in ways that contest that right, its extent, limits, or exercise; or by seeking to influence the authoritative allocation of values conducted within a state. A leader may set the pattern of action using a range of means such as charisma, incentives, coercion, or by claims to knowledge or formal authority, all of which may be understood as resources of power. It is tempting to want to distinguish the exercise of power from leadership, as James M. Burns does by defining leaders as those who induce "followers to act for certain goals that represent the values and the motivations . . . *of both leaders and followers*" and by characterizing Hitler as "an absolute wielder of brutal power" and thus as not displaying leadership,[4] but, although forcing someone to do something is not the same as leading them, political leaders do draw on a wide range of resources, including coercion, in exercising their authority. It would also be wrong (dangerously so) to believe that Hitler relied solely on the brutal exercise of power and showed no leadership. Leadership can be exercised for good or for ill, and those who obey can do so from either love or fear. It is leadership if you can set the pattern of action for others, where *action* implies the exercise of the will (which cannot be wholly the product of brute force), but there are many degrees of voluntariness.

Leadership is built into politics because politics involves the attempt by some to gain power and to command the distribution or deployment of resources within the state. In vying for power, in building coalitions of support, and in justifying their policies and activities, politicians attempt to legitimate their commitments and establish their authority with at least some proportion of the population. To gain the support of others involves more than representing their interests since these may be diverse, conflicting, or inchoate; to lead one needs the ability to interpret, express, aggregate, and render tangible those interests. In this sense, leaders necessarily shape the aspirations and self-understanding of those whom they lead and when they fail to do so, they will fail to lead. Moreover, those who gain power and exercise rule control resources to which the rest of the population may be denied access; this is why Weber emphasized the state as "the sole source of the 'right' to use violence."[5] States tax citizens, determine property rights, police behavior, oversee key rites of passage (from entry into the world to departure from it), manage the armed forces, and exercise the right to declare and fight war. Their control of resources, and their right to use means that are prohibited to citizens, reinforces both their distinctive role and the need to legitimate that rule to those subordinate to it. Built into that relationship is the imperative that those in power must dominate and frame the actions of those they rule. Simultaneously, the potential for perverse relationships is also created: The interests of leaders and those they rule may diverge; the control of coercive resources may be used to ensure the dominance of those who rule, with scant regard for securing their legitimacy; and authoritative leadership can become eclipsed by manipulation or force.

Most people's sense of their goals and their values (and their ordering of them) is imperfectly formed. Each of us has many potential identities that may assume political significance: class, age, gender, ethnicity, race, source of income, occupation, religion, type of home ownership, and so on. Not every potential identity will become salient in a lifetime, many lie dormant and lines of cleavage evolve over time. Some identities are dormant because they are suppressed; others just lack significance. Under some conditions we do find explosive expressions of popular commitments occurring without leadership, but in most cases political organizations and activists play a substantial role in identifying and making prominent particular identities and, as they project their political aims, they inevitably also shape people's interpretation of their interests. Vying for power requires that we attempt to set the pattern of action for others in ways that focus and delimit people's choices, and inform and render concrete their beliefs and commitments. Generating shared purposes and commitments takes a complex mix of organization, conviction, shrewdness of judgment, political "touch," the capacity to inspire trust or confidence, a degree of dominance over one's opponents, and, sometimes charisma. The performances by which politicians create and reinforce a sense of shared purpose and establish their authority invariably involve a gamble. To say and do nothing new is to risk nothing and to leave the situation unchanged; to overreach, and thereby fail to carry one's public, is to leave oneself vulnerable and exposed; to try to give people just what they want is to become hostage to their demands and will fail to conciliate conflicting interests. This essential indeterminacy of political action and the associated "decisionism"—in which the rightness of the decision is partly established by its being made and acted on, rather than by it meeting a set of antecedent standards—makes it inevitable that a few will frame the ambitions and activities of the many.

Despite the fact that the subject of leadership is largely ignored in contemporary liberal political theory it is clear that it is of abiding importance in politics and in the realization of the kinds of values with which liberals are centrally concerned. The opportunities for political innovation and leadership may be greater or lesser depending on the degree of state autonomy, its institutional structure, and the character of its social and economic order, and states with roughly equivalent degrees of autonomy will not necessarily find leadership in equal degrees or of a similar character. But we are not looking for a comprehensive set of generalizations about what kinds of leaders certain political systems have, since path-dependency plus luck (good or bad) would seem to play a pretty large role in such matters. Rather, given the inevitability of political leadership in the political process, we need a clearer sense of what sort of motivation on the part of those who lead is compatible with the character of the political rule they attempt to exercise and of how far we can expect that motivation to resemble the motives politicians and leaders actually claim for or recognize in themselves. We need this to help us understand why (and when) we are not complete fools to trust ourselves to political rule—and to retain a sense of how far we should do so.

*   *   *

Max Weber, in "Politics as a Vocation," directly addresses the nature of leadership and the motives that men and women bring to politics. He recognizes the attraction of power and fame and of having one's finger "on the pulse of historically important events," and asks:

> What kind of man must one be if he is to be allowed to put his hand on the wheel of history? . . . Politics, just as economic pursuits, may be man's avocation or his vocation. . . . Politics as an avocation is today practised by all those party agents and heads of voluntary political associations who, as a rule, are politically active only in the case of need and for whom politics is, neither materially nor ideally, "their life" in the first place. . . . There are two ways of making politics one's vocation: Either one lives "for" politics or one lives "off" politics. By no means is this contrast an exclusive one. . . . He who lives "for" politics makes politics his life in an internal sense. Either he enjoys the naked possession of the power he exerts, or he nourishes his inner balance and self-feeling by the consciousness that his life has meaning in the service of a "cause." . . . He who strives to make politics a permanent *source of income* lives "off" politics as a vocation, whereas he who does not do this lives "for" politics.[6]

For Weber, in contrast to the civil servant whose duty is to administer his office and conscientiously execute the orders received from his superior, the politician's role is "to take a stand, to be passionate," and to take full personal responsibility for his actions.[7] A political career raises for the politician the question of how it is possible to do justice to the responsibility that power imposes upon him. The answer Weber gives is three-fold: passion, or devotion to a cause; a sense of proportion, judgment, or detachment—"the ability to let realities work on him with inner concentration and calmness;" and a sense of responsibility to the cause. Set against these qualities is the ever-present temptation of vanity—"the need personally to stand in the foreground as clearly as possible"—which threatens to subvert the vocation by undermining the politician's sense of realism or responsibility. To seek power for its own sake is to fall prey to vanity: the pure "power politician may get strong effects, but actually his work leads nowhere and is senseless. . . . It is the product of a shoddy and superficially blasé attitude to the meaning of human conduct; and it has no relation whatsoever to the knowledge of tragedy with which all action, especially political action, is truly interwoven."[8]

Weber holds that the politician must have some kind of faith, some cause that he follows. Without a sense of a cause, the action would lack "inner strength." He needs this because "the final result of political action often, no, even regularly, stands in completely inadequate and often even paradoxical relation to its original meaning." Weber here endorses a semi-tragic view of political action: Because intentions often have a perverse relation to outcomes in politics, only a commitment to a cause and a sense of proportion and responsibility can give meaning to political action. Without it we are ruled by illusions. With commitment we can invest the chaotic world in which we act with meaning, even if its best result is often to reveal to us only the limits of our efforts to impose order. Moreover, for Weber, only this sense of proportionality and responsibility can adequately prepare us for the fact that politics revolves around violence. Violence is the decisive means for politics—it is what the state must exercise in its struggles with other states, it is a central instrument in the conflicts that threaten the security of a regime, and it is the final recourse of those who wish to resist or revolutionize the state.[9] Crucially, it is not something from which those engaged in politics can walk away, since it is both an instrument and a potential inherent in every form of conflict that must be negotiated, and those who enter politics must do so fully aware that they must encounter and exercise it.

Weber's sense of proportionality and responsibility involves resisting a commitment to an ethic of ultimate ends, which he discusses predominantly with regard to Christianity. The injunctions of the Christian religion are absolute, they admit no exception, and, as such, they are unconcerned with the consequences of conduct. "The believer in an ethic of ultimate ends feels 'responsible' only for seeing to it that the flame of pure intentions is not quenched;" but a politician who lived by such an ethic would act without responsibility or proportion.[10] What is decisive in the character of the politician, according to Weber, is the trained relentlessness in viewing the realities of life, the recognition that politics involves the employment of force, and the ability to face such realities and measure up to them inwardly. "Politics is a strong and slow boring of hard boards. It takes both passion and perspective."[11]

It is not possible to do justice here to the extensive concerns current within Western democracies with religious fanaticism and the threats it poses, not least through terrorism, but Weber's distinction is certainly apposite. The perspective he sets out is one in which the actions of those in politics must be conditioned by a sense of responsibility and proportion, where that sense grows out of one's involvement in and feeling for the political order. True fanaticism, where the purity of intention is unconditioned by the need to compromise, negotiate, exercise authority over others, or conciliate competing demands, essentially denies all legitimacy and autonomy to politics. In its extreme, it is antipolitical—although there is a complex issue about how far those who lead such movements can or do sustain such a commitment, and how far the very process of leadership invokes issues of strategy in which objectives become less absolute, even if there is every incentive to look for complete devotion from those who follow. Weber's position shrewdly draws attention to a line that marks the difference between those who engage with politics as a set of activities that involve commitment and an orientation to the future alongside the need for compromise and conciliation, and those whose actions are essentially antipolitical, who focus on the purity of intention, and who acknowledge neither the demands that politics makes nor the abilities or virtues of those who respond to those demands appropriately.

Weber's account stands firmly on the side of political virtue. Given the demands of politics, as he understands them, the agent acts virtuously only insofar as he is open to and responds to the facts of the situation imaginatively and with commitment, but also with responsibility and a recognition of the limits of what any individual can achieve. Nonetheless, if it is clear that Weber demands stability of commitment, integrity of character, and a healthy degree of realism from his politicians, it is less clear what kinds of *cause* are acceptable within the parameters of politics or what counts as a cause rather than simply a set of personal preferences.[12] To understand a cause as simply some project to which the agent is committed ignores Weber's rooting of the politician's cause within the domain of politics. A cause in politics is a *political* project, one that takes its bearings and rationale from the political order even if it aims ultimately to transform or transcend elements of that order. It is also implicitly an attempt to make that project normative for others, and to rule through the exercise and deepening of authority. Egoism may be a part of the drive to rule, but it cannot be the sole end. To be in politics wholly for oneself is to become a parasite who lives off politics, not for it; it is to fail to see the point of the activity and one's place in it. The idea of a cause is, then, an ideal-typical postulate: it is a minimum requirement for making intelligible the will to exercise political leadership and rule. The idea of a cause starts from the motives that most men and women in politics have, and that the institutions and practices of most states implicitly (and democratic states explicitly and systematically) demand of them by requiring direction, the justification of objectives, and the instigation of and commitment to implement policy (which, in democracies, issue in a panoply of manifestos, platforms, and electoral pledges). The commitment to a cause makes political agency intelligible as a general category of action, but the particular causes that drive men and women are rooted in their specific political contexts: politicians project their own ends, but they do so from materials that are not of their own choosing. Leadership is not wholly rule- and norm-bound; it requires innovation, the interpretation of norms, and an ordering of values and commitments that are not completely governed by some further set of norms. The force of the decisionism of élite theorists lies in their recognition that political leadership involves being committed to a cause or certain ends that their activity either succeeds or fails in making right, rather than in conforming to established standards of right. While this view is extremely persuasive in its sense of the open-ended character of politics, it comes with the recognition that the standard of evaluation for political conduct cannot be wholly external to the agent's commitments, purposes, and achievements (and their context).

Weber's harshest comments are reserved for those who are driven by vanity: "the need to stand personally in the foreground as clearly as possible."[13] As with Machiavelli's prince, it is self-defeating to be committed only to one's own glory; the alternative is possession of the qualities of passion, responsibility, and proportion.[14]

Caesar was driven, in part, by a concern for his *dignitas,* just as Machiavelli offers his prince the rewards of glory for his activities. In both cases there is something that the "prince" wants; but there also is a problem about the direct pursuit of these ends. In neither case are their motives entirely disinterested since both want the recognition to which they believe their conduct entitles them. This might seem to set them against Weber's more stringent demand; however, it is misleading to model their actions as motivated by their desire for either *dignitas* or glory since neither is a discrete, external good, identifiable independently of the practices within which they act or of the excellence of character that the agent displays. *Dignitas* and glory are ways in which others see us, the standing one has in the eyes of others, and both imply the recognition by others of qualities in the agent that his conduct expresses in response to the exigencies he faces, that he himself sets store by. Caesar had a right to expect that his *dignitas* would be respected. It was something due him, by birth, by his career, by the offices he had held and those he continued to hold in the republic, and by virtue of his achievements for the republic. It marked him out as different from others, and their recognition of that difference and its elevated standing was a token of the respect his conduct commanded. He did not do these things solely to achieve that result (because of the self-defeating objection), but rather because he believed the ends he pursued to be of value: he thought them worthy, fitting to his station and commitments, appropriate to the demands of the situation, and in keeping with the traditions of republic. Similarly, the prince's achievements entitle him to the respect, deference, and acknowledgments of others not simply because of what he brings about, but in recognition of the value that the prince himself places on those achievements and the integrity and commitment with which he pursues them. Weber shares this more complex connection between motive and reward, and between self-evaluation and external evaluation: when he talks about the honor of the political leader or statesman being rooted in his personal responsibility for what he does, that honor (as distinct from vanity) is something with which the politician is rightly but not exclusively concerned. It is a function of the respect that the individual commands among others who understand the demands of politics and who share the evaluation of his conduct as a response to those demands. Indeed, the other side of honor is shame, which involves being seen by others as weak or failing in one's response.[15] These "goods" of honor and reputation can and do form part of the agent's motives but not in the form of egoism. The standing that good politicians seek is one whose underlying valuations of actions they essentially share, so that when they act in these ways they commit themselves to these actions as "choice-worthy." Insofar as they break from more classical accounts of the virtues it is by emphasizing that the choice-worthiness of the act is not wholly intrinsic to the act (in the vast majority of cases) but is partly a function of the cause or end served by these chains and sequences of acts or practices.

The connection between the objectives and the motives of the agent, the way in which the agent is judged by others, and the way that the agent's self-evaluation is partly connected to that assessment play an important role in rendering commensurate political ambition, leadership, and political rule. *Dignitas*, glory, and honor are not simply cases of conforming to the expectations of others (what Gouldner refers to as the source of self-esteem), nor do they derive from the sense of self we get from challenging the expectations of others (Gouldner's self-regard).[16] They involve a complex interplay between innovation and setting the pattern of action for others in the pursuit of certain goals, where the pursuit of those goals is intelligible to those within the political context and where the qualities shown in that pursuit are acknowledged and respected by those involved.[17] Those who attempt to lead others in politics may do so with various motives, ranging from altruism through to self-interest, but their actions are admirable as political conduct if they make their purposes normative and thereby authoritative for others; if they do so responsibly and with a sense of proportion, and by doing so are accorded a certain standing and respect; and if they judge themselves at least in part in relation to this appraisal. It is this context, coupled with the role politics plays in the authoritative ordering of conflict, that provides the ground for thinking of this appraisal as potentially an ethical one, rather than being simply a process of admiring someone's skills.

A complicating factor in this process, however, is that politicians do not value all individuals' judgments equally. What matters to them is the standing they have in relation to their particular reference group, since it is this that is regulative for the politician's sense of self and achievement. The stability of the reference group is another concern. To change one's reference group to avoid criticism and secure sycophancy is pretty self-defeating (although not unknown), but it is not unusual for politicians to move from pleasing the crowd, to soliciting the respect of their colleagues, to estimating their standing in relation to those who have gone before or may follow. Crowds are easier to please in the short rather than the long run: there are incentives to valuing one's colleagues' judgments as one climbs the ladder of success and to ignoring them the more they threaten to constrain one's career; and the historical judgments of politicians can have a substantially self-serving character without them really being aware that this is so. Nonetheless, there are some pressures that work to emphasize the links between self-esteem and self-regard and the political order. Those who lead attempt to make their purposes normative for others; completely to disdain the views of those one attempts to influence and guide is to court failure. We may seek to impose our leadership while valuing the respect of others only instrumentally so that it plays no part in our sense of self, but this too threatens unwelcome results since those who are led follow a cause that they believe is shared with their leader and disdain for their judgment may undermine their sense of the congruence in objectives. While we need a clear sense of the demands of politics to recognize when people demonstrate abilities and virtues, that sense is not the exclusive prerogative of any particular reference group, let alone that chosen by the leader, and competing evaluations may threaten one's capacity to set the pattern of action for others.

The desire for fame, honor, and glory has its nemesis in the temptations of greed, hubris, and vanity. What holds a performance together, and more broadly what holds a political life together and gives it some integrity, is the agent's ability to continue to endorse it as an expression of his or her commitments and to continue reflectively to endorse those commitments. To fall prey to vanity or greed is to reveal one's weakness, to lose one's thread, to sacrifice one's integrity, and to abandon one's cause. Nothing guarantees that the pursuit of self-esteem and self-regard will always go the right way. That there are pitfalls and temptations does not make the idea of a cause irrelevant, it simply underlines the challenge that devotion to a political life involves for those who aim high.

Where they exist, political virtues are expressions of a politician's character and will. In contrast, some politicians experience the demands of other virtues such as fidelity as external constraints or demands; hence the capacity of good politicians to be caught out by scandals associated with their sex lives.[18] But demands for political virtue—for direction, a degree of vision, a sense of purpose, and a basic political integrity—are not demands for qualities that one could have in spite of oneself. The disposition to *virtú* has a similar character to other ethical virtues: it is not exclusively self-seeking, it is not something we do mechanically or as a result of habit, nor is it "a causal force making me choose; it is the way I have made myself, the way I have chosen to be, and in deciding [to act] in accordance with it, I endorse the way I have become."[19]

Good politicians are not simply good in terms of effectiveness, or in terms of wanting the right things; the judgment we make is one concerned with the integrity and ability with which they conduct their lives in politics. Part of what it is to have the right kind of character for politics is for the agent to have the right virtues (courage, self-control, a sense of proportion, and so on). Moreover, for those for whom politics is a vocation, political *virtú* is not merely the means to achieve certain ends, it is what they must have if they are to identify and achieve the ends that someone with political *virtú* would pursue. To have these virtues is, as Williams puts it, "for certain ranges of fact [to] become ethical considerations for that agent."[20] Having the virtue of tolerance means that one acts in ways that take account of and show respect for the views of others. A good politician has such virtues, recognizes certain ranges of fact as ethical considerations, and acts only after weighing these considerations. A central part of that process must involve a sense of restraint toward the ends pursued, and the ability to see that there are limits to what it is reasonable to attempt to make normative for others. Being a good politician, then, is not just a matter of being able to bring certain things off, or of being effective (it is not, that is, to be a good politician in the way some might claim Hitler or Mussolini were good politicians because they were able to usurp and retain power); it entails that the politician recognizes the salience of certain ranges of facts in the process of determining how to act, facts that are not simply instrumental to antecedent purposes but that play a constitutive or critical role in framing those purposes. The responsiveness to such facts as considerations with ethical weight results in commitments to certain delimited ends that exemplify certain virtues, including a sense of proportion and responsibility. The suggestion that the virtues are to be understood in terms of "certain ranges of fact becom[ing] ethical considerations for that agent" might seem obscure; or it might suggest that the crucial issue concerns the type or range of facts that surround the situation. This would mean that the assessment of political behavior should be based, not on an account of individual character or virtues, but on prior commitments as to what the relevant facts are for decision making in politics. For example, a political leader who fails to take into account the costs that his or her actions impose on a certain group of individuals might be blamed not for lacking a particular virtue, but for failing to give due weight to those individuals' interests on the grounds that all interests ought to be accorded equal weight. That principle is an abstract commitment, and the facts to which politicians respond are rooted in their context, with more abstract values reached through that context. We can make sense of the idea of receptivity to certain facts by recognizing that those in politics have formal and informal roles and responsibilities that identify and delimit the particular ranges of fact to which they should be receptive and that they should weigh as considerations in determining how to act. Moreover, being engaged in politics in general renders certain issues, information, and considerations relevant to individuals, where that relevance may imply responses or responsibilities that if we ignored them, would compromise our claim to be politically engaged and politically serious. The integrity of a pri-

vate individual is not automatically harmed by the existence of poverty in
society, although there are ways in which the individual can give ethical
weight to such facts and thereby change one's conduct in ways we can regard as virtuous and as showing enhanced integrity. However, the holder of
a ministerial office associated with welfare has as a result of the positional
duties associated with that office, and as a function of the authority she attempts to exercise, a duty to recognize certain facts as ones to which she
must attempt to respond (even if the response must fall short of the ideal).
For President George W. Bush or Prime Minister Tony Blair not to have
taken any account of the interests of the Iraqi people in the determination
of war in 2003 would impugn their integrity. How much weight they
should have given those facts is a different issue. If Iraq had weapons of
mass destruction capable of posing an immediate threat to neighboring
countries or to the world at large then that concern should have been taken
into account, and Bush and Blair would be lacking political integrity if they
did not. The balancing of information, probabilities, and possible outcomes
is one that involves considerable and careful judgment, and observers
should judge their conduct based on the extent to which the decision was
thought through in all its ramifications (for example, with appropriate
weight being given to the impact on stability in the Middle East, the costs to
civilians in Iraq, the United Kingdom, the United States, and elsewhere, the
effects on terrorism, the credibility of intelligence information, and so on).
That no weapons of mass destruction were found does not automatically
mean that they acted without integrity. Nor, indeed, does the suggestion
that they knowingly used inaccurate information in reaching their decision—since this simply raises the question of what really drove their commitment to war if it was not this information. It is not clear that that question has, at the time of writing, been fully resolved; but what we do know
certainly does not suggest that the multiple dimensions of the issue were
weighed with much care. If there were a deeper, less public, set of objectives
it seems increasingly unlikely that these will prove more credible or cred-
itable than those they purported to be following.

Different dimensions of facts will influence judgments about the degree
to which certain virtues—such as tolerance, shrewdness, prudence, imagi-
native projection, political responsibility, honesty, or courage—have been
demonstrated and the sum of these different dimensions will contribute to
judgments about both political integrity (in relation to the roles they played
and responsibilities they sought to meet) and the agent's character more

generally, since aspects of personal judgment or conviction contribute to bridging gaps between such facts and considerations and the individual's responses and decisions. From those judgments issue praise and blame, honor and shame. Part of our sense of an individual's integrity concerns whose audit of conduct the leader acknowledges and whether he or she finds comfort in their praise and dishonor and shame in their contempt, rather than than just feeling resentment in their failure to respect his or her *dignitas*. Not to care how we are seen by those who bear the costs of our actions—not to give ethical weight to that set of facts—must also figure in our assessment. Contempt for the judgment of one's enemies may sometimes (in war perhaps often) be warranted, but to be found lacking in mercy, charity, or common humanity toward those defeated may also be taken as a deep ethical failing and as shameful.[21]

It is by understanding political agency in this way that we can recognize the source of ethical constraints on political action, even if it is clear that such constraints are open to wide interpretation. With this model, what counts as acting well depends heavily on context and on what is politically possible; what is politically possible depends on what political agents can bring about within a wide range of casual constraints; and what agents can bring about depends, in turn, both on the agents' abilities and purposes and on the range of considerations they bring to bear in forming and pursing those ends. In contrast to the kind of absolute injunctions of the Christian ethical tradition that have so influenced liberal political theory (with prohibitions on certain classes of act, such as killing, lying, cheating, and so on), this political conduct-centered account understands political agency in terms of the virtues, integrity, and abilities of those who act in politics. What holds the good politician's performance together is not a strict moral law or consequentialism; rather, it is a degree of integrity of character as a player in politics and of the commitments and performances that flow from this standing.

For various complex reasons, including quite fundamental changes in the character of reflection, the integrity of the good life in which ethics and politics are effortlessly linked seems a utopian aspiration.[22] This is not to counsel the abandonment of the virtues and considerations of character, so much as to recognize that the modern society is simply too pluralist and fragmented to provide a unified and coherent ethical language that unites politics and morality. Moreover, as Weber argued, there are elements of sheer luck and contingency in politics, especially in relation to outcomes, and that contingency provides powerful reasons for placing the greatest weight on the avoidance of certain consequences—certain types of harm or conflict—as a basic ethical demand in politics. There may be no ideal of human flourishing that can command universal support but failures of human governance are more easily identified. Starvation; brutality; insecurity; the absence of fundamental provisions for health care, housing, and education, and so forth do militate against crossing a basic threshold for human well-being even if they do not designate an ultimate ideal, and such facts have become increasingly relevant for those who purport to act conscientiously in politics.[23]

Political leaders inhabit to greater or lesser degrees a political culture (of greater or lesser degrees of concreteness) that provides an essential element for their sense of themselves as having standing with their fellows. We should not be naive about the ethical integrity of political leaders—some are, without doubt, pretty appalling people—and, as we shall see in Chapters, exercising power can place considerable strain on people's integrity. Furthermore, we should not be naïve about the standards of integrity it is appropriate to apply. To succeed in politics generally requires a degree of ruthlessness in the pursuit of power: tactical alliances must be formed and tactically broken, deep friendships in modern politics are rare because of the costs they can impose on the pursuit of ambition, and often one must act toward one's opponents with a cunning that is not easily reconciled with liberal norms. Still more discomfiting is the fact that the actions of politicians have profound consequences for their own citizens, and often for those of other states. At least some of the time politicians must act in ways that cost lives, damage people's futures, impoverish some and benefit others, and enormously influence the experiences of individuals in their own and other states. As Weber insists, their conduct cannot be evaluated by a rigid code of absolute ethical injunctions. They may lie, connive, and cheat in ways that at least some of Machiavelli's critics would associate with the sure road to hell, and while some doubtless deserve such a destination it is naive to think that it is possible to act in the political world without risking some such stain or sin. Accordingly, our judgment as to whether a politician acted shamefully is not covered by a mere description of the act or ensuing consequences. We have to know in what character the agent acted: we must ascertain, that is, if there was a claim to authority, if the person acted authoritatively to set the pattern of action for others, and whether the action was in keeping both with that authority and its ends and with the purposes brought to the office. The person may have acted ruthlessly, but it is possible to do so with a sense of proportion, responsibility, and passion; that is, with an acute sense of the value of the ends one's actions were intended to deliver.

Political philosophers (and playwrights) worry about the problem of "dirty hands"—cases where, no matter what one decides, a wrong is committed and there is blood on one's hands.[24] The problem arises because sometimes politicians have responsibilities that require them to act in ways that violate important moral standards.[25] One needs only a bare acquaintance with the history of, for example, national security services to recognize that the responsibilities of politicians to protect the state can be taken as a warrant to engage in activities that may violate people's (both citizens and those outside the state) fundamental moral and civil rights. Of course, politicians have used such powers for a very wide range of purposes, in the too well-founded belief that they can shield their activities from public scrutiny. But the very fact that politicians are in a position to make such decisions underlines the point that such choices are inescapable. The torture of terrorist suspects is deeply abhorrent, but it is impossible wholly to eliminate the opportunity for it, and when that opportunity is coupled with a major threat to the lives of citizens in a state, someone has to decide how to proceed. The discussion surrounding the U.S. administration over the use of torture in recent years with respect to Afghan and Iraqi insurgents, despite the United States being a signatory to the United Nation's Convention Against Torture, demonstrates the choices that face those in power and suggests how easily politicians can be persuaded of the necessity to act in ways that are inhumane, have little pay-off, and have a dehumanizing effect on all involved. More importantly, it shows that the UN prohibition cannot rule out the opportunity for torture, and where opportunities exist, judgments must be made. We can lay down rules about how decisions should be made and we can enshrine them in international conventions, but politicians faced with such judgments must decide what weight to accord such conventions in the particular circumstances they face. The tendency for politicians to think that they face a really exceptional case is only one instance of the cognitive failure that often attends such decisions, leading to violations of conventions, but this does not mean that there never are exceptional cases.[26]

There are two accounts, however, where there should be no problem of dirty hands. A strict consequentialist will weigh the costs and benefits of an action, and the right action will be the one that maximizes overall benefit (on some calculus of utility, welfare, preference-satisfaction, or whatever). It does not make sense for such a calculation to worry about costs that are essential to attain the outcome if the outcome is indeed optimal. In contrast, a strict deontologist or rights-based thinker will take the view that politicians simply have a duty not to act in ways that violate the rights of citizens, or those of members of other states, thereby eliminating the quasi-consequentialist judgments that Machiavelli appears to be make in allowing *virtù* to trump virtue. Moreover, these two positions suggest that the dirty hands problem is generated by attempting to combine two incommensurable worldviews—a deontological view of the rights and duties of individuals, on the one hand, and a consequentialist view of how politicians must sometimes act on the other. However, since each position denies the validity of the other there is something odd in thinking that they combine to generate a tension; which suggests that it is only if we are prepared to think that both consequences and deontological constraints matter that we have a problem. If both do matter, then neither can claim to be absolute, and the problem diminishes even if it does not disappear.

Men and women in public office and political life, by virtue of their powers and responsibilities, are sometimes required to take (or order) actions that ordinary citizens and everyday morality would condemn. In particular, the connection of political office to violence, emphasized by Weber, is such that politicians must sometimes set in motion actions that will harm or kill others, and must do so if they are to fulfill their political office. It is because of the special responsibilities associated with their office that they have to act in this way; whereas, because politicians must, ordinary citizens need not and should not. This means that they (politicians) are expected to act (or commit others to act) in ways we find repugnant and, in that sense, they are being asked to do something we think wrong in itself, even if it is the right thing for them to do as someone holding that office. The problem of dirty hands is not simply that politicians are placed in this situation and must make such decisions and take such actions if they are to be true to their office and associated responsibilities, but that they should nonetheless recognize that in doing so they have done something regrettable.[27]

The issue of regret is important. We may agree that what needs to be done should be done, and further acknowledge the costs that doing so imposes on those who decide and who undertake what needs to be done. Unlike strict consequentialism, in which actions are right if they result in a balance of good (and in which there is no place for regret, which would be morally self-indulgent), we can hold on to the idea that doing the best and responsible thing may nonetheless impose moral harms and costs (not just on the victims but also on the perpetrators) that it is rational to regret. Someone who acts in this way does not simply dismiss the moral costs imposed once the decision to act has been made; rather, part of what it is to act conscientiously is to recognize those costs, to regret that they have to be paid, to see them as costs that are in part paid by the agent, and to recognize that the choice is, in some sense, a tragic one. Political leaders are sometimes required to act in ways that on some dimension diminish them as human beings, not just to others (since they may never know) but to themselves. Their regret is not self-indulgent—it is their bad luck that they faced a particular situation, and so had to act in ways that on some dimension are repugnant to them.[28] Although Machiavelli tends to celebrate the disjunction between *virtú* and virtue, he does occasionally recognize the moment, in which what we do in contending with disordered humanity is sickening to us.[29] This does not deny our political virtues, nor does it subordinate them to moral principles. On the contrary, it serves to emphasize that ordinary morality will not see us through such cases, and that political virtue must do that responsibly and with proportion, even while recognizing that the outcome cannot avoid damaging the individual (because of what he must do to others) in some way.

With such a take on political ethics one must see political agency and decision making as a matter of judgment about what the political situation demands and of having the character to make those judgments, to see them through, and to accept responsibility for them.[30] As politically committed people we need to address the basic question of what it is in (political) life we should struggle to achieve. We should regret, in undertaking that struggle, that it cannot be achieved wholly without cost to others.[31] To be incapacitated by regret would be inappropriate and self-destructive, but to count these costs as wholly cancelled by the benefits would be to lack a true sense of the price that conflict and human frailty and evil impose upon the world and a true sense of the worth of the human goods for which we strive. It would be to claim immunity to certain facts to which we, as human beings as well as politicians, should remain open. Consequences and costs as well as norms and principles must inform the agent's judgment but it remains a judgment about what it is right and appropriate for the politician to do in that situation and with the responsibilities he or she has. Those responsibilities do not simply cancel any other claims, not least political commitments based on Weber's sense of responsibility and proportion, which are themselves fuelled by and intertwined with commitments to deep human values. Ordering escaping terrorist suspects to be shot for fear that they will use themselves as human bombs kills in the hope of saving others; but the decision is not simply a quantitative or balancing one. It is not about probability and the risk of getting it wrong (although this matters); it is one in which the full enormity of our doing some of the very things we are striving to prevent must abide with us and, even if we get it right, doing so must leave us in some degree diminished. In this sense political virtue is not only not rooted in the good life, it is in its nature exposed to demands that may compromise some of our most cherished commitments.

Tough political decisions need to be experienced as just that. What must see us through them is our commitment to what it is worthy or unworthy to do or want, our reflective judgments as to the relevance or irrelevance of certain facts, an accompanying sense of responsibility for one's actions, and a responsiveness to the demands of the situation. What keeps those judgments clear is our own capacity for reflection; our continence with respect to our emotions; our recognition that it is with reference to the consistency of the will and the intent of our agency that the success or failure of our actions should be judged; our ability to reference our will and judgment to those of others who have similar responsibilities and who will judge of us as we believe we should judge ourselves; our recognition that others may exaggerate or otherwise misrepresent the situation on the basis of their own anxieties and concerns; and our ability to remain grieved by what we have, nonetheless, to do. If it is inevitable that politicians will sometimes have to make hard choices that impose tragic costs on some people with the aim of avoiding something worse, then it is crucial both that we have people in power who can make such decisions and that these people do not take such decisions lightly. As Williams has pointed out, "fruitful thought should be directed to the aspects of a political system which make it less likely that the only persons attracted to a profession which undoubtedly involves some such (disagreeable) acts will be persons who are insufficiently disposed to find them disagreeable."[32] Institutional design begins to matter greatly.

This suggestion certainly sets an agenda, but there are at least five factors that make Williams's requirement difficult to meet.

First, the innovatory character of political leadership and of how one sees an action through affects whether the action takes effect and has legitimacy, and can result in someone giving the authenticity of his political will greater weight than considerations of the rights of others and the importance of observing rule-constraints. Especially in rapidly changing political circumstances, where the survival of the political system is at stake, innovation may be more than ordinarily called for and the moderating and constraining elements within the system may be substantially more fragile.

Second, the differences among getting power, keeping it, and exercising it are critical to leadership (although the condition the political order is in is equally important). The qualities that ensure the acquisition of power do not necessarily enable one to rule well. In systems subject to political competition, politicians who have won office always have some incentive to use their position to consolidate their hold on it and to ward off competitors. Hereditary succession carries different risks, but it does not usually involve systematic training in the competitive wooing of popular favor coupled with a struggle to reach the top of a political organization, and a powerful interest in using the resources of office to increase one's chances of retaining ascendancy within the political system.

A third factor is that the rule-bound character of political office offers both a set of constraints on conduct and a set of permissions. Above all, the rules sometimes allow politicians to act in ways that members of the public cannot. That such permissions exist does not thereby cancel the duty to act responsibly; but for some people it can have a corrosive impact on their sense of how they should act. Having power over others can be an exhilarating feeling with frightening consequences.

Fourth, as we have seen, problems develop where the political culture is disjoint from the broader public culture.[33] Political action may be about commitment and cause, but it is also about legitimacy and judgment. The more the legitimacy of political action is referenced to a small political élite, and the more restricted the group among whom decisions are discussed and assessed, the greater the prospect of that élite taking decisions that are rogue.[34]

Finally, as I discuss further in Chapter 10, institutional design is a matter of politics; it is not an activity insulated from it. As such it cannot provide an Archimedean point for structuring the political domain.

Collectively, these factors make it difficult "to find politicians who will hold on to the idea that there are actions which remain morally disagreeable even when politically justified."[35] Only those who are reluctant or disinclined to do the morally disagreeable when it is really necessary have much chance of not doing it when it is not necessary. Nonetheless, politics by its nature puts people in demanding and complex situations and they have to have the right kind of character to make responsible and proportionate choices. It is a case of trying to ensure that people act conscientiously; that we do not have institutions that make it less likely that they will have the right sort of character; that we have political regimes in which those in power are served by men and women who retain some independence of judgment; and that these inner circles are themselves held to account.

CHAPTER 5

Must Power Corrupt?

Success in politics is subject to *fortuna.* Some politicians mean well and create chaos; others with much less laudable motives govern states that provide their citizens with peace, stability, and prosperity. It is disconcerting that good men and women can fail while bad succeed, but more troubling is the suggestion that anyone who wields political power will find his or her virtues tested (and often wanting) in distinctive ways. There are a great many reasons why people behave badly in politics but two of the most discomfiting theories are that in the process of achieving and/or exercising political power the chances that it will be exercised well diminish dramatically, and that those who are drawn to exercise power are inherently inclined to exercise it poorly.

Under both theories, good behavior in politics would be the exceptional, not the standard case.[1] If acting well is the exception rather than the rule, this raises serious issues about the role that we accord politics. We should conclude that public office is too heavy a responsibility for most men and women to bear well, and we should attempt to limit and minimize the scope of such offices and their powers at all costs.[2] A still more pessimistic conclusion emerges if we think of power as deriving not solely from the office held but from the personal qualities and abilities of particular men and women. Writers from Homer onwards have a recognized that part of what empowers men (and, much later, women) is the respect that their abilities command. As the poet says at the opening of *Beowulf:* "Behaviour that is admired is the path to power among people everywhere."[3] The suggestion that power corrupts, then, is especially disturbing because it implies that the very qualities that generate power may be corrupted or destroyed in its exercise.

The idea that there is something about holding and exercising political power that in itself systematically undercuts the chances that it will be ex-

ercised well is substantially more troubling than the idea that those attracted to politics are especially weak, disturbed, or otherwise delinquent
individuals because it suggests that corruption is a fate that will befall even
the best. The theory that power attracts the weak troubles me less because,
although there are concerns about the motives of politicians and public office holders, it is not clear that we can really sustain a case for saying that
they are distinctively deviant as an occupational group. I suspect they are
simply characteristically human.

The nature of the classical presumption that power corrupts and concerns
about the absolute character of certain forms of political rule provide the
focus of this chapter. To examine these issues, I must first define what is
meant by power *corrupting* those who exercise it, and that will involve recognizing that corruption is only a subset of ways in which power may be
abused. A second line of inquiry begins from the recognition that with the
development of modern constitutional states and democratic participation
in the wake of the Enlightenment, absolute power is a rarer phenomenon,
which raises the question of whether such states need have the same concerns as those that animated the classical tradition. Finally, I analyze the
roots of political motivation, which reveal a set of enduring tensions between the nature of political power and the motives of those who aspire
to it.

> How can a monarchy be an orderly affair, when a monarch has a licence to
> do whatever he wants, without being accountable to anyone? Make a man
> a monarch, and even if he is the most moral person in the world, he will
> leave his customary ways of thinking. All the advantages of his position
> breed arrogant abusiveness in him, and envy is ingrained in human nature
> anyway. . . . Now you might think that an absolute ruler is bound to be
> free from envy, since there is nothing good he lacks, but in fact his natural
> attitude towards his people is the opposite of what you would expect. He
> resents the existence of the best men, while the worst of them make him
> happy.[4]

Herodotus's characterization encourages Juvenal's conclusion that "Few
monarchs go down to Ceres's son-in-law [Hades] free from bloody wounds;
few tyrants avoid a sticky death,"[5] which reassuringly suggests that failure
of character delivers retribution as a matter of course. The opinion that
kingship has an especially destructive effect on individual character retained
its power over subsequent centuries. Writing very shortly before the execu-

tion of Louis XVI, William Godwin noted as a commonplace that "Every king is a despot in his heart."[6] That judgment, at least in Godwin's case, is not as glib as the epigram implies. He does not assume that only those with tyranny in their hearts become kings and hence despots, so much as that tyranny is what is introduced into one's heart by kingship. That is also the sentiment that Herodotus voices through Otanes and, while Michel de Montaigne's view of monarchy is somewhat more sympathetic, he too concludes that the position of king is one that makes continence in rule especially challenging: "I can excuse more shortcomings in kings than men commonly do, out of consideration for the horrifying weight of their office, which stuns me. It is difficult for such disproportionate power to act with a sense of proportion." Further difficulties arise because, while the character of their office may require extraordinary ability and self-restraint, the education of kings is least likely to equip them for this. Montaigne acknowledges Carneades's suggestion that only in horsemanship can kings excel, since in any contest with other men, the ruler's subordinates will prefer to betray their own glory than to challenge that of their king, whereas a horse is neither a flatterer nor a courtier![7]

Yet the route from kingship to despotism is not self-evident, and theories abound. Some writers claim that the opportunities created by kingship are such that the temptation to exploit them to one's personal advantage is often overwhelming. Others note that that the reactions of others (notably courtiers and advisors) to the king distort his judgment, since he is told only what people believe he wants to hear, or what it is in the interests of those seeking to influence him to tell him. Flattery and dissimulation can lead kings to overvalue their own judgment, to become the dupes of those who flatter them, and to act on woefully inadequate and inaccurate information. These suggestions are commonplace in Enlightenment literature on monarchy. Less common, but certainly present, is the more basic claim that the inequality between ruler and ruled ensures that cognitive failure over proportion is the inevitable lot of the ruler, and sullen resentment and resistance the lot of those who are ruled.

Lord Acton famously claimed that "Power tends to corrupt and absolute power corrupts absolutely." He goes on: "Great men are almost always bad men, even when they exercise influence and not authority: still more so when you superadd the tendency or the certainty of corruption by authority." But Acton is pressing a particular brief concerning historical judgment. His prime concern is to deny that it is sometimes necessary for those who rule to be bad and the associated relativist judgment that "the office sanctifies the holder," in favor of a view of history that judges in absolute terms. "The inflexible integrity of the moral code is, to me, the secret of the authority, the dignity, the utility of history." So Acton's case is really for what he calls "conscientious history" in contrast to "apologetic history." Nonetheless, it is surprising that the argument for his claim that power tends to corrupt is never really spelled out, not least since his suggestion that authority itself corrupts would suggest a more sympathetic approach.[8]

Judging political behavior depends on how we are to understand the terms *power* and *corruption*. In its broadest sense, power refers to the ability to bring about effects; it is a form of causality in the social world. Within this broad definition lies a subset of cases in which the ability to bring about effects depends on being able to get other people to do things they would not otherwise do, and to accomplish this one can draw on a range of resources, from persuasion, through offers, to coercion. Control of such resources may come from the formal office that one holds within a political system, or may derive from the personal qualities, loyalties, or capacities (in extreme cases the brute strength) of the individual. In identifying why power might tend to corrupt those who exercise it, two distinctions are relevant: power to/power over and with limit/without limit. "Power to" refers to capacities to attain one's ends;[9] while "power over" concerns the capacity to get people to do things they would not otherwise do. "Power over" is seen as the more troubling form of power; what is troubling is not the power per se, but the particular methods used to get people to do things they wouldn't otherwise do. Linked to this is the second issue concerning the extent or limit of the ascendancy of one person over another which in many respects, is the more crucial question.

A critical element in having power over another is having the capacity to overcome their resistance. Power increases when the relationship of domination overcomes the most extreme resistance. As the capacity for resistance is systematically weakened or broken, power can be exercised with relatively low costs and few limits. Furthermore, to make others subject to one's will, not just in accord with it in some respect, or to make others the instrument of one's will by bending or breaking their will and overcoming their resistance produces a significantly different type of ascendancy than does persuasion or making offers. Those in power no longer simply influence the actions of others, they force them to serve against their will. Moreover, the power to rule others is not a series of encounters in which any participant may emerge the victor, but a relationship in which the ascendancy over another is systematic and assured. The more pervasive that relationship, the more complete and systematic the domination.

When writers have voiced concerns about the tendency of power to corrupt they have done so mostly in relation to absolute power. Something is absolute when it is perfect, disengaged, or free from imperfection or qualification. *Absolute power* is, precisely, not relative or conditioned. Nonetheless, despite the literature, there are grounds for doubting that there is such a thing as absolute power wielded by a single individual. It is more likely a figment of the literary imagination, since those who rule need others to rule with. So what is a plausible version of the claim that one person's power over another can be absolute?

My power over someone else is absolute when it is without limit, but "without limit" seems logically to have two components: the ability to determine completely how a person acts or thinks and that such action is costless to the ruler. The significance of the second condition is that it allows us to refine the earlier claim that no one's power is absolute. For example, I may have perfect domination of B, but I cannot simultaneously have the same degree of domination over every other agent under my rule. Limits and costs need to be understood both in respect to specific individual and in respect to all other individuals within the domain of control. My exercise of power over B will involve costs with respect to alternative uses of that power.[10] In examining absolutism, then, unlimited power is unlimited specifically with respect to the victim's capacity to resist, but in overcoming all resistance in one person, the ruler must use some resources and that limits his or her ability simultaneously to dominate all others. Absolute rulers need others to execute their will, and in ruling absolutely (that is, without limit) they face the problem of who is to coerce those coercing the coerced. Rule is absolute with respect to the particular subordinated agent, but it is not absolute *tout court*. Moreover, to insist on absolute sovereignty as a matter of right creates a fundamental tension at the heart of absolutism, which pushes it further toward tyranny. The ruler who simultaneously insists on the boundless and unquestionable character of his rule and on its legitimacy, bases his legitimacy on the claim that he rules by right. However, he cannot be the sole arbiter of in what that right consists, and to be absolute is to be unaccountable.[11] Thus the claim for legitimacy most imply criteria with respect to which others may audit the ruler.

The claim for absolute supremacy and the illegitimacy of questioning it are grounds for the view that kings are despots in their hearts. Subjects who show their independence implicitly claim a standing that a ruler cannot acknowledge because it necessarily implies a boundary to the ruler's power and superiority—one that the ruler cannot admit consistently with claiming absolute power. There is no proportionate response to such a claim; the offense can be assuaged only by a reassertion and demonstration of the sovereign's unlimited power over the offender to the rest of the community. Kings become tyrants and corrupt when they insist on absolute supremacy. The less secure and continent the character of the ruler, the more sensitive will he or she be to slights, the more enraged by them, and the more correspondingly extreme will the retaliation be. Once extremism is used with satisfying results (that is, with the elimination of carping and criticism, as well as ensuring the increased subordination of the rest of the population), the more habitual does recourse to it become. For this reason it is difficult to see how someone could both claim absolute power and remain continent in exercising it.

In ancient tyrannies, appeals to birth, descent, and the will of the gods often helped support brutal and corrupt forms of rule. In modern tyrannies, political ascendancy has been coupled with powerful legitimating ideologies, with leaders buttressing their claim to rule by insisting on its historical inevitability. Those who obstruct this course face a ruthless ideological logic—they lose their standing as authentic human agents by becoming symptoms of an obsolete historical moment. The full power of the system is directed most against those who are seen as sharing this historical destiny but who betray it, and by doing so confess to a degeneracy that is worse than historically reactionary. The elimination of these traitors involves a demonstration of the ascendancy of the future over the past and the true over the false. When such conflicts are coupled with personal struggles for political ascendancy, rule becomes increasingly deadly. The arrogance of power is to think itself legitimate without limit—both in respect to the depth of its reach (captured in the dystopic novels of the 1940s and 1950s) and to the extent that the whole population is covered by that reach (mass society). That arrogance corrupts because, while those in supreme office may claim simply to bow to the demands of history, their personal anxieties, passions, and irrationalities inevitably feed their vision and guide their judgment. The weight of their position and their sense of their historic role will press every character flaw, every want of self-control, every unreasoned anxiety or fear, and any sense of insecurity in their claim to supremacy. In this sense, there are some pretensions to power that do seem inevitably corrupting.

In constitutional political systems, challenges to holders of high public office rarely attack simultaneously the personal qualities of the office holder, their political program, the legitimacy of the office, the legitimacy of the administration of which that office forms a part, and the legitimacy of the system of government and of the nation-state. Indeed, what it is for there to be a consolidated political order is for these different elements to be separated so that those in power are not existentially threatened by challenges in the way that they are in tyrannies. Within such a system the tendency to respond tyrannically is weaker, the impact of responding poorly is narrower, and leaders face countervailing forces who can resist them. Democratic rule is profoundly more egalitarian, which makes it harder to sustain the delusions of grandeur that animate the tyrant and ensures the persistence of opposition—which is strengthened by formal protections for the individual in the broader legal and political system. Petty tyrannies are far from rare, but the political system itself is less susceptible to tyrannical tendencies among those in its highest offices so long as the constitutional order is preserved. Once it begins to crumble the safeguards disappear fast, and democracies can prove as savage as any other regime, sometimes more so because of their mass character.[12]

Thus far, I have treated what it means for power to corrupt as involving despotism—for rulers to claim for themselves more than their entitlement and invasively to dominate and control others. There are, however, difficulties with this understanding of corruption that should be addressed if we are to frame with sufficient precision the issue of whether power *must* corrupt.

The driving force behind the claim that power corrupts is the sense that a natural standard is decaying or is being eroded. A corrupt fruit is one that has moved from ripeness to decay. The idea that there is a natural standard in politics is difficult to spell out in concise terms but at the least it assumes an attempt to act authoritatively and in a public capacity that is referenced to a set of norms, rules, and institutions that give more precise content to the practice of politics and identify certain goals or ends as legitimate objectives. Such a standard assumes that political power is an instrument to such ends, rather than an end in itself. The claim that power corrupts is therefore multilayered: it concerns the tendency for personal ends to supplant political ends, for the exercise of power and authority and the distributions of benefits and burdens to escape from their regulative procedures and norms so as to ride roughshod over such constraints, and for the struggle for power to become an end in itself. At its strongest, the claim is that the struggle for and exercise of power corrupts politics itself; that the very institutions that are used to secure the compliance of others generate activity that subverts those institutions; and that those who exercise political power will tend to act in ways that subvert the ends for which that power exists.

This set of ends is hardly self-evident. The indeterminacy of the objectives and of the point of politics, and the central role that political agency plays in interpreting that point and legitimating that interpretation, both demands a lot from those in politics and increases the risk that men and women will pursue ends that elude those objectives. It is misleading to suggest that all action that damages those ends is corrupt since we have an additional range of terms for those who act badly in politics—irresponsible, incompetent, self-serving, shortsighted, treacherous, arrogant, and faithless, for example. In the modern lexicon of political science *corruption* is taken as properly concerning only a specific subset of cases in which rule is distorted: those where people in public office use their office illegitimately for personal or private benefit.[13] Acton does not recognize the distinction, but it is essential to see that while using the resources of office to kill an enemy so as to protect the state is not necessarily corrupt, doing so to advance one's personal interests or to strengthen one's position for one's own private ends, is. The distinction can be very difficult to draw in practice, and Acton was rather committed to seeing cases of the former as essentially instances of the latter (which involves a claim about the way that great men are almost entirely incapable of viewing politics except in personal terms). However, if the claim that power corrupts is to make sense, it must be that power distorts the character and moral judgments of those who rule and that the ends, procedures, or principles of politics (not necessarily or immediately those of morality; again, this is a distinction Acton resists) tend consistently to be subverted by self-serving actions on the part of those who act within it—the more so the more power they wield.

Absolute power or power without limit is something that constitutionalism and the safeguards of liberal-democracy and pluralism constrain both by formally prescribing limits and by nourishing a civic culture that undercuts the ability of power to transgress boundaries. This suggests that corruption will decline as absolute power is curtailed and implies that power can be purged of its tendency to corrupt. Of course, insofar as there is power in politics, the possibility of its misuse must remain, but we might ascribe this to morally weak or opportunistic individuals and regard it as having only minor significance. On this view, the regulated character of the powers associated with public office in liberal democracies, the existence of political accountability and checks and balances, the counterweight of an established civil society, and the absence of any inherited claim to rule all serve to constrain blatantly arbitrary power even if they do not eliminate corruption altogether.

However, in examining failures in control we must distinguish between misconduct where the officeholder intentionally perverts the exercise of his or her office to achieve certain private ends, and misconduct where the officeholder interprets and exercises his or her powers for political ends that go beyond the common understanding of the bounds of that office. That distinction is foreign to tyrannies, which merge both types of misrule by considering the state as the personal domain of the ruler. Yet the distinction is important since the two problems are different: one is concerned with what we now tend to regard as corrupt practices, opportunism, and political delinquency; the other focuses on the transgression of the limits of legitimate political power. In the former account, it is inevitable that some politicians will be corrupt, incompetent, avaricious, and idle, and in such cases office is exercised poorly and individual weaknesses are revealed. Gaining office may have created the opportunities for these flaws to exhibit themselves, the opportunities may simply have increased in number and size, or those with such flaws may be more than ordinarily attracted to such offices, but office in itself does not actively to create the flaws.[14] In the latter case, the suggestion is that there is something in the attempt to restrict political power by liberal and constitutional constraints that may itself motivate men and women to press their power to its limits in their own interests. On this view, some politicians are venal, sleazy, and contemptibly self-serving, while others overreach themselves and act in their official capacity in ways that go beyond the boundaries of their office. The line between these two groups is not always easily drawn but the phenomenon of someone misusing his or her office for personal profit is clearly distinct from that of someone exercising it for recognizably collective ends in ways that are of doubtful legitimacy. Instances of this second class of cases might include President Richard Nixon with the Watergate bugging and subsequent cover-up; Prime Minister Margaret Thatcher and the sinking of the *Belgrano* and its subsequent justification; Chancellor Helmut Kohl with respect to the party finances of the Christian Democrats; Premier Nick Greiner, in New South Wales, on patronage and the civil service; President Ronald Reagan on the funding of the Nicaraguan Contras; Prime Minister Tony Blair and his conviction that war against Iraq was politically legitimate and fully justified; and President George W. Bush and his willingness to use terrorism as a pretext for war with Iraq. In these situations those involved appeared to believe that they were right to act as they did. They believed not only that their action was compatible with their office (as surprisingly many who are charged with corruption tend to claim), but that it was demanded by their interpretation of their office—that it was the right thing for them to do, which in turn settled the question of whether they had the right to do it. This suggests that there are instances where politicians' judgments as to how to act become distorted by the positions they hold and the power they wield, not simply by the presence of opportunities coupled with flaws in their character.

I have said that the two types of modern examples (the sleazy politician versus the overreaching one) seem distinct, but there is a deeper connection. In liberal democracies, institutional balances, accountability mechanisms, transparency, and the professionalization of public administration all work to combat corruption (in the sleazy sense) in modern democratic states. They do so by creating formal constraints, regulatory mechanisms, and disincentives that delimit the formal scope of political agency, but they thereby increase the probability that those in political office will find themselves hamstrung and will chafe against the constraints. Many of these institutions and practices are designed to help create and sustain a public culture in which certain standards of conduct are widely supported, endorsed, and internalized, the aim being that we can trust those who rule to act with propriety because they have taken to heart these norms of conduct.[15] However, while the internalization of norms does militate against sleaze, it does not necessarily act as a disincentive to action that frets at the limits on political authority, in large part because pressing political exigencies demand innovative political responses—responses that may formally lack authority but can nevertheless be widely legitimated. One feature of such cases is that those involved will believe that they are acting appropriately given the remit of their office, even if they do not have a distinct warrant. Since political office involves trust and discretion, the very open-ended character of such positions lends support to the belief that statesmen must do what statesmen must do. We cannot eradicate this open-ended character, and yet it is this that builds the risk of transgression into political office and the exercise of its accompanying powers.

This point might be made more strongly: because of the open-ended character of political office, we need leading politicians who have the character and personal qualities that enable them to make decisions and see them through. Part of what it is for office to be open-ended is for it to be a matter of judgment as to what decisions are made and acted on. This means that there will be cases where someone goes beyond the normal limits of their office not because they are weak or because their character is flawed, but because they are convinced that they are acting for the best.[16] An additional difficulty in these situations is that acting in this way in a political system that puts a high premium on accountability gives one good reason for protecting certain actions from subsequent scrutiny and criticism. Those who act in such ways do not think of themselves as corrupt or despotic in intent, yet they recognize that their actions may look altogether different to members of the broader political culture.[17] Moreover, unlike those who occupy formal regulatory roles, those with an interest in challenging the authority of those in high public office may have little corresponding sense of political responsibility: Newspaper publishers want to sell more copies, muckraking journalists want to build a reputation, opposition politicians want to weaken their opponents, and members of a ruling political party may have an interest in undercutting the standing of their rivals within the party.[18] In such cases, there is little incentive for those challenging the actions of those in office to ensure that their own conduct is directed to the public good; and in the absence of a robust, substantive discourse of the public good that is shared by all parties, it becomes correspondingly difficult for those in office to defend their actions in such terms, and equally difficult for them to accept as legitimate the forces that attempt to hold them to account for their actions.

All this suggests that a case does exist for a special democratic anxiety about power corrupting the hearts of presidents and premiers. The concern is less one of turning the state into a private domain, and more one of coming to believe that one's office confers, to some degree, the right to act as one sees fit. Overstepping the boundaries of office involves a certain hubris. This is *hubris* in the modern, English sense of pride or arrogance and involves overreaching—claiming for oneself and one's position more than can properly be claimed.[19] In modern politics it affects those who assume office (especially high office within the state) and who come to believe that their office places a responsibility on them to act broadly as they see fit. But, if we can see that this might happen, is there anything in the relationship between politics and individual character that makes it a likely occurrence?

The basis for this pressure to push the powers of high office to the limit and beyond turns out to have a number of features in common with classical accounts of why kings become despots. It is in part the estrangement—

the distinction—from others that weakens the sense of solidarity, friend-ship, and loyalty upon which depend the prospects for genuine communi-cation between those at the apex of the political system. The range of sources of advice diminishes. Equally, the perspective of those who advise and serve changes: from having strong incentives, based on both loyalty and self-interest, to promote the success of their patron, the growing power that the patron comes to exercise encourages, if not fawning servility and dumb flattery, at least a tendency not to create obstacles for one's leader. True candor may be as little welcomed by those who have power in modern democracies as it was by classical tyrants. Supporters who are seen as re-sistant to innovation become less welcome where there is enthusiasm to test the full limits of one's authority, with the result that those promoted are often the supporters who encourage the broadest interpretation of those powers. People in positions of power need an honest fool; few want what they need.

The attitude of the broader public outside the immediate circle of those in power also changes. In many Western democracies there is considerable cynicism and hostility to those in politics but this is often coupled with a willingness to look to politicians for solutions to the society's problems. This can come in the form of expectations that leadership will frame people's in-terpretation of an issue, or the desire for someone to articulate national sen-timent on occasions of national tragedy, crisis, or success. Moreover, these demands, because of their inarticulate and often emotive character, and their widespread nature, sometimes enjoin action that is insensitive to the precise responsibilities of office and the proper limits of political power. In turn, this exacerbates the feeling among those who are the target of such expectations that the constraints of their office against which they chafe lack real legitimacy or justification. As Tocqueville recognized, the concen-tration and extension of power in the democratic state is largely driven by the demands of the people, and it takes considerable continence on the part of democratic leaders to resist responding to popular feeling in the name of the proper limits to political authority.

A further element in democratic politics that encourages hubris is the dis-junction between gaining power and exercising it. The struggle for office and, above all, for supreme office, requires a high level of investment and ambition. That struggle raises two problems: personal and political debts and costs in terms of betrayals and actions taken to avoid exposure are in-curred on the path to high office; alongside such costs arises a difficulty in retaining a sense of proportionality about the objective and the means to attain it. In the struggle to attain office there is a tendency to inflate its value, and in doing so to inflate one's expectations of its powers. Most offices, once attained, probably seem very short-term in character; insecure because of the need to campaign for re-election; limited in scope, since they are hemmed in by a panoply of political and civil institutions and instruments of public scrutiny; and unnecessarily—indeed illegitimately—constrained. It is not inconsistent both to find it difficult to believe how constrained one's actions are as the head of a government or state and to believe that one must have a right to act as the occasion and necessity demand, even if this sometimes means some undercutting of other aspects of the democratic process. The struggle to achieve high office provides reasons not to minimize either one's achievement in securing it or one's interpretation of the powers conferred by it.

In fact, such offices usually do bestow considerable powers (even though they also may confer fewer rights than hoped for) with patronage in appointments, the right to hire and fire, investigative initiative, legislative initiative, and considerable control of the public service and one's own staff. Even if the office is not as well-equipped and staffed as the incumbent would like, it is likely to be better equipped than are rival offices in government, over which one might be keen to assert dominance. Political leaders with clear agendas, facing groups within their party working toward different objectives, have every incentive and often the means to circumvent opposition, to undermine its public standing, and to challenge outright certain prominent individuals. Much of this is perfectly legitimate, but it also contributes to the tendency of such innovators to overreach themselves and to alienate their political support.

Finally, democratic states offer multiple opportunities for populist appeals by their leadership. Populism can legitimate the suspension of formal procedures, can dramatically empower political leaders over the short to medium term, and can frequently sacrifice the interests of certain minorities to the populist bandwagon. A little war can go a long way in distracting public opinion from failings at home; attacks on welfare scroungers and single mothers can mollify better-off supporters; a high profile campaign against drugs and crime can garner wide support from those fearful for their families, while doing little or nothing to attack the roots of either problem; and campaigns against various elite or professional groups—such as teachers, lawyers, bureaucrats, doctors, and so on—can give the impression of a dynamic egalitarian commitment to achieve electoral support despite the potential damaging effect of such campaigns on institutions that people value. In short, there are considerable incentives to strike politically opportunistic poses, to enhance one's power in ways that can undercut some of the more prosaic but nonetheless central responsibilities of high political office, and to use office to retain office rather than to pursue widely legitimated ends or objectives.

These several possibilities do not add up to absolutism or corruption but they can weaken the legitimacy of democratic states and fray the edges of liberal institutions, and in states with fragile authority they can push the political order in less liberal and constitutionalist directions. The lack of absolute power, the relative independence of judicial and police powers, the countervailing elements of a free press and media, and the existence of a plural political and civic culture may limit the impact of hubris by those who rule, but may also stimulate it since the very limits that they place on power may urge transgression.

Does the desire for power itself betray a weakness? Why do people seek to rule? If for honor, glory, or reputation, why are these important, and can they be continently willed? Can we want them as badly as many apparently do, while still requiring of ourselves that we should fully deserve them? Are they goods we can pursue directly, or can we gain them only if we are virtuous, where *virtuous* means acting without direct concern for these sorts of reward?[20] For Montaigne, it would seem that "virtue is a vain and frivolous thing if she draws her commendation from glory: then, for nothing should we undertake to make her hold her rank apart and detach her from Fortune: for what is there more fortuitous than reputation."[21]

In Leo Strauss's commentary on Xenephon in *On Tyranny*, he points out that the dialogue between Hiero and Simonides emphasizes a contrast between two ways of life, ruling and wisdom. Those who want to rule demand something from those they rule—fame, recognition, respect, love. These goods are wanted for the pleasures and rewards they bring, but this means that those who want to rule are not guided solely by what is intrinsic to the purposes of rule. Moreover, their neediness leads them astray, generating resentment and intemperance when what they see as their just desserts are not recognized, or encouraging them to play to the crowd rather than pursue the harder road of the public good. Because they want something for themselves out of ruling, not just the achievement of justice or the common good, their struggles for ascendancy make convergence on the best policy inherently unlikely. In this case both policy and objectives become instrumental to the personal ends of those in politics so that their investment in them ceases to be a function of the balance of reasons. In contrast, the wise ask for nothing, and insofar as they are admired it is not for the services they render, but simply for being what they are.[22]

If those who enter politics are attracted by something other than the intrinsic value and ends of the activity, then to that extent those ends will not systematically be pursued unless we ensure that the countervailing forces are sufficient (and sufficiently balanced) to ensure that they get what they want only if they also deliver on the proper ends of politics. Philosopher-rulers are an implausible option in modern democracies. If they do not care about whether they please the people, they will face competition from contenders who do. If they do care about pleasing their people, they will cease to act on the basis of the common good. Politics, then, will govern philosophers; and where power governs virtue, it corrupts it. This makes even the just liberal state a utopia: It is one we can imagine but that is inevitably compromised in the practical process of translating the ideal into political reality for the utterly prosaic reason that political conduct is driven by motives and desires that, while they can be contained, disciplined, and to some extent laundered through political procedures and institutions and through deliberation and debate, cannot ever be wholly expunged of personal desires and ambitions. The result is that we have no way to guarantee that the ends of politics will wholly and enduringly supplant the ends of those individuals who struggle for ascendancy and satisfaction within the political process. Hence, then, the fragility of the distinction between public and private ends and the sense that political power is attractive only to those who seek it, in at least some sense, for their own rather than public ends.

Philosopher-rulers are an implausible option in modern democracies but they may not even be a desirable one. Although Simonides portrays the philosopher-ruler as a seductive option, the attraction rests on his incorruptibility and that must remain doubtful (unless we make it a matter of definition). I argued earlier that one force behind hubris in modern states is the belief among those who rule that they have the right and responsibility to act as they see fit in certain cases. The corresponding difficulty for the wise is that they know best. One potential understanding of the claim that power corrupts is precisely the claim that power implies inequality: it makes some subordinate to others, it allows some to impose upon others a vision of how they should live, and it generates a conviction among those who rule that they do so by right. If democracies are sometimes pretty sorry political spectacles because of the transparently craven character of those who aim to rule and those who criticize them or compete with them, a community run by the wise may be little better. Rule by philosophers may mean rule without regard to the grubby exigencies of human life that makes politics necessary. Such rule corrupts politics because it rules where politics must rule—because there are conflicts, disputes, disagreements, and a need for compromise and conciliation that have to be acknowledged. The philosopher-ruler may have difficulty in seeing the value of the many things over which men and women, neighborhoods, communities, cities, and states struggle and will find it hard to see the rationality of these conflicting purposes and ends. Someone so distant from us, wielding the sovereign power of the state, might well be experienced as a despot irrespective of his intent. More worryingly, there needs to be some proportionality between those who exercise power and those who are ruled by it: the wisdom of the philosopher needs to guide his or her exercise of power in ways that can legitimated to the ruled, and it is far from clear that this demand can be met. This is so not just in cases where (as is common enough) a ruler's confidence in his or her beliefs is unwarranted, or where the confidence has some warrant but the beliefs do not take into account the fact that the imposition of solutions creates supplementary problems. It is probably also true in cases (unlikely though they may be) where the confidence is warranted and the beliefs are truly and deeply wise. In such cases, the truly wise will not want to rule because they can see the impossibility of their engaging in an activity that rests not on knowledge but on the creative brokering of interests and the moving of the hearts and minds of men and women—an activity that cannot be wholly rational. And if they did rule, could they do so in a way that was true to their perfect knowledge of the imperfect world over which they exercised power without becoming caught up in that world and its entanglements?

For those involved in politics, who are mired in its practices and who want certain things out of it for themselves and, on the preceding argument, even for those (if they exist) whose ends attempt to track the public good, political integrity is a complex and challenging requirement. To take seriously the activity of politics involves (following Weber) an attempt to live for it rather than off it. This demands that those who devote themselves to politics show some awareness of what drives them and that they find some way of reconciling what they want from politics with the ends that politics serves within the community as a whole. That reconciliation is inevitably fragile because the pleasures of politics—its excitements, the plaudits and loyalties it can generate, and the opportunities for mastery and for determining the shape of the world for others—may subvert its ends. It takes strength of character to resist hubris in success; it demands self-control not to relish revenge against one's opponents; and it requires a rare integrity to hold fast to one's principles and ends when they will lose you the rewards for which you entered politics. To achieve such integrity it is necessary to retain some ability to weigh at its true value what we want for ourselves from politics, while giving due weight to the interests of those whose lives our actions will affect. This is a challenging conception of the demands of political power, since the opportunities for conflict between the two sets of demands are numerous, while the capacity to subordinate our own interests to the responsibilities associated with our position is one that is cultivated neither in the struggle for office nor in the expectations that are then focused on the office holder. To this extent, while there may be little absolute power in modern liberal democratic states, the powers that there are might plausibly be said to tend to corrupt those who thirst to exercise them.

At the beginning of this chapter[23] I identified two ways in which we might think that acting well in politics might be the exceptional rather than the standard case. In the first case, the bulk of political behavior falls to one side of the middle point of the full range of cases, producing a lopsided distribution. In the second case, the judgment is made on the basis that the range of cases, which has a normal distribution, is substandard with respect to a set of external criteria. One such basis might be gained from the recognition that corruption is predicated on an implicit natural standard of politics, but it is also clear that the abstract components identified in such a teleology need to be given concrete form in highly complex contexts, and this lends a considerable degree of indeterminacy to what kind of political conduct may be said to meet the natural standards of politics. Although this teleology guides the concept of corruption, it does not rigidly fix its content, and it argues against the second approach to why acting well in politics might be the exceptional rather than the standard case. Rather than applying external criteria to assess the range of cases, we should examine the way that the distribution in actual cases tends disproportionately to favor poor behavior. On this view, the claim that power corrupts is a claim about a tendency. If power always corrupts then it could only be by an external standard that we could make that judgment, since the claim is that all cases appear on one side of an externally identified line. The subtler claim, and the one I have defended here, is that power of certain kinds does tend to corrupt, but that we mark that tendency by the fact that it does not necessarily corrupt, and that there are politicians who are not corrupted by their power, who retain their integrity, and who act with responsibility and proportion. That such cases exist provides both normative political theorists and political scientists with a challenge—to consider the personal qualities and the contexts that make such conduct more rather than less likely. That such cases are perceived to be rare, and that this perception in democratic states results in a sense of disillusion and cynicism toward politics, gives that task a degree of urgency.

PART II

Servants, Followers, and Officials

CHAPTER 6

Loyalty in Politics

Commitment to a cause or ideal, to one's country, to one's community or family, to organizations and parties, or to other individuals, is commonplace. Indeed, each of us has some sense of what we hope we would have the courage to fight for and, if need be, die to defend. Thomas Hobbes's axiom that death is the greatest evil since it involves the extinction of all desire misses (probably intentionally) the point that there are things to which we will hold true even at the cost of our lives. And those who would not die for a cause might nonetheless fall in defense of those they love. Indeed, to have nothing more important than one's own personal interests and desires, to have no sense that there are things in the world of a value greater than oneself, is to live an emotionally impoverished and solipsistic life. Yet powerful loyalties may demand a high price from those who embrace them, and from those who fail to do so. In his speech to the Central Committee plenum of the Soviet Communist Party in January 1933, Nikolai Bukharin denounced the Smirnov group—accused of right-wing factionalism in the party—which Bukharin admitted had drawn on his own earlier writings in developing their position.

> Both our internal and external situation is such that this iron discipline must not under any circumstances be relaxed. . . . That is why such factions [*gruppirovki*] must be hacked off without the slightest mercy, without [our] being in the slightest troubled by any sentimental considerations concerning the past, concerning personal friendships, relationships, concerning respect for a person as such, and so forth. These are totally abstract formulations, which cannot serve the interests of an army that is storming the fortress of the enemy.[1]

Nearly five years later Bukharin wrote to Stalin from prison to assure him of his personal loyalty and his loyalty to the Soviet cause.

> This is perhaps the last letter I shall write to you before my death. . . . In order to avoid any misunderstandings, I will say to you from the outset that, as far as the *world at large* (society) is concerned: a) I have no intention of recanting anything I have written down [confessed]; b) In *this* sense (or in connection with this), I have no intention of asking you or of pleading with you for anything that might derail my case from the direction in which it is heading. . . . Standing on the edge of a precipice, from which there is no return, I tell you on my word of honor, as I await my death, that I am innocent of those crimes which I admitted at the investigation. . . . I know all too well that *great* plans, *great* ideas, and *great* interests take precedence over everything, and I know that it would be petty for me to place the question of my own person *on a par* with the *universal-historical* tasks resting, first and foremost, on your shoulders. But it is here that I feel my *deepest* agony and find myself facing my chief, agonizing paradox. . . . *If* I were absolutely sure that your thoughts ran precisely along this path, then I would feel so much more at peace with myself. . . . But believe me, my heart boils over when I think that you might *believe* that I am guilty of these crimes and that in your heart of hearts you *yourself* think that I am really guilty of all these horrors.[2] (emphases in original)

Bukharin's willingness to sacrifice personal friendships, relationships, and self-respect, and subsequently both his own life and the facts of the matter in the name of the cause for which he had fought as a Bolshevik revolutionary is shocking, and mundane. It is shocking because of the Stalinist terror's insatiable appetite for victims, despite their abiding loyalty to its architect. It is mundane because in the history of politics there are many examples of such loyalty. But Bukharin's public acknowledgement of guilt also shocks us because his partisanship and loyalty seem to have no inherent restraint or proportion. Our willingness to die for causes or for other things we value (as with our families) is only narrowly separated from a willingness to kill for them, and that willingness may be hard to keep proportional. Bukharin's case is tragic not because he was committed to a cause, but because his acceptance of Stalin as the authoritative interpreter of what that cause demanded of him seems now so plainly ill-judged. His loyalty is not unusual; the ruthlessness with which it was exploited may be.

The literature on Soviet and Nazi ideological domination tends to assume their distinctiveness as experiences. Historians and social-scientists look for what it is about the ideology that drew such intense devotion and resulted in such extremism, albeit they tend to couple this with a considerable degree of cynicism in their accounts of the motives of those who led these movements. More generally, we are less comfortable seeing such commitments—to organizations, states, causes, or ideals—as on a par with personal loyalties to individuals, and we tend to claim that ordinary, personal loyalties have a fundamentally different character to the fanaticism that seems to dominate in more extreme cases such as Bukharin's. This objection, however, relies on an essentialism about loyalty (and an associated restriction of scope to personal relations) that is extremely difficult to sustain. Moreover, it is often accompanied by the assumption that loyal behavior always expresses a virtue and is always deserving of respect. Viewing loyalty as a positive or at worst as a benign element in political relationships is a reassuring perspective, but there is little warrant for such a stipulative move. Loyalty has a number of dimensions that may prompt, under certain conditions, extremes that are fundamentally destructive of political order and people's well-being. Nonetheless, these dimensions are best understood as forms of loyalty, rather than as something wholly other. Taking this route has one disquieting consequence—that all political and social life must be seen as harboring the resources for such extremism—and one encouraging one—that different structures, institutions, and political cultures might prove to be differentially suited to handling these powerful commitments in constructive rather than destructive ways. To support this stance, a better understanding of the nature of loyalty and its impact on politics is needed.

There are two primary reasons for focusing on the issue of loyalty. The first concerns the contrasting demands of impartiality or neutrality. Many think of civil servants and their masters as appropriately guided by reasons that are general in form. Many want policies to be formulated in terms of what it is best to do, where best implies some impartiality in the judgment. In contrast, to think of politics in terms of relationships, organizations, and causes rooted in loyalties is to introduce a largely nonrational, nongeneralizable, and partial motivation into an account of how democratic politics works that is dramatically at odds with the more common picture, but considerably more persuasive.

The second reason for considering the nature of loyalty is that it is often referred to as a virtue. Indeed, loyalty to a friend has been extolled as among the highest virtues, and as offering the most complete happiness. Aristotle is clearly one source for this, but his linking together of friendship and the good life, and the sense of the goodness, rationality, *and* the particularity of one's relationship to a friend is best exemplified in Montaigne's essay "On Affectionate Relationships." In that essay, Montaigne raises the case of Caius Blosius, who was interrogated by the Roman consuls for his connections with Tiberius Gracchus. Gaius Laelius, who was assisting the consuls, asked Blosius how much he would have done for Gracchus: " 'Anything.' 'What anything,' Laelius continued: 'And what if he had ordered you to set fire to our temples?'—'He would never have asked me to,' retorted Blosius. 'But supposing he had,' Laelius added. 'Then I would have obeyed,' he replied."[3] Montaigne thinks Blosius should have resisted this conclusion and persevered with his deeper sense of the character of his friend:

> They were more friends than citizens; friends, more than friends or foes of their country or friends of ambition and civil strife. Having completely committed themselves to each other, they each completely held the reins of each other's desires; grant that this pair were guided by virtue and led by reason (without which it would have been impossible to harness them together) Blosius' reply is what it should have been. If their actions broke the traces, then they were, by my measure, neither friends of each other nor friends of themselves. . . . I do not doubt what my will is, any more than I doubt the will of such a friend. All the arguments in the world have no power to dislodge me from the certainty which I have of the intentions and decisions of my friend. (p. 213)

In Montaigne's account, my loyalty to my friend is a loyalty to something that is so much a part of myself that I cannot be mistaken about its character and tendency. If this is the virtue of loyalty, when does virtue become vicious or excessive? At what point does the mean lie? How can we hit that mean? And, what institutional and cultural frameworks facilitate that attempt, or militate against its success?

There is some resistance in the literature to defining loyalty. In Hirschman's *Exit, Voice, and Loyalty* there is little in the way of a definition of the term *loyalty* (save reference to "a special attachment to an organisation")[4] although he does supply an account of its behavioral manifestation: that is, a reluctance to exit in spite of disagreement with the organization of which one is a member.[5] Yet, while loyalty will almost always have a behavioral manifestation (without ruling out someone who is mentally loyal but unable to act through some restraint or disability), it cannot be defined simply by its behavioral concomitants; its primary reference is to a set of independently defined mental states that provide the underlying consistency for the behavior in question.

A similar focus on behavioral components can be recognized in George Fletcher's insistence that loyalty is always a triadic relation; that is, between A and B, where B's loyalty to A is dependent on the contrast with the lack of loyalty to C.[6] In practice, however, it seems that B's loyalty to A does not need to rely on any contrast—although it might not be possible to *observe* that B is loyal to A except in the presence of C. B is loyal because he has the appropriate motivational set with respect to A, it is only a contingent truth that he does not have it with respect to C.

Although recent philosophical literature has not dwelt on the definition of loyalty, Josiah Royce's work at the beginning of the twentieth century is admirably forthright and provides a basis for a preliminary definition of *loyalty*: The willing, practical, and thoroughgoing devotion of a person to a cause. Royce states that "A man is loyal when, first, he has some *cause* to which he is loyal, when secondly, he *willingly* and *thorough-goingly* devotes himself to this cause: and when, thirdly, he expresses his devotion in some *sustained and practical way.*"[7] Although Royce's account comes with a considerable amount of excess baggage, motivated by his desire to subsume the whole of morality under the idea of loyalty, the core of his definition is astute: loyalty involves the devotion of a person to some other person, cause, or ideal. *Devotion* implies willing, in the sense of being freely and fully chosen, although there remains the issue of how far devotion can be wholly willed. Royce sees the willing as prior to the devotion, thereby insisting that loyalty is more than blind obedience or passion. For example, we must distinguish between love and the loyalty we often associate with devotion to the one we love. My loyalty to the person I love is, for Royce, a loyalty to love itself, of which my particular relationship is, for me, the salient instantiation: "You can love an individual. But you can be loyal only to a tie that binds you and others into some sort of unity, and loyal to individuals only through that tie. . . . Loyal lovers, for instance, are loyal not merely to one another as separate individuals, but to their love, to their union, which is something more than either of them, or even than both of them viewed as distinct individuals."[8] Similarly, for Royce, loyalty more generally has some component of willed commitment that takes it beyond a passion; integrates an element of judgment; and, by fastening onto some individual, cause, or value that stands outside ourselves, gives our lives a ground and purpose they would otherwise lack. On this account, loyalty is not simply a passion; it requires will and commitment. Moreover, as with other virtues, our loyalties identify certain ranges of fact as ethical considerations for us.[9] For example, to be loyal to X is for certain facts in relation to X to have ethical significance for us. Our commitment, then, both identifies objects of value that stand outside the individual, and alerts us to a range of considerations that have a cognitive dimension and inform our judgments as to how we should act with respect to those objects. These two features combine to explain why we regard loyalty as grounded in a deeper way than are our first-order preferences or interests.

One might object that loyalty is more like love than respect and that love is more like brute hunger, being resistant to judgment. Love, like hunger, certainly can take a genuinely physiological form (in pretty much any form it has physiological concomitants), but unlike hunger it is relational and involves judgments about the object of attachment. There may be all kinds of things that people are prepared to regard as unimportant on the part of those they love, but this does not mean that they will accept everything and, if they are prepared to do so, we may no longer be talking about love but about an especially acute case of psychological dependency. There is a similar bottom line for loyalty—it is not entirely immune from reasons or facts about the world no matter what complex emotional attachments may be involved in the devotion one shows to another, or to an organization or a cause. One may be willing to die for a cause (or a party or person), but that willingness is underpinned by attitudes that are linked to judgment in two ways. That is, I *behave* loyally in response to facts regarding X that I judge to be ethically salient for me; and my loyalty to X has some judgment sensitivity, it is an identification with X not Y, on ground W not Z: different facts of the matter would affect the identification.

That said, loyalty is certainly not *wholly* rational. It is not, for example, a case of having an agent-neutral reason for action.[10] Loyalty to a friend, cause, or ideal is loyalty only if it goes beyond what agent-neutral reasons would demand, "if you are loyal to a person, it appears that you cannot be moved by considerations that recommend themselves generally."[11] Similarly, Andrew Oldenquist points to the fact that if individuals are willing to defend their country, they have a *prima facie* loyalty; if they are prepared to substitute "a liberal-democratic state" for "their country," then they have a value or ideal rather than a loyalty, since they are committed to no particular instantiation.[12] So it is possible to distinguish two distinct types of attachment: one based on a balance of reasons, which provide agent-neutral grounds for others to share the evaluation of the object; the other based on loyalty, where having the appropriate psychological state with respect to an object (a person, valve, or organization) is sufficient to identify certain facts in the world as ethical considerations. If I am right in interpreting Bukharin as instancing loyalty, it is because the intensity of his Bolshevism was not just a matter of a commitment to a cause or ideal but was deeply particularized through commitments to his party, his revolutionary comrades, and his country. But there may be other forms of fanaticism that are properly distinct from loyalty in virtue of being associated with a commitment to a general cause only rather than involving any attachments to particular instantiations of that ideal.

On this account, loyalty has some judgment sensitivity, but it is not "judgment dominated" in the sense of providing agent-neutral reasons. Indeed, loyalty often seems to require a degree of insulation for certain commitments from the potentially corrosive impact of certain facts or reasons—a willingness to suspend a degree of critical scrutiny of select aspects of the world and of one's attitudes to them. Indeed, in some spheres, such as English football,[13] and some faiths or ideologies, loyalty is often recognizable largely by its apparent ability to withstand evidence to the contrary.

Royce recognizes that our loyalties may involve us in destructive conflict with others being equally loyal to their own causes and he offers the formula, "loyal to loyalty," as a meta-rule for evaluating our own loyal commitments: "In so far as it lies in your power, so choose your cause and so serve it, that, by reason of your choice and of your service, there shall be more loyalty in the world rather than less. . . . More briefly: *In choosing and in serving the cause to which you are loyal, be, in any case, loyal to loyalty.*"[14] But it is difficult to see where the motivation for this higher-order commitment is to come from. Loyalty may involve beliefs (hence its judgment sensitivity), but it also involves less rational elements that help lock our beliefs to a cause or an ideal. Once focused in this way it is simply hard to see why we should be moved by a general injunction to act so that loyalty is itself maximized. Our loyalties are motivationally powerful but incompletely judgment sensitive, while "loyal to loyalty" looks to be weak on motivation and strong on judgment sensitivity. Royce assumes that loyalty enters into the agent's own deliberation as to how to act—as if we want to act loyally, independently of wanting to do for the object we value what others would describe in terms of our acting loyally. In contrast to this view we might more properly see loyalty as like courage and modesty, where their standing as virtues can be recognized by others, but the agent need not think of himself as acting in ways that are so describable.

A third objection to Royce's account is that he sees loyalty as always having a positive moral value. Yet the grounds for taking this route are weak. Loyalty describes a psychological, dispositional, and action set that may serve good or bad ends and may be of positive or negative moral value. Insofar as we refer to it as a virtue it must, like other virtues, exist in appropriate quantity, be responsive to appropriate facts, and be dedicated to appropriate purposes. Curiously, Royce's attempt to turn loyalty into the paradigmatic virtue results in an amoral decisionism.[15] What matters is that we commit ourselves to loyalty, a commitment where the act of commitment is more important than its object. Hence the slogan: "Decide, knowingly if you can, ignorantly if you must, but in any case decide, and have no fear."[16]

This decisionism is symptomatic of the difficulties we often have in justifying our loyalties: why should I be more committed to this person, cause, or organization than any another? In being loyal, we demonstrate that we have this distinctive commitment, but the root difficulty is that there is a fundamentally nonrational component to such commitments. They have an agent-relative, context-specific, and essentially possessive character because we identify with an object (person, organization, principle, or cause) that we take as integral to our sense of self. The commitment is particularizing, possessive, and self-subordinating. That is, we are loyal to X because we see our commitment to X as a commitment to what we fundamentally are and stand for. To fail X is to fail oneself and to feel diminished. We are loyal to *our* friends; *our* cause; and *our* party, organization, or ideology; And, in being loyal to them, we express our commitment to what we see as ours.[17]

These elements of possession and self-subordination limit the judgment-sensitivity of our loyalties. By integrating the concerns of the object of my loyalty with my own, the rationality of my commitments to that object coincides with that of my own personal preferences and decisions. At the same time, unlike strictly personal preferences, the process of self-subordination results in the agent relating to these commitments as to a duty that gives them preemptive priority over his or her personal preferences because they have the status of regulative or normative claims on (or sets of dispositions for) the agent.[18] Yet because that dispositional set remains particularized to *my* friends, family, or cause, and because I defend my commitment to my cause as *my* commitment rather than on the basis of the general validity of the cause, my loyalties are substantially less susceptible to rational criticism.[19] Of course, our judgments have some factual basis and they may be susceptible to counterevidence and criticism, but few are strongly factually based. Football supporters cheer for their team because it is theirs, just as loyal partisans support their party, not because doing so is instrumental to their goals but because it is their party, and they define their goals in terms of that identity. Loyalty, then, may not be wholly irrational but neither can it be claimed to be wholly rational.[20]

Rational-choice accounts propose that loyalty be understood as a problem of agent irrationality with respect to sunk costs; that is, as expenses that have been incurred that cannot subsequently be recovered, and that it is irrational to care about.[21] Those who stay in the theater during an awful play just because they have paid for the tickets are acting irrationally because they cannot recover the cost of the tickets. If they are rational, they would question whether they are spending their time in the way that produces the most utility. If not, they should leave. To see loyalty as a sunk cost is to see one's commitments to others as past costs and benefits that are paid and unrecouperable. For the economist, losing one's arm in fighting for Pompey is a sunk cost when it comes to weighing whether one should now defect to Caesar; the time, emotional disturbance, and pain incurred in a fracturing marital relationship is a sunk cost in determining whether one should continue to invest in the relationship; and the hours the activist has spent walking the streets, knocking on doors, stuffing envelopes (or ballot boxes), and ruining his or her social and personal life for a candidate are also sunk costs when it comes to determining whether he or she should stick with that candidate.

Hirschman suggests that there is a higher degree of rationality involved in decisions about loyalty than is generally acknowledged,[22] on the grounds that loyalty is motivated by a belief that "voice" (the capacity to protest to those in authority in the organization) can improve the state of affairs that would otherwise encourage defection. However, the rationality of that belief does not bear on whether or not the individual is loyal. The soldier might mistakenly believe that the loss of his arm will give him more voice in

Pompey's council than any benefit he can derive from defecting to Caesar's camp, where it is simply a disability; the pain two people have shared together might be considered by each to constitute the starting capital to reforge their relationship founded on some alternative set of principles; and one might believe that the credibility that has developed from one's commitment as a supporter may be the basis for a voice in the candidate's campaign, but, in each case, such an interpretation treats these costs as no longer wholly sunk. If it is these kinds of judgments that motivate people's behavior then self-interest is the motive rather than loyalty. This is true too when past acts are treated as generating reputational effects or a social and political capital that will lose their value when we transfer contexts. A lost arm is no good to Caesar, the emotional baggage of a failed marriage is of no value to one's new partner (and may be worse), and the dedication to a candidate or party in the past may be grounds for suspicion on the part of rival candidates or campaigns.

Yet to interpret these cases in this way equally abandons the framework of loyalty. Indeed, the emphasis on the particularity of loyalties underlines the fact that we value those who are loyal to *us* (friends, colleagues, subordinates) rather than those who have demonstrated that they can demonstrate loyalty per se. When Pompey is dead, the marriage irreparable, and the candidate has retired from politics, there is little or nothing left to show for one's loyalty—and that little is likely to have a very modest value in other potential markets, be they alternative armies, new relationships, or other parties. Indeed, that value may be lower than it would have been had one defected earlier and shown less loyalty. The proper rational calculation would be to quit at the point at which the potential returns from the costs incurred fall below the value that one can secure for those costs in alternative markets. By picking exactly the right point, we can be recognized as having done our duty and as having an appropriate sense of when enough is enough. But this is precisely what loyalty precludes, providing another instance of the way that loyalties retain a basic insensitivity to judgment and dominate our personal interests rather than serving them.

In essence, what matters to us, if we are loyal, is our value to the domain, not what our general market value would be. As a result, it is inevitable that those who act from a sense of loyalty will fail to recoup their costs. They will stick to their commitments past the point at which they can maximize their market value and, in doing so, they instance precisely their loyalty. To quit at the optimal time requires that one assess the value of loyalty instrumentally, and insofar as a person can do that it is no longer a loyalty—or a virtue.

There is a basic distinction between loyalty among equals and among un-equals. Egalitarian loyalties are essentially reciprocal and concern mutual attachments such as love, comradeship, and fraternity.[23] Because they are tied to reciprocity there are limits to the extent of the overdraft that can be tolerated in the relationship. Someone who always counts on your loyalty and never reciprocates fundamentally changes the nature of the relation-ship; not to keep faith with those who keep faith with us destroys the char-acter of the relationship. In an important sense, these people turn out not to be who we thought they were. As Montaigne recognized, there is some-thing about truly knowing one's friend that makes it inconceivable that ei-ther of you could act in certain ways—either with respect to each other or with respect to other parties.

Loyalties in inegalitarian relationships appear to be different, not least in that we usually use the term loyalty to refer to the subordinate's attitude to his or her superior, not vice versa. That position is classically captured in Lyndon B. Johnson's demand for loyalty: "I don't want loyalty. I want *loy-alty*. I want him to kiss my ass in Macy's window at high noon and tell me it smells like roses. I want his pecker in my pocket."[24] A superior may have duties, obligations, and responsibilities associated with family, birth, place, or office, but there is something odd in thinking of a lord being loyal to his vassals—the pocketing of peckers is not strictly reciprocal. Can both people in an hierarchical relationship completely commit themselves to each other? While the subordinate can, the superior may have many subordi-nates and so commitment cannot be exclusive. The personal interests of a loyal subordinate are delimited by those of the superior, but the superior's concerns may well encompass the relevant interests of all the subordinates; so the intensity of the commitment cannot be the same. This is one reason why people often remain loyal even when their leaders abandon them. King Lear may banish Kent, but Kent remains loyal to the king. Lear no longer recognizes Kent as essential to his interests (and sees him as in con-flict with them), but Kent's commitments are a function of his unshakeable belief that his duty is to be at Lear's service—a sense that abides until Lear's death, and which is unaffected by Lear's attitude to him. "My life I never held but as a pawn, To wage against thine enemies; nor fear to lose it, Thy safety being motive."[25]

This asymmetry raises the further question of whether hierarchical loyalties attach to the person, or to the position that the superior occupies in the social and political system. Does the flunky devote himself to LBJ the individual, or to LBJ the President of the United States? What would the basis of the more personal loyalty be? LBJ certainly did expect something extraordinary from those working for him, but it remains opaque as to how he justified that expectation (to himself or to them). Certainly, he did not think it was something owed exclusively to the presidency since he asked for it long before he reached that office and had little interest in people's loyalties to other presidents.[26]

It is also possible that hierarchical loyalties may differ in the degree to which loyalty is personalized, depending in part on the stability of the order. Instability serves to accentuate dependence upon others, highlight the importance of the person in contrast to the formal position, and increase the reciprocal character of such dependence (making people more equal); whereas, in stable orders, personal loyalty makes fewer practical demands and becomes more associated with attachment to the political order more generally. As the king transmutes into the formal office of the crown, so do his loyal servants come to derive similarly formal functions with responsibilities as servants of the crown and claims and duties against those who seek to subvert those responsibilities, including the king. This does not account for LBJ, and while those who demand or cultivate intensely personal subordinate loyalties may just be psychologically needier than most, it is also the case, as is discussed in Chapter 7, that there are strong incentives for those in politics to seek personal loyalties among subordinates even in bureaucratic systems.

In modern democratic politics, loyalties are subject to special strain because of the stability and meritocratic character of the system. Stability reduces the need for unstinting loyalty to particular people, and opportunities for careerism weaken the interest in it. In addition, the more successful a politician is, the less need for any particular person's loyalty. This needs some qualification: we may need A's compliance because A has information or skills which could be harmful or essential, but, in these cases, we do not need what is distinctive to loyalty itself. The institutionally weak position of the U.S. presidency and the need to prevent staff and appointees going over to congressional or federal bureaucracies, or to support lobby group's, makes the demands for loyalty from U.S. presidents more understandable (although it certainly does not account for Johnson's demands on his staff).

Moreover, in stable, democratic orders, political success generates rewards and incentives for subordinates that can substitute for loyalty, albeit these dispositions remain conditional. In contrast, the personal rewards for loyalty on the part of the follower seem to be greater the *less* securely the leader is established. Here the relationship of loyalty is likely to be a much more intense experience because the leader's needs are acute, the people available to meet those needs are dramatically fewer, and as a result, the recognition one receives for one's contribution is more targeted and specific. We do not act this way because of that recognition; rather, if loyalty involves both possession and self-subordination, then the vulnerability of the object of one's loyalty must necessarily call forth a greater endeavor to protect it, and the identification is likely to be dramatically more intense and self-reinforcing. Similarly, loyal people in an organization whose other members begin to defect will find both that they are valued more and that the consequences of their defection become multiplied, so that the cost they would inflict by quitting rises fast. The former may be a source of pleasure, but what distinguishes the latter from self-interest maximizing is that it weighs costs and benefits not in personal terms, but in terms of the object of its loyalty. Political parties, organizations, and firms that can generate loyalty may, then, be able to brake and reverse collapse in a way that those who rely on interest cannot.

This is a distinct concern from that raised by the way that public goods or evils can complicate the possibilities for exit. With public goods, the incentive for contributing is greatest if a person is distinctively unable to protect himself (or herself) from the costs arising from the collapse of a public good, and the more convinced that person is that the good cannot be sustained without his or her contribution. For example, I may want to quit my political party because it is going against what I want done (and there is no party closer to my preferences); if I quit it will go further in the direction I oppose and, if it does, the things I want will also suffer. That problem is one of rational choice. In distinct contrast, consider what I call the psychological version, in which we experience maximal guilt over exiting an organization when it seems to need us most, and where one's identification with the organization is such that we will "put up" and sometimes "shut up" to preserve it even when we fear it may be moving in an ill-advised direction. The public good/evils account concerns incentives and costs; the psychological version implies loyalty. The former appeals to the costs to the individual; the latter to the costs to the cause.[27]

Egalitarian personal loyalty in modern politics is rendered fragile partly because it can clash with ideological and institutional loyalties, and partly because politics is essentially both hierarchical (if not in aspiration then, following Michels, at least in organization) and involves mobility. Loyalty to colleagues is strained by the inequality that results from differential political success. Moreover, the equality of individuals in the initial stages of friendship is harder to maintain once they achieve political success. It is harder to make time; advice comes from a much wider circle; and others are accorded responsibilities which preempt domains in which the services of friends used to occupy a central role (prosaically, for example, one no longer trades practical favors). The wider the circle of acquaintances, the more likely it is that the successful participant will be subjected to an increasing range of information that reflects on their old friend's honesty, integrity, reliability, and so on. Given that political careers can be jeopardized by standing by someone whose activities are suspect, it is hard to bracket out such information.[28] The result is likely to be a weakening of loyalty on the part of those who succeed without any automatic concomitant weakening on the part of those who are less successful—with the consequence that the former can be embarrassed by accusations of disloyalty or treachery by those who retain a stronger sense of identification.

A related set of considerations concerns the psychological mechanisms that kick in to relationships of loyalty. One such mechanism is that the cognitive content of loyalty can develop perverse relationships with its emotional content, so that, instead of cognitive judgments shaping the formation of emotional attachments, those emotional attachments systematically derail our cognitive judgments. When Montaigne talks about Blosius knowing that Tiberius could never advocate setting fire to the temples, he expresses a view of friendship in which the judgment sensitivity of Blosius's beliefs provide him with a grounding for his identification with Tiberius—so that in being loyal to his friend he is being loyal to someone upon whom he has a clear cognitive grip. But it is difficult to think that all loyalties are so grounded. Indeed, in Hume's discussion of ideological loyalties he is clear that the basic motivation for the commitment to "parties of principle" is nothing more rational that our tendency to over-react positively to those we see as like ourselves, and to do so negatively to those we see as different.[29]

Our loyalties may also generate a considerable stake in self-deception.[30] It is self-deceiving if Blosius's loyalty makes him more likely to overlook anomalies, to look for confirming rather than disconfirming evidence, and to interpret neutral evidence as favorable—just as if, by having paid to see a play, we may become more likely to judge it favorably. Similarly, employees may develop a loyalty to their firm that goes beyond its objective standing relative to those of other firms or organizations, with knock-on effects: a pat on the back from one's manager may be valued disproportionately to a raise in pay and status in another firm. Indeed, status considerations tend to be strongly domain related. In making the firm their own, the employees adopt its criteria for success and the markers by which it recognizes such success; similar markers in other domains simply do not mean the same. Certain elements of psychological adaptation may follow from loyalty to individuals or organizations: one may adapt one's speech and dress codes, social aspirations, cultural tastes, and so on, so that they conform more closely to those of one's manager, or to those who are perceived as dominant within the organization, or as required by the ideology. We laugh at the boss's jokes, identify with the values of the corporate culture, and indulge in the austerity recommended by the ideology. Moreover, as Hirschman suggests, the higher the entry or initiation costs one pays, the higher our tolerance of the institution—often the most reactionary members of an institution will tend to be those who had to fight hardest to get in![31] These considerations are very difficult to categorize. On the one hand, they seem to be derailments of cognitive judgment; on the other, they are part of what it is to be loyal. One's identification with an organization should not be understood in instrumental terms, as if we could straightforwardly compare what we get from our organization with that which is offered by another, simply because what it is to be loyal is to have a sense that it is *our* organization, and the other is not; that is, markers in *my* organization have a significance for me that those in other firms do not. The line, then, between elements of identification that are open to cognitive scrutiny, and those that are not, is partly determined by the character and intensity of one's loyalty. This makes Montaigne's position both difficult to substantiate, in that the claim for the cognitive character of our understanding of our friends is difficult to prove, and difficult to falsify since the identification with the other in loyalty literally makes the other my own, and that possessive character differentiates this person, organization, or set of beliefs from others in a way that makes it impossible to compare their respective merits. Someone who attempts to weigh the benefits of moving to another company against his loyalty to his present company is, in a real sense, lacking a basis for comparison. This does not mean he cannot quit, just that the benefits of quitting are not strictly commensurate to the loss of his attachment to and identification with his existing firm.

This feature of loyalty confirms the earlier suggestion that the term is used to describe a person's dispositions and behavior from a third person point of view. There is something like a solecism involved in the agent appealing to loyalty in explaining why he acted, since the explanation for why he acted involves an appeal to reasons and emotions that he has as someone who identifies in a particular way with some person, organization, or ideal. These particular components account for his action, and the action, from a third person position, can be described as exhibiting loyalty. But loyalty is not some extra thing in addition to these particular elements that plays an independent role in the actions of the agent. That makes it difficult to weigh up one's loyalty against other possible benefits—one can only recognize the fact that we value and identify with some person, organization or set of ideals in such a way that they form part of our sense of who and what we essentially are. This necessarily rules out certain types of judgment as irrelevant. Just as what it is most essentially to be me is not something I can calculate in a cost-benefit analysis, so too my identification with others cannot be assessed in this way. In this respect, such commitments are in the driving seat of judgment, rather than something over which judgment can be exercised.

That dominance of commitment over judgment is particularly evident in respect to causes and systems of belief: a commitment to a cause or ideal will frame the way people relate to the world and will tend to confirm their attitudes, increase their attachment, and explain away anomalies and resist counter-examples or evidence. Moreover, as in many ideologies, the beliefs to which a person is loyal often provide a fertile resource for interpreting interventions by others in a way that downgrades, and treats as ill-motivated, claims that undermine one's cause. In revolutions, treachery becomes the byword for those who are seen to deviate from the cause, and loyalty often becomes judged by the intensity and extremity of one's zeal. The paradigm of true revolutionary loyalty is to be found in the uncompromising austerity of the French revolutionary Saint-Just, while the complex and shifting balance of loyalty to individuals and to ideals is exemplified in the ideological debates of the Central Committee of the Soviet Communist Party in the 1920s and 1930s. Such debates have often been dismissed by treating the leaders as engaged in a cynical, tactical jockeying for position while exploiting the gullibility of their subordinates, but this sort of account looks considerably weaker in light of the evidence we now have of people's deep fear that the revolution was at risk.[32]

Loyalty is not by nature a moderate virtue since it gives priority to a particular person, cause, or institution over similar persons, causes, and institutions. I suggested earlier that loyalty in politics is likely to be more urgent the less stable the order and the position of the politician. If this is true, this suggests that periods in which the political system is most fragile will tend to generate relationships that militate against neutrality, impartiality, and a respect for procedures over individual concerns. Where the system is stable, loyalty is less demanding and less necessary, and attachments to the more abstract claims of procedures and their neutrality are more easily generated. The difficulty is in making the transition between the two conditions, given that the former generates relationships that are fundamentally inimical to the latter. A further, and equally troubling thought is that nearly every politician, irrespective of the stability of the political order, will start his or her political life needing support from others, and needing to secure the patronage of others through his or her own loyalties, which means that a consistent undercurrent of nonneutral and partisan relationships is endemic to political life. As a result, many politicians will find themselves compromised by activities and relationships that were essential in the early stages of their careers but that subsequently prove incompatible with attempts to establish their commitment to established procedures and rules.[33]

A final dimension of loyalty that demands attention is the problem of conflicting loyalties. For example, a bureaucrat may understand her responsibilities in terms of any one (or some combination) of at least five different views of the object of her loyalty and the nature of its claims. She may work within a hierarchical model in which loyalty is owed to her superior and the demands that loyalty makes are equated with the orders she receives; she may have a sense of loyalty to her values, conscience, and personal ethical code; she may see herself as owing loyalty to her peers and the social norms they share; she may have a loyalty to her profession and its ethical code of conduct; or she may see her role as demanding a loyalty to her fellow citizens which she meets by acting in accordance with civic values.[34] While these conceptions of the nature of a bureaucrat's responsibilities can be associated with different models of responsibility, it is plausible to think that most bureaucrats work with several different models simultaneously, and then come face-to-face with certain types of conflict. For example, both Daniel Ellsberg, the U.S. Defense Department employee who leaked part of the Pentagon Papers in 1971, and Clive Ponting, a senior British civil servant whose abilities were recognized by an accelerated path of promotion under Prime Minister Margaret Thatcher and who released a document revealing that his minister, Michael Heseltine, had misled the House of Commons over the arrival of Cruise missiles in Britain, may have acted out of a sense of the basic loyalty they owed as citizens to their fellow citizens, but it is implausible to think that every one of their actions as public servants was similarly motivated. Like most of us, they probably worked with a number of different models of their responsibilities. Only when facing a major conflict between models does it become necessary to nail one's colors to a particular mast. Similarly, in personal loyalties to family and friends, we often need to make trade-offs between conflicting demands in which we implicitly make judgments about the respective claims that each object/person/cause can make of us. Our decisions will be affected by the types of loyalty we have, which will take one of three basic forms:

1. Loyalties may be *conditional*—that is, each on its own may be a sufficient reason for acting, but may be overridden by a more weighty reason, although they do not thereby lose their weight or status as reasons. Equally, a loyalty may outweigh other reasons, without those reasons losing their weight or status as reasons. (I am assuming here that two or more loyalties are being compared, but this is not the case, for example, when comparing a preference with a loyalty).

2. Loyalty to a particular object/person/cause may *exclude* any other potential loyalties to others. For example, an *exclusive* loyalty is such that in sticking by X, I cannot stick by Y, and in choosing X, I deny that Y really has a claim of loyalty against me. This judgment may involve a re-evaluation of my sense of self and of where my commitments most fundamentally lie.

3. One may have a *partially exclusive* loyalty; that is, by virtue of my loyalty to X, I cannot be a friend of or loyal to Y, but it leaves open the prospect of further loyalties to Z.

It is debatable whether a conditional loyalty can ever be completely nonexclusive. That is, can one have a loyalty that does not necessarily exclude certain types of reasons for action? Fletcher's suggestion that loyalties are tri-adic—A's loyalty to B, rather than C—implies that every loyalty is always at least partially exclusive; however, it may be that we need to understand at least some triadic relations as involving only conditional loyalties—my loyalty to B is more weighty than my loyalty to C, but it does not exclude my having a loyalty to C or to D.

Conditional and nonexclusive loyalties can be trumped or outweighed by stronger loyalties; for example, my decision to stay at work and support my colleagues in a protest when I had promised to be at home to help with the children does not deny my loyalty to my partner or my children. My sense of loyalty to my superiors, exhibited in my carrying out of commands received, may nonetheless have strict limits, perhaps defined by personal conscience, or by a sense of civic responsibility. Similarly, intrafamilial conflicting loyalties (between one's parents, spouse, siblings, and children) may force us to recognize one claim as of greater weight, but without our feeling that the overridden claims have no weight; indeed they would have had sufficient weight to motivate us in the absence of the conflict. This explains why we might have feelings of betrayal and guilt simply because it is not always easy to do justice to those whose claims on us we recognize as legitimate but insufficient to override other claims.

In contrast, the development of exclusive loyalties may lead to the denial that anything is owed to someone who might have counted on support in the past, without any feelings of betrayal—even though the abandoned person is left feeling betrayed. For example, when a political party splits, those defecting to set up a new party tend to deny that they have any obligation to the old party or that they betrayed the cause. They may claim that their loyalty has always been to a set of ideals and that in moving to the new party they retain that loyalty, and in doing so it became clear that the subsidiary loyalties they once felt to individuals, constituents, and party organization no longer have weight for them. Similarly, members of certain religious sects expect that those who join their sect will not only regard their loyalties to the new sect as trumping other loyalties (even those to their families), but will come to exclude those past loyalties as weightless.

Conditional loyalties seem to be, on the whole, an essential ingredient of political life. Without such loyalties we would have little connection with the social or political world, save self-interest, which can be deeply destructive, and reasonableness, which is often in deficit. Loyalties relate us to the world in a way that connects us with its ideals, institutions, practices, and associated comradeship; they do so in a way that recognizes that hard decisions have to be made, and have to be made with something like Weber's "ethic of responsibility."[35] In such decisions it is necessary to recognize that certain loyalties are outweighed by others, but it is also important to weigh the competing claims carefully. In contrast, exclusionary loyalties are more suspect, the more so the broader their exclusion. Orwell's *1984* depicts a nation in which the loyalty to the state is assumed to exclude other loyalties: it is not just that it trumps them, it is that they cannot be understood as retaining their status as independent reasons for action. Although the story is fictional, history reveals that loyalty to a political system in both the East and West has occasionally excluded other loyalties (such as those to family and friends).[36] In authoritarian regimes, even if people were not so brainwashed as theorists of totalitarianism once argued, citizens sometimes behaved as if their loyalty to the state excluded, rather than simply trumped, other forms of loyalty.

Loyalties become more troubling the more exclusionary their nature, the more encompassing their scope, and the more intensely they are experienced. Loyalty to some individuals may be partially exclusionary of certain loyalties to others, but as long as the individual remains involved in plural relationships that make competing demands, it is harder for one such relationship systematically to trump (rather than exclude) all others.[37] One potential problem that arises from identifying with a person or object is that the identification assumes greater importance as more features of the relationship become entwined. Loyalty to an organization can be more potent than loyalty to an individual if the organization comes to dominate every aspect of life. Moreover, the shift from one loyalty trumping others, to loyalty becoming exclusionary, is in part a function of the way that the object of one's identification represents the nature of its claims. A revolutionary ideology that is open and inclusive when struggling against a regime may subsequently demand more exclusive and finely honed ideological commitment when it assumes power.[38] Equally, organizations that recruit widely may subsequently increase the demands they make on their staff, turning issues of compatible loyalty into issues of trumping, and subsequently into issues of exclusion. And loyalty to an ideal or an ideology that influences nearly every aspect of one's daily life and behavior can be still more demanding and exclusionary. But I must emphasize the difference among conditional, partially exclusionary, and exclusionary loyalties: While many political loyalties can trump certain conditional personal and social loyalties, by not denying their relevance as reasons the pluralism of social and political life is sustained and some judgment sensitivity is also preserved.[39] When political loyalties exclude such loyalties, pluralism is seriously under threat—the more so because exclusive loyalties on the part of some will tend to generate similarly exclusive loyalties among others.

Montaigne's belief that Blosius's knowledge of his friend Tiberius Gracchus was such that he knew that Tiberius would not ask him to burn down the temples offers one line of argument about how "true" loyalty may have resources to resist extremism. Underlying his account is the view that, while a person's attachment to a friend is particular to that particular friend, it is not devoid of cognitive components. That is, to value that friend is to value him for what he is, not for what he is to me; to be loyal to him is to be loyal to what we are to each other. In both components, cognitive elements have precedence over the emotional attachment. To repeat the passage quoted earlier, "If their actions broke the traces, then they were, by my measure, neither friends of each other nor friends of themselves. . . . I do not doubt what my will is, any more than I doubt the will of such a friend." That is, not only would "breaking the traces" indicate that my friend was not the man I thought him to be, but in doing so it would betray the mistake I had made in conferring on him my affection, and in betraying that it would undercut the relationship upon which my loyalty was founded.

Montaigne's account of friendship and loyalty offers a model of the kind of mean between attachment and belief that renders loyalty always a virtue. One's devotion to a cause, a professional calling, or a friend, is a case of loyalty (following Royce and others) when it identifies certain ranges of facts as ethical considerations for the agent. Loyalty becomes less particularistic as one recognizes that others similarly take a certain range of facts as ethical considerations; for example, this can move from recognizing that my loyalty to X is matched by Y because Y takes a similar range of facts as having ethical weight, to recognizing that my loyalty to X has something in common with Y's loyalty to W, because we treat similar facts as having ethical weight for us with respect to different particulars. In that process we can move from a particular attachment to a cause, calling, or friend to recognizing in that attachment an instance of a more general value. More general values (such as the existence of ideals and the causes that pursue them, the ideal of professional service, or the ideal of friendship) may result in critical reflection on the range of facts that we regard as relevant to our attachment. An ideal cannot be merely self-serving, a conception of professional service cannot involve intentional harm to those who need it, and a friend must be someone whose qualities (and defects) are known. These cognitive components are pretty abstract and are not necessarily robust when we have to decide between competing claims in the heat of the moment, but they give us a basis for identifying the point at which loyalty becomes dysfunctional and ceases to be a virtue (although that does not mean that it ceases to be a case of loyalty). The point at which loyalty becomes a vice is the point at which the emotional attachment begins wholly to drive a person's beliefs. This is not to say that people's attachments are wholly grounded on their beliefs since that would eradicate the emotional and particular identification that loyalty involves. Nor does it deny the earlier claim that the sense of one's possession of, and by, the ideal, organization, or friend makes certain sorts of evaluative weighting simply inappropriate. Rather, beliefs and attachments must continue to run hand in hand; that is, John's commitment expresses his belief that his identification is warranted by the values that his ideals, organization, or friends embody. To insulate one's attachments from evidence and argument, to ignore disconfirming instances, or to interpret the world wholly through an attachment to a particular cause is to abandon the cognitive dimension which underlies the individual's sense of the worth of the thing with which he or she identifies. It is, in effect, to narrow the range of information to which one is open.

As the discussion in this chapter has shown, political virtues can be especially difficult to instantiate consistently. We need loyalty, commitment, and judgment in politics. We want people to care about others and about issues and matters of principle, but we want their loyalties to be conditional or partially exclusionary in form rather than exclusionary, and we do not want them to undermine their own implicit cognitive content.[40] Similarly, we want professionals to be loyal to their profession and its basic values and principles, but we want that loyalty to be reflective and conditional, rather than blind and exclusionary. Civil servants, judges, and politicians should reflect on the way their activities in office conform to the values and ends of public service to which they should be committed. They need not deny that their loyalties to their families are stronger than to strangers, but those stronger loyalties should not undermine their conduct in their official or professional capacity. When the conflict is great, rather than one loyalty simply winning over the other, those in politics must accept the rules that restrain them from using their official standing to pursue personal loyalties.

In looking for this kind of solution we seem to be asking for loyalty to be trumped not by other loyalties, but by more general normative principles, procedural rules, or considerations of impartiality—principles that are difficult to derive in anything more than a very attenuated form from the cognitive components of loyalty. Even if we value people's loyalties, on their own they are inadequate as constraints on people's conduct. Were we only ever the sum of our loyalties and commitments, in the way some communitarians have suggested, then policy decisions and the execution and administration of policy would be relatively tribal—and tribal politics can be vicious even when not radically exclusionary. The natural alternative seems to be the creation of more abstract loyalties to the political system itself, or the insistence that those in public office act in ways in keeping with impartiality and liberal neutrality. Yet these options depend on such principles being able to constrain the often dramatically more powerful motivation of particular loyalties to particular individuals, groups, or identities.

Would we then be better off without loyalties in politics? It is tempting to think that we would and that politics could become simply a process of the concertation and ordering of interests so as to maximize aggregate welfare, utility, or some similar standard. But, without loyalties, it is doubtful that this result could be produced. Our loyalties play a major role in defining for us where our interests lie and in identifying what most fundamentally matters to us. Moreover, we rely on those in politics to have some identification with the values and ends for which they stand such that they will stick to them under certain types of pressure. But we do not, for the most part, want them to put their loyalties before everything and it is by no means clear that there is an optimal balance between loyalties, on the one hand, and a more principled commitment to (for example) the norms of the political system, on the other. Nonetheless, because loyalty to a cause can in itself influence our sense of the legitimacy of certain procedures and practices in politics, it is easy to see how such trade-offs might be dominated by loyalty.

In this sense, while there is a need for loyalty, it carries risks for political systems in which it is generated. I have suggested that competing conditional loyalties might help to sustain the judgment sensitivity of our commitments and create a context in which judgments between loyalties are made with care. Those judgments do not serve to abolish the claims which others make on us and the allegiances we feel toward them, but preserve them by ranking and ordering them, just as we do with our own preferences and interests. Although such loyalties are not deduced from a rational code of ethics they are, through such judgments, partly rationalized and moderated. If there is any chance that we will find the mean in loyalty, I think it likely to be in dealing with conditional commitments, in a pluralist order, and with professional loyalties and values dominating the conduct in the political order. That achievement will depend on certain causal preconditions and cultural and institutional arrangements that are not easily identified or realized, but only under these conditions will our loyalties qualify unconditionally as political virtues.

CHAPTER 7

Officials and Public Servants

Does loyalty have any place in the relationship between politicians and those who serve them, either in a personal, political capacity or in the capacity of servants or officials of the state? Why not conceive of such relationships as entirely contractual in character? Or should professionalism be seen as an alternative to both loyalty and contractualism? Why should loyalty, or any other form of emotional involvement or identification, have a place, or, indeed, be an essential requirement in public service? In this chapter I explore the types of loyalty that public service demands, the systematic problems modern states have in consistently generating this loyalty, and whether the demands of loyalty are compatible with whistle-blowing.

The classical Greek world had rather little sense of service, distinct from that of slavery. Selling one's labor in an ongoing relationship with an employer was largely foreign to the Greeks and was seen as incompatible with one's standing as a citizen and free man. There were official positions whose function was to serve the community, but these were construed essentially as positions of rule, awarded by lot, of restricted tenure (usually a year), and not renewable. Although service to the state was not a feature of ancient republics, the idea clearly does arise under Imperial rule. The emergence of single rulers in Rome created some initial difficulties in that there was no official residence or public office for the ruler to occupy. They had a military escort and ceremonial attendants, but there was no staff specifically established to do the bidding of the emperor. What gradually emerged was an entourage made up of domestic employees and freedmen; those assigned by military duty; and a group of friends and advisors, often skilled in law, rhetoric, and literature, who came from the equestrian and senatorial orders.[1] The public attendants who served the emperor were largely drawn from the freedmen of his household, and as such served to link private service to the person of the emperor with service to the state through service to the emperor as a form of patrimonial bureaucracy.[2] This immediately raises the question of where one's primary loyalty lay: to the state and its offices, or to the person of the emperor? In fact, the uncertainties of rule, the threat of political competition, and the partial deification of the emperor to place him above the remnants of republican institutions encouraged rulers to put their trust in those whose loyalty was personal, rather those who might lean to the political order or public good. A further tension emerged as those who had the trust of the emperor often became the source of scandal and outrage within Rome, not least for the wealth they accumulated and the influence they exerted. This phenomenon marks an early indication of a parting of the ways between the norms, mores, and expectations of the wider society, and those that develop around the exercise of power by the state. One of the most extreme instances of both conflicts is the emergence, in Rome's Byzantine Empire of the fourth and fifth centuries, of a group of court eunuchs who rose from their roles as slaves and ex-slaves initially serving as domestic attendants to the emperor to positions of considerable power and influence in the Imperial court.[3] Their emergence provided a mechanism for an increasingly sacred but isolated emperor (pushed in that direction to legitimate his claims to superiority over potential rivals from the nobility) to communicate with his state without being beholden to it. This development is not an isolated case; there are parallels in the roles of eunuchs in the late Ming court.[4]

For our purposes, the central issue is the tie between the eunuchs and the emperor. Eunuchs, unlike many of the other groups who came into the Imperial service from the body of the Roman citizenry, "could never be assimilated into the aristocracy. Their origins as slaves and barbarians, their physical deformity and the emotions it aroused, their easy identification, and their lack of family, were all against it. They were completely dependent on the emperor and had no natural allies in society, no other retreat than his protection."[5] They had no sons to achieve social mobility, no possibility of transmitting wealth, and their position was entirely in the gift of the emperor, who could dismiss them, confiscate their property, exile them, or execute them at will.

The Roman Imperial world, like the Chinese Ming dynasty, raises in stark form the issue of how to organize and exercise power and authority in a state where there are many rival contenders for power, where levels of trust are correspondingly low, and where there is a concerted attempt to elevate the emperor above the rest of society. In both cases there is a need for an efficient and disciplined financial and military system, but there are difficulties in assuming direct control of those organizations without becoming hostage to their demands. To avoid this one requires the absolute dependence and loyalty of those managing relations with these organizations and running those areas of one's life in which one is most vulnerable. The combination in the Roman empire of drawing from the equestrian ranks to staff the military and administrative leadership of the state (so as to develop a rival power to that of the nobility), while entrusting to one's household considerable responsibilities for the management of the court and its interface with imperial and state bodies, was an attempt to forge on the one side an efficient bureaucratic apparatus and on the other a cadre of servants with deep personal loyalty who could implement the commands of the emperor and resist the demands of administrative system.

The eunuch is an interesting metaphor for the public servant: he is someone whose personal interests were brutally curtailed; he posed no threat to the sexual security (and by extension to the physical and emotional security) of the household to which he was admitted with complete intimacy (especially important in the late Roman world of high official morality);[6] and the rewards that he received were compensation for the (enforced) sacrifice made. The rewards consisted of tokens of esteem and recognition of service rather than payment for services rendered. Indeed, although the riches lavished on certain eunuchs were sometimes immense, there was a general contempt for their wealth and for their concern for wealth among their contemporaries—as if the coin of their reward was somehow demeaning (the nobles regarded the desire for wealth for its own sake as incompatible with dignity). But it is significant that there is a degree of "blocked exchange" in relation to the eunuchs' rewards (they cannot pass them on, nor translate them into a broader social status), just as there is to the status and honors awarded to public servants in a court or government (their value is largely limited to the domain within which they are received).[7] Indeed, the eunuch symbolizes the subordination of the private to the public.[8] However, another dimension to the employment of eunuchs was their utter personal dependence on the emperor—they did not act impartially, they served faithfully and in important respects selflessly as the instruments of the emperor's will. (Of course, things sometimes go wrong, as when the eunuchs conspired to secure the execution of Caesar Gallus,[9] or when Wen Zhongxian orchestrated a reign of terror against senior public officials in the Donglin movement for reform in the 1620s Ming court.) Common interests among the eunuchs were relatively unstable and collectively they were strong only to the extent that the emperor was weak, otherwise they were wholly dependent on his will. This meant that their loyalties were not to the laws, to the state, or to the public good, but were intensely personal. Furthermore, the eunuch's standing and success was rarely transferred from one emperor to another. Such intensely personal loyalties are, then, exclusionary, and they encompass all elements of the agent's life since they stand and fall with their leader's fortunes.

The tension between impersonal public service and personal fidelity has remained throughout the long and uneven development of public officialdom and has greatly added to the complexity of the political process: Those who rule want personal loyalty *and* efficient bureaucratic administrations, but those demands are never easily reconciled. Moreover, the two dimensions pose potentially competing standards of conduct for those who serve.

While Imperial rule betrays this uneasy tension between formal bureaucratic authority and a cadre of personally loyal servants, the smaller, less structured, and less ambitious forms of rule associated with medieval courts and principalities found more moderate mechanisms for combining personal loyalty and institutional service through the model of the household, and by the development of offices that allowed the incorporation of men and women from outside the family for tactical or strategic purposes or in recognition of their potential contribution to the management of the "estate." This model of the state as a variant of household management has a powerful influence in European history. The prince's officers were his *serjeants* (his *servientes* or servants), who held their lands in virtue of the performance of some specified service in war or more generally, or those with knight-service who held tenancy in return for payment (or *scutage*). Again, the history of these arrangements is partly a story of administrative organization and partly a story about the need for loyal support for the throne and its occupant. For both purposes the household provided an apt model— a system of freighted exchange, where the subordinate is bound in service to the master in return for a range of benefits and rights. It is not an exchange between equals, or an exchange of equivalents. The inequality of the exchange is central to the demand for loyalty from the subordinate: becoming part of the household is not a strictly monetary and contractual matter, it is a process that simultaneously subordinates the individual to the master, while conferring status and standing within the household. The duties of members of the king's household are similarly personal honors that the king confers, that mark one's standing in the court, and which, if denied or contravened, would give rise to serious complaint.[10] The subordinate pays the price of loyalty and service for the standing and recognition that the role confers. Indeed, even when the service is commuted to payment, the payment is not a market price for the benefits received so much as a symbolic recognition that the agent receives his standing from the hands of the king.

The loyalty of eunuchs in Imperial courts was primarily personal, rather than to the office; for serjeants and members of the royal household there was a willingness to run both elements together, in much the same way that, in many traditional communities, servants were incorporated into the household of the master and could expect to remain in the household and to serve the master and his family for their lifetime and often for those of their children. As such, the concerns of the household also become their concerns, and the order of the household becomes an order with which they identify, in which they find their place, in which they can develop their own private lives, and in which they may hope to find preferment. However, as traditional communities became part of a more national and centralized order, and simultaneously became penetrated by more pluralistic market and contractual relations, a structure of service emerged that transcended individual households, opening wider vistas of aspiration for servants—such as to serve in a more noble or greater house—and providing a more systematic organization of functions so that roles and positions became similarly differentiated within major households. These developments increased the tension between the sense of one's duties as a particular officeholder and those arising from one's duties and loyalty to one's master, and encouraged an embryonic articulation of the concept that there are standards that should be met by those who govern the household. A master who acts inappropriately risks forfeiting the loyalty of his servants, once that loyalty becomes a commitment to the master by virtue of his place or position within an order extending beyond the household to the wider political and social world—a judgment that the prospect of mobility would encourage. Of course, the servant's subordination within the household in many respects militates against such judgments, but that service is not wholly uncritical or unreflective. Indeed, insofar as a servant aims to serve his master, this wider context is something to which he should be alert so as to provide support and guidance if he identifies potential harms to his master's interests. The development of a sense of office as part of a broader system involving rights and responsibilities creates the potential for the loyalties of the officeholder to move from the person to the order in a way that can generate criticism of those to whom one is formally subject. In that development there is a shift from exclusive personal loyalty to a loyalty to office that is likely to be partly exclusionary of interests and loyalties that run against the performance of the formally defined role.

The spread of contractual and market relationships, and of wage labor, also had an impact on public (and private) service. In England, culminating in the eighteenth century, there was a gradual change from work undertaken as members of households to wage labor.[11] A central dimension of this change was the greater freedom of the individual to contract to whomever they wished, to work set hours, and to pursue their own interests, coupled with a greater responsibility to provide for oneself in all domains (food, clothing, lodging, tools) and a greater vulnerability to market forces. Moreover, the market assumes no normative relationship between an employer and employee since neither owes loyalty to the other, and the worker's interests and those of his employer can be sharply distinct. In contrast, public office evolved from more personal and patronage-based service, where allegiance was owed to the individual into whose service one entered, to a more impersonal form in which it is to the service itself, a sense of one's responsibilities and ends framed by one's institutional location, that one's loyalty is primarily owed. The possession of and self-subordination to office and its associated standing remains central to this sense of service and is linked to an awareness of one's place within a larger network of responsibilities and activities within the institution and state. The roles of those in public service are no longer personal, nor are they employed in a strictly professional/technical capacity (in which they own their craft and retain fully their independence of judgment) or in a wholly contractual or wage-relationship. The state demands from its officials something more than a particular type of professional expertise or a certain amount of labor for hire. It does so because public officials remain the instruments that implement the outcomes of the political process. The end of their activity (unlike those of most professions) is not ultimately for them to decide; in that sense, they remain in service to political masters who determine and legitimate such ends.

The parallel between domestic and public servants goes beyond their sharing a term: underlying both is a sense of loyalty and commitment that links the agent closely to those who command him and to his office, and this is expected as part of the ethos of public service. We want officials to show responsibility and integrity not because of their financial or reputational interests, but because they identify with their role and its place within the larger machinery of government and consider it a matter of integrity that they put the interests of the state before their own. According to Weber, the official is part of an order to which he or she must be normatively subordinate: "In the great majority of cases he is only a small cog in a ceaselessly moving mechanism which prescribes to him an essentially fixed route of march. . . . The individual bureaucrat is, above all, forged to the common interest of all the functionaries in the perpetuation of the apparatus and the persistence of its rationally organised domination."[12]

The idea of the individual bureaucrat as only a small cog in a ceaselessly moving mechanism is an ideal-typical account that for many political philosophers captures at least some elements of a normative ideal. Indeed, most liberals, and some who are profoundly illiberal such as Machiavelli or Schmitt, concur that it is centrally important that the state not be controlled or suborned by forces within society (or outside), and that public servants must be prevented from exercising their office for their own ends. The view of the bureaucrat as merely a cog in the hierarchical machine depicts a disciplined system of administration subordinate to the sovereign and independent from other groups or agents.[13]

Although diverse perspectives converge in emphasizing that the demands of public office must trump the private concerns or interests of the official, there is less agreement on the exact nature of these demands. Some emphasize subordination to the rules that govern public office, some stress the subordination of officials to those who rule, and others emphasize the ends that office serves. Hobbes and Schmitt, for example, take the second route by suggesting that it is subservience to the sovereign that really matters. In contrast, liberals stress justice or natural law constraints and republicans emphasize the sovereignty of the common good, both of which are seen by realists as potentially destabilizing, a threat to sovereignty, and as disguising self-serving (Hobbes) or group-serving (Schmitt) interests. For Hobbes, because proximity to power breeds ambition and only absolute sovereignty can protect the political system from competition and the lust for glory, officers, bureaucrats, servants, and others must be welded together and rendered subservient and loyal to the sovereign so that they pursue without question the ends he sets. An impartial bureaucracy will not meet this need. For both Hobbes and Schmitt, those who are not absolutely with the state and prepared to bend to its will, are against it. With Lyndon Johnson, they want absolute loyalty; they want our peckers in their pockets—or a eunuch class.

The persuasiveness of this view depends partly on its claims about the fragility of the political order; principally, the suggestion that without absolute sovereignty (or something akin to it) order will be undermined by faction, or domestic or foreign subversion. Where disorder looms, as we have seen, unswerving service, dedication, and loyalty become essential and central to identifying oneself as friend not foe to that sovereignty. Such views deny, by induction from contingent experience to a foundational philosophical anthropology, that the state and its servants can make the transition from this order to one in which loyalty translates into compliance with public norms, rules, and standards of impartiality. While this opinion is extreme, it signals an abiding problem. As Bentham notes, there is a built-in interest in monarchical rule to want the state to serve the (personal) ends of the monarch, thereby encouraging the demand for loyalty and the subjection of officials to the monarch (qua person) rather than to the crown (qua institution).[14] But there seems to be no reason for anyone in political power to want less than such service—hence the vexed issue of the degree of politicization that can be permitted of civil servants. The British tradition of civil service neutrality runs up hard against the demand by ministers for people committed to their programs; the U.S. tradition of political appointment runs up equally hard against the need for expert and impartial advice. The historical story behind the emergence of different types of bureaucratic order is complex, but one major recurrent issue is how to ensure that officials of the state perform their office while also recognizing that those in power have, to some degree, a legitimate right to determine the standards for what that entails and for assessing how far their officials meet those standards.[15] However much liberal democratic states rely on appeals to higher-order values of justice and fairness, formal procedures, service values of impartiality and neutrality, and natural and international law constraints, the interpretation and implementation of such values is determined by the political process. The loyalties of public servants cannot be wholly detached from that process and transferred to these more abstract values. The rapid growth in the size of the public service in most states in recent decades has profoundly changed the setting for public officials, demanding more independent action from them while also introducing greater scope for both personal judgment and ethical scruple than Weber ever imagined. But these developments do not eradicate politics, and the public service, especially in its upper echelons, unlike other professions, must remain governed by the goals and values set by the political process. In this sense, loyalty cannot simply be narrowly to one's office (a type of bureaucratic formalism), nor to the person of one's minister (not least since the occupants of office change frequently). Loyal service remains necessary, but it is a loyalty owed not to abstract values such as impartiality but to the public service and the broader political system itself.

How do we ensure that those in public office work in the public interest, rather than in their own (either directly self-servingly or in pursuit of group, partisan, or sectional advantage)?

Many accounts look to corruption control mechanisms, as well as regulatory and accountability systems; others focus on ways to build integrity in those in public office. Despite their common objective, they are two very different routes. To use rules and incentives to create integrity risks being self-defeating since *integrity* (by definition) concerns the extent to which agents demonstrate a certain consistency of character that is rooted in morally serious commitments to ends and values that are felt strongly enough to enable them to resist pressure to act otherwise; someone who merely responds to external incentives lacks integrity.[16]

One objection to appeals to integrity is that becoming a public servant is an act of will that commits one to undertake an office or fill a role, rather than to having a certain character; yet the demand for integrity implies an intense identification with the office involving deep commitment. Clearly, the depth of that commitment varies, but the reason that loyalty and the virtues seem appropriate concepts in discussing public officials is that (at the upper reaches) we expect their identification with, and their commitment and subordination to, the political service and their place within it to become central to their sense of themselves, and to provide the basis for deep and reflective judgments in respect to the demands of public office.

Integrity is not just a case of manifesting the right behavior but involves doing the right things for the right reasons. Regulation that relies wholly on incentives and penalties to ensure good conduct produces conformity not integrity. Of course, pay and conditions of service affect people's incentives to reject bribes and avoid risk, and they may even provide essential background conditions for self-respect and a sense of professional responsibility and status,[17] but they do not directly promote integrity. The integrity-based approach expects people to be guided by the desire to act in keeping with their responsibilities and fundamental commitments and the practices by which these are framed. Reputation, status, income, and respect may acknowledge the person's commitments, but the model holds that these commitments should not themselves be motivated solely by the reputation, status, or income that they earn for the agent.

In contrast, the compliance-based model portrays public office as a potential source of temptation that must be guarded against by establishing incentives for conformity and penalties for opportunism. This approach, in which principal-agent models are prominent, treat the public official or politician as an interest-maximizer for whom a system of incentives and rewards is required to ensure that they act in the public interest. The assumed default position is that citizens should expect the worst of their officials and design incentives to ensure that politicians, by pursuing their own interests, end up serving those of the public.

If the distinction between these two approaches is intuitively clear, its implications may be less obvious. In broad terms, democracies ask their publics to support institutions and procedures that constrain the pursuit of individual and group interests. To do so successfully (with maximum legitimacy and minimum recourse to state violence) these institutions and procedures must be justifiable in terms of their impartiality, fairness, probity, and reliability. Yet these institutions cannot have these qualities if they are lacking in those who exercise authority and power in them. If civil servants are to be regulated by a compliance model then another set of institutions must ensure that compliance, and why should that set be any more reliable? If we make civil servants directly answerable to the people, then we are trusting the people to demonstrate the very virtues that the model assumes that those in office lack. Yet, in many cases, we create public offices—such as the police—to remedy the shortfall in certain virtues among the public—which cousnels against giving the public a controlling role in such offices. Any political system needs some on-going locus of integrity. Even the best balanced and best designed system needs interpretation and judgment, and those who interpret and judge must do so authoritatively and impartially, not just in the interests of some section of the community; for that we need integrity.

There is evidence of growing dissatisfaction with the performance of governments in the Western world during the 1980s and 1990s, even if it is less clear whether this is a long-term trend.[18] I do not wish to review the evidence for this (which is not for the most part of great depth) but, if true, its implications for public office are serious. Declining confidence saps democratic political systems of one of their major sources of reward and reinforcement for politicians and public officials; systems that expressly disdain public valuation are not similarly threatened. When, for example, political honors become derided or treated with suspicion, their value to individuals correspondingly declines. While civil servants in the past worked with an administrative ethos that emphasized a life-long commitment to the service, the encouragement of the French system of *pantouflage*[19] exposes those in the service more directly to the judgments and expectations of others, weakens the institutional ethos of the service, and reduces the self-reinforcing nature of public service norms. The result is not so much corruption as a decline in the institutional resources for resisting corruption and malpractice, with an erosion of the institutional and cultural framework that reinforces the virtue of integrity and an undermining of the ethos of public service and institutional loyalty. If the valuation of one's activity is linked to the valuation of others, and if that is declining, the job becomes less attractive, ceases to attract high caliber candidates, and tends to produce a less able and less dedicated staff. This process of demoralization further weakens institutions' resistance to corruption and maladministration.

Moreover, declining confidence tends to result in pressure for increased accountability and scrutiny, which pushes the context further toward a compliance culture. That trend is not in itself disastrous: it encourages rule-bound systems that further erode loyalty and confidence and exacerbates the need for an ethically sound institution to enforce the compliance model; however, while it may not lead to corruption if enforcement is efficient and there are good rewards for conformity, enforcement mechanisms themselves are likely to become weaker and more populist, officials will increasingly face a range of incompatible demands, and rewards will be assessed against the gains of converting their "capital" to the private sector. Under such pressures, we should expect diminishing commitments to public service; difficulties in recruitment; and increasing levels of maladministration, incompetence, and corruption.

This is not an argument about the moral frailty of officials. It derives from the view that status is a public and (to some extent) collectively allocated good. Its value to individuals is the standing it accords them in the eyes of their culture and in society more broadly. Such standing, as discussed in Chapter 4, matters both for people's self-regard and their self-esteem.[20] This is less of a problem where the key reference group for civil servants is their colleagues and where the status rewards are internal to the service (or where they are internal to the household or court), but modern democratic systems, by their nature, demand greater openness and accountability, and public officials no longer exist as a distinct caste with distinct mores and distinctive institutional loyalties that embed them in the system of administrative rule. Their openness exposes them to other pressures, loyalties weaken and become more conditional, monetary rewards become more important, and regulation tends to grow. Karl Marx may have exaggerated the speed with which market relations undermine all other forms of communal and hierarchical relation, but the thrust of his argument still seems pertinent: "All fast frozen relations, with their train of ancient and venerable prejudices and opinions are swept away, all new formed ones become antiquated before they can ossify. All that is solid melts into air."[21]

The central problem facing the organization of government is that those involved in the everyday tasks of government—public administration, regulatory bodies, and so on—cannot approach their responsibilities within the political arena in the spirit of taking for themselves what they can. *Cannot* because doing so denies the responsibilities and duties of the position that the system relies on them to fulfil, thereby systematically destabilizing the system.[22] This does not mean that public officials must be entirely selfless. It is not a matter of choosing between incentives and education or indoctrination;[23] it is a case of recognizing that public office cannot function if people do not fully understand that they are accepting a public trust. Their integrity as repositories of that trust must matter to them. The practices, norms, and rules of their office must have some grip on their minds and must generate an identification with the public service, and thereby some loyalty.[24] Incentives and recognition have a role, but these must themselves ride on the back of a more basic disposition in relation to office, and that disposition must not be undermined by encouraging calculations of interest or by de-

valuing or demeaning the features of the service that those who serve identify with and value.

The resilience of conformity to public office norms is partly a function of
the continuing conformity of others with those norms—not least since it
ensures that the costs of conforming are widely shared. Resilience thus may
rest as much on trust and solidarity among public officials as it does on trust
between them and those who command them or are administered by them.
Various forms of social solidarity, such as caste, clan, class, familial or patrimonial relations, and shared ideological commitments, have in the past
contributed to the trust upon which such commitments were built, but
often raised problems of conflicting loyalties.[25] Partly in response, modern
liberal democratic states have made double transition in their public services. The first involved shifting from personal to institutional loyalties and
thus altering the focus of loyalty from the master to the office and the institutional system in which it functions, but leaving unstable and contested
the interface between the administrative elite and their political masters.
The second transition was from a system of recognition that revolved
around status and standing in relation to a cadre built around the ruler, to a
system in which the public service has become an occupation and career
choice, rather than a status group. This latter process is still working itself
out in many states and the effects of the process are uncertain but, in rejecting bureaucratic orders based on class and status with their solidaristic
culture that explicitly spurned commercial and market norms in favor of a
patrician sense of responsibility to the state, modern democratic societies
risk further weakening the ground for the institutional loyalty required to
sustain an effective and committed public service.

A core responsibility of public office is to ensure that one's conduct is consistent with the demands of that office. Interpretations of what this means
differ. At least some part of the motivation for recent moves toward codes of
conduct in public office, even in commercial organizations, is the desire to
make explicit those norms that the organization believes are vital but that
are not codified elsewhere. The sudden fashion for stipulating rules may
speak to the disappearance of deeper forms of social solidarity among public
servants as a group as recruitment has become more heterogeneous and
more egalitarian, but it may also represent a more political agenda, directed
at tightening control of bureaucrats and technocrats in an era marked by
political attacks on the activities and increasing costs of ruling administra-

tions. Either way, there is now consistent pressure in many Western countries to make these practices and norms explicit rather than implicit. (Which is not to accept that this is a feasible objective; any moderately complex practice requires a degree of tacit knowledge that can never be completely codified.)

However, there are several areas where it is extremely difficult to codify practice; such as passive resistance, unauthorized (and authorized) leaking, bureaucratic obstructionism, and whistle-blowing.[26] In each case there may be tensions between formal responsibilities and what best serves the interests and ends of the institution, and there is both a potential for those acting in these ways to do so in their own rather than in the institution's interests, and for them to do so in the institution's (or public's) interest but in a way that runs against formal responsibilities. Bureaucratic obstructionism can be self-serving, but it can also be a way of slowing down precipitate action on the part of eager but poorly informed politicians. Covert leaking of information may be incompatible with the need for politicians to take responsibility for political decisions, but it may also be done to draw attention to issues of public concern that might otherwise be hidden. Although whistle-blowing is not distinctive in its negotiation of the tensions among formal responsibilities, a sense of duty, and potentially self-serving action, it illustrates some of the difficulties that arise in performing one's official duties loyally and with integrity. Moreover, as I conclude, it may be a category of diminishing salience as those in public office come increasingly to identify their responsibilities as owed more directly to the public, as against working through a conception of the particular demands and responsibilities of office. If so, it is further evidence of the impact of democratic regulation and of the decline of loyalty in the public service.

Whistle-blowing involves confronting or reporting others who work within one's organization for activities that involve derelictions of duty; especially, but not exclusively, corrupt derelictions. Auditors, scrutineers, and security officers are not whistle-blowing when they act in their formal capacities; rather, whistle-blowing arises where commitments over and above the formal rules and requirements that define their particular office lead people to expose the misconduct of colleagues.

That it might be someone's responsibility to whistle-blow rests on the claim that standards of conduct within the political system cannot be sustained unless those within the system themselves both conform *and* expect (and work to ensure) that others will do so, whether in lower, higher, or equivalent positions. If politics is to order conflict authoritatively, then its various associated institutions must resist being suborned by the forces that they order. When the exercise of administrative responsibilities is self-serving or is undertaken with no sense of obligation toward the values, norms, and rules of politics, then the system becomes deeply vulnerable to corruption, authoritarianism, and other forms of misconduct. To become vulnerable to something is not necessarily to experience it, but it does increase the probability that it will be experienced. There are of course ways of reducing that probability: greater scrutiny and control and diminished latitude for public servants in their work will reduce the opportunities for corruption (although they dramatically increase the need for probity elsewhere in the system). Nonetheless, if we had wholly to discount members of the bureaucracy themselves as potential checks on those who rule and on their own members, the resources for resisting corruption and authoritarianism would look very thin indeed.

This more general subscription to political and administrative norms is important both in relation to one's fellow bureaucrats, and in relation to those who exercise the right to rule. In neither case is it an easy function to perform, especially when there is concern that others do not share one's acceptance of the rules and ethos of office. Again, those with formal responsibility for the conduct of others—section or department heads, for example—have a built-in requirement that they undertake this role with more junior colleagues and, while it can be an uncomfortable role to fulfil on occasion, the formal standing of the official does make the process easier, as does the possibility of referring higher up for additional authority or support. The more difficult cases are undoubtedly those that involve one's peers and those with greater authority (whether senior bureaucrats or politicians) and where the responsibility is not formal.

When there is rather little common culture inside an organization; for example, where role and function differentiation is very precise and there is little collaborative work or contact with other members of the organization, sustaining a commitment to organizational norms relies most heavily on those with the formal responsibility to do so. Whistle-blowing issues arise most acutely in institutions that operate with networks of informal relations. These relationships give those employed a strong sense of allegiance to their colleagues, play a major part in job satisfaction, and provide an indispensable mechanism for the flow of information within the organization. They also commonly involve ties of affection, gratitude, and reciprocity that bind people of similar standing together in a group. In some organizations which face high stress, police forces for example, very close informal relations can develop. The group develops an identity that is partly independent from that derived from their formal standing and that provides certain resources to tackle deviant behavior by members of the group—such as ridicule and ostracism. This self regulation can be highly beneficial for the organization if the mores of the group are not set in opposition to those of the organization, and extremely harmful where there is such a divergence. Most critically, for our discussion here, it can make it very difficult—emotionally painful and costly because of reprisals from the group—for individuals to criticize or expose derelict behavior on the part of other members of their group.

Internal criticism becomes even more difficult when those in authority (rather than one's peers) are involved, since the risks are substantial, and are greater the less complete one's information. Not being sure how high up the corruption goes, or who is implicated, makes disclosure a risky venture. Yet remaining silent allows the continuation of corrupt practices and may encourage their spread. It may also become increasingly difficult to avoid being implicated—not least because if those engaged in corrupt activities know that someone has potentially damaging information about them, they have every incentive to ensure that that information will not be used. Although they can use threats or intimidation to achieve this, those who act corruptly in ways that are not easily disguised from one's peers will often find it safer to implicate new members of the organization in corrupt activity than to try to avoid them finding out about it. This certainly seems to have been a common practice in corrupt police departments.[27]

The difficulties of resisting collusion with corruption are exacerbated when the activities are ones that the individual is formally instructed to undertake by his or her superior. Two variants need distinguishing: in the first the formal relationship between the official and the subordinate is subverted by the content of the order, as when an official makes various personal or sexual advances toward the subordinate. These are disturbing experiences and can be costly to resist, but it is relatively easy in principle to recognize this use of authority as inappropriate. The situation is more complex in the second version, where someone is ordered to do things that he or she is formally responsible for doing. Should a man working in the accounts section of a public department refuse to issue a payment because he believes that, while his authorization to do so is complete, the person who orders it is acting in some way improperly? Should a woman working in the central office of a political party question her superior about the origins of certain donations she is asked to process? Should civil servants question the use of powers to achieve ends that have not been publicly legitimated? Should they reveal information that shows that their minister has been lying to parliamentary or judicial institutions? Should junior military personnel question orders that seem to them to violate norms of conduct in war?

There are no easy answers in these circumstances, but the structure of the ethical situation is reasonably clear. The responsibility of an officeholder (Ms. Smith, for example) is, in the first instance, to fulfil the responsibilities of office. These include the duty to execute instructions from her superior (Mr. Jones). Jones's authority over Smith derives from his hierarchical position, and that authority has its raison d'être in the role it plays within the broader organization, as well as the role that organization plays within the broader political system. Clearly, the most immediate context for Smith is the organization and her subordinate status to Jones. She is there to do her job, but the job is ultimately linked to the goals of that organization and to its place and function within the political order. The distance of these deeper ethical issues, and their relatively abstract character, means that they are rarely easily translated into clear moral imperatives. The complex character of judgments as to what the most pressing imperatives facing the political system are, and what is politically possible, ensure that some situations are very difficult to call—strictly in the sense of it being unclear as to what Jones (and thereby Smith) should do. The difficulty of Jones' decision, and Smith's subsequent disagreement with it, cannot in itself be grounds for Smith rejecting it, since it is Jones's responsibility to make the call and Smith's job as his subordinate is to follow Jones's judgment. Problems arise when Smith is convinced that Jones's call is made, not in the spirit of fulfilling his duties as a public official, but to serve some personal end or to pursue objectives that cannot be legitimated by the terms of his office. This is a difficult judgment to make and to act upon. It is one thing for Smith to believe that in acting under formal orders from Jones she is furthering a policy or practice that is of doubtful validity; it is another to feel confident that she ought to refuse to act, or that she has the grounds and obligation to blow the whistle on Jones, either to his superior or in the public domain. The paradox is that Jones's issuing of the instruction, and the implicit appeal to his authority in the matter, implies that he has the right to have it carried out, and in questioning Jones's judgment Smith risks insubordination. This is not trivial since Jones's superior position to Smith must have some influence on her judgment as to whether the order is legitimate. That Jones has ordered her to do something gives Smith at least a *prima facie* reason for action. Jones's authority does not absolve Smith from every responsibility, but it must have some weight for Smith in determining how to act, and it should influence our understanding of how she should act.

Smith cannot simply judge the situation on the basis of her own personal or moral views and act accordingly.[28] Her holding of public office gives her a responsibility to her superiors to comply with their orders, even if it also implies certain broader duties to reflect upon the consistency of her conduct (whether ordered or discretionary) with the ends of the office. Moral beliefs can make it difficult to undertake some official responsibilities; for example, being a pacifist might make one unsuitable for office in the Ministry of Defence, having very strong views on abortion might make some positions in the Department of Health difficult, and strong views on capital punishment might counsel against a career in certain U.S. state prison services. In such cases the conflict is between personal, moral views and publicly legitimated practices, so there is no question of blowing the whistle on such practices, and individual cases of refusal are best understood as instances of conscientious objection.[29]

Conscientious objection also occurs in authoritarian regimes. A number of officers in the German army refused to execute Hitler's order that Communists and Jews should be summarily slaughtered on the Eastern front.[30] Their behavior falls short of whistle-blowing because their objection remained essentially private in character; that is, they did not publicly denounce the orders, but simply stated they could not comply with them (an understandably limited response given the potential costs and the absence of a public arena in which to blow the whistle). Whistle-blowing thus requires a particular type of political regime to generate the "space" necessary to exercise it.

Our interest, then, is in cases where Smith might have a duty as a civil servant or public official (not as an individual moral agent) to resist orders because of the way they threaten to subvert the practices and ends of the political system of which she is a part, and to act to ensure those orders are not carried out by others, by, for example, making public her refusal. Such a duty would be "positional," in that it arises from the office she has undertaken to fulfil, where that office has a claim on her that goes beyond the mere execution of her formal orders by being a part of a system that has ethical weight in virtue of the ends it serves.[31] The commitment to undertake an office is one that entails that the ends of the office must inform one's understanding of the associated responsibilities. It is a sense of such ends that is evident in codes of conduct and principles for officeholders—responsibilities that go beyond compliance with the formal rules and procedures that frame the office.[32] One symptom of this commitment to one's service is the conformity of those who blow the whistle on their corrupt colleagues. In their study of whistle-blowers, Glazer and Glazer found that those they studied were

> conservative people devoted to their work and their organizations (who) . . . had built their careers—whether as professionals, managers, or workers—by conforming to the requirements of bureaucratic life. Most had been successful until they were asked to violate their own standards of workplace behavior. Invariably, they believed that they were defending the true mission of their organization by resisting illicit practices and could not comprehend how their superiors could risk the good name of their company by producing defective products, the reputation of their hospital by abusing or neglecting patients, or the integrity of their agency by allowing their safety reports to be tampered with or distorted.[33]

Such cases are complex because, in the wider sense, one's responsibility as a public official is not often spelled out fully and concretely in advance. The principles and norms appealed to in modern codes of conduct remain abstract and in need of interpretation, which means that there is inevitably a case-by-case character to the judgment. Moreover, there remains a still more difficult issue of the respective weight to be given to roles and rules as against these more general principles. The subordinate position in which Smith is placed gives her a *prima facie* duty to act as instructed, and yet if the *prima facie* duty to comply is never overridden we dramatically increase the chances that those in office will behave badly—sometimes appallingly so— and we effectively abandon the possibility that either corrupt leadership or political corruption in lower levels of the public service will find any resistance within the very institutions that are most suited to recognizing when the ends of politics are being subverted.

Whistle-blowing can be extremely costly; people lose their jobs, their professional standing, their families, their health, and occasionally their lives from unauthorized disclosure of wrongdoing in firms or public service agencies.[34] Indeed, Western liberal democracies differ dramatically in their willingness to tolerate, protect, support, or reward whistle-blowers,[35] and there is disagreement within the academic community as to whether whistle-blowing should be understood as a valued addition to standards of openness in a democratic society or condemned as disloyal, maliciously motivated, or morally self-indulgent behavior.[36] From the perspective I have developed here, however, people in positions of trust have a duty to act in accordance with the *full* demands of that trust, and cannot settle for doing only what they are told. There are undoubtedly ways in which this can be made easier—codes of conduct, open discussion of the expectations of the standards to which members of the organization should adhere, the creation of informal and formal internal mechanisms for hearing complaints, public compensation systems for those discriminated against when challenging illegal practices, publicly funded advice services for companies and public departments, and, when necessary, witness protection programs and so forth. These elements are much more likely to be found in liberal democracies, especially those with strong traditions of freedom of information, public accountability of government, and a commitment to sustaining high levels of legitimacy. Where, however, there is little freedom of information, no access to a free press, and fears of preemptive elimination of complainants (or their reallocation), then the costs of disclosure are high and the prospects of success poor. This does not mean that the duty of public officials to challenge corrupt and illegal practices within government is contingent on it being wholly safe so to do, since few such actions are costless (although a U.S. judge did award Christopher Urda $3.75 million for whistle-blowing on defense contract swindling by the Singer Corporation, which employed him as internal auditor),[37] but there are some costs that make the expectation of disclosure unreasonable (as in the case of individual German generals on the Eastern front), even if we would find supererogation praiseworthy.

Whistle-blowing is motivated not directly by one's personal or moral values, but by one's sense that an instruction (or someone's behavior in office) is incompatible with one's official responsibilities. The issue is complicated because what it is to act in line with one's responsibilities as a public official involves an implicit commitment to do one's job in keeping with the ends of political rule. If there was no ethical weight to the practices of politics, we could distinguish the demands of morality and those of office and expect public officials to do as they were instructed except where they conscientiously objected to those instructions—just as an actor might do whatever a film director asks in playing a role, but might draw a line (motivated by personal moral convictions) at certain forms of nudity or language.[38] But the trust of public office implies that they have a responsibility on occasion to refuse to act as instructed because the instruction goes against, not their own moral position, but their responsibilities as officials. When a public official acts as a whistle-blower he or she does so on the basis of the office and projects an understanding of the role that he or she implicitly believes ought to be recognized by the political system.

Some researchers have argued that whistle-blowing is properly an expression of democratic citizenship, that those in public office act both as civil servants and as citizens and where the requirements of these roles clash, the role of citizen motivates behavior that challenges the right of those who command to the kind of compliance they seek.[39] This raises an empirical question: How do those who whistle-blow conceive of their responsibilities? If Glazer and Glazer's study is a basis for generalization, the conflict is experienced as between an order and one's sense of one's responsibilities to the organization and practices in which one works and in the context of which one's commitments and choices as an officeholder are intelligible, rather than to one's citizenship. This view understands whistle-blowing, somewhat paradoxically, as involving loyalty to one's organization and/or calling: It is the deep identification with the office and its ends, and the resulting sense of commitment to it and to what it stands for, that explains why otherwise conservative members of an organization may blow the whistle on others in their organization, and why they do not simply exit. It also underlines the real emotional costs incurred by whistle-blowers, since they necessarily inflict costs on the organization with which they identify, and they will be extremely lucky if their loyalty is recognized as that.

Glazer and Glazer point out that post-war liberal democracies have seen the emergence of a new phenomenon of ethical resisters—those who are prepared to blow the whistle on their workmates and superiors because of their powerful commitment to their professional responsibilities and moral principles, and who expect their states to live up to their liberal and democratic claims and to recognize their actions as praiseworthy and appropriate. This clearly is an appeal to democratic citizenship. It is evidence of a changing culture within bureaucracies, and of increasing identification with profession standards that are not framed by the practices of the political system. The opportunity for such action is also assisted by the ease of access to the public through the growth and democratization of the mass media. But such resistance is not whistle-blowing; it is the coupling of a straightforward moral protest with an implicit appeal to democratic values and citizenship. As such, it derives the opportunity for protest from the situation, but the duty to protest is derived from a far more general claim to moral and civic justification than in whistle-blowing proper. Unsurprisingly such ethical resisters are unlikely to be conservatives! Moreover, the emergence of such actors in the public service is further evidence of the dissolution of personal and institutional loyalties in favor of commitments to more general moral and political principles.

In contrast to court eunuchs, *serjeants*, and others absorbed in the households of their rulers, most people involved in modern democratic polities are not wholly dominated by the political process and, with more plural social orders and a range of fields for action, the criteria for probity in political conduct become more fragmented, issuing in conflicting views of how one should act to be in good standing. If there is some fragmentation of value, there is also likely to be some loosening of political norms. This is not necessarily harmful. Indeed, there seem to be two equally plausible hypotheses. One is that fragmentation opens up those who act in a public capacity to influences from outside politics in ways that make them more susceptible to personal or monetary motives, thereby increasing the probability that they will, in Bentham's terms, commit a "sinister sacrifice" and act corruptly. Alternatively, the complete absorption of people within bureaucratic and political structures, producing high levels of conformity, can result in the perpetuation of intensely corrupt practices, whereas an openness to extra-organizational values and principles can help the individual gain critical purchase on the tasks undertaken in one's official capacity. What does seem clear is that fragmentation and the development of a democratic public culture may be changing the demands of political conduct for those with formal administrative office, and in doing so it is also changing the nature of whistle-blowing. With increasing demands for transparency and accountability for all forms of public office, and with a language of democratic accountability that implies the existence of a clear set of ethical norms and standards underpinning liberal democratic culture, public office is increasingly assumed to be wholly beholden to general public norms. The result is that those who protest against the demands made of them, or about the conduct of others, do so with reference to those norms, not to the distinctive claims and responsibilities of office and its particular institutional loyalties.

In modern liberal-democratic states with pluralist social orders, the conception of public servants and officials as well-tooled cogs in an inexorably driven machine is simply untenable. The more pluralist character of the social order necessarily influences what it is reasonable to demand of public servants, even as it threatens to weaken their loyalties and attachments to the political order. I have thus far emphasized loyalty and other virtues with respect to public servants because I am arguing that we must understand the practices and institutions in which the official serves if we are to have an adequate grasp of what moves the agent, and because we are trying to capture features of character and conduct that run deep. Of course, the commitments of those in office are not *necessarily* deep, since the virtues, by their nature, can be present to greater or lesser degrees; nor do I deny that, at any given moment, an individual public servant can walk away from such commitments. The strains of public office are considerable, the alternatives in the modern world are increasingly wide and increasingly attractive, and the loyalty that people show is often poorly rewarded in democratic states, not least because public servants are often resented as a distanced elite. So the cross-pressures can be considerable. But we need to distinguish actions on the part of public officials that are consistent with their office, and those that involve to varying extents the repudiation of that office and of the implicit standards and expectations of politics. In the former case we are concerned with dimensions of loyalty and related virtues of office; in the latter, we are dealing with individuals who turn their back on the practices and demands of political service. Such shifts in allegiance are more existential in form the fewer the options and the more separate (and conflicting) their spheres are; they are more ordinary where spheres are cross cutting and the alternatives are several. That people can give up a way of life and its associated virtues does not mean that we are dealing with superficial roles that can be traded in at will rather than with the virtues associated with complex practices. There is a moral gamble, and moral luck has considerable weight in determining whether the decision gains some justification, but not all such choices are necessarily shallow (although for some they may be). However, my principal concern here has been with those who do not walk away but who use their office as the basis for challenging the conduct of others within politics.

Loyalty does not demand unconditional obedience. The distance between what the office stands for and the ends it serves, and what the subordinate is asked or required to do, holds the potential that one's loyalty will be exercised by questioning the order, or by whistle-blowing on the source of the order. But the justification that Smith gives in the earlier example is one internal to the practices of politics and political office, it is a justification in terms of the responsibilities of office and the ends that the office serves. Any such justification is capable of being more or less contentious. Resisting corrupt instructions in a stable, rule-governed, constitutional order lies at the less contentious end of the spectrum; doing so where the rules are unclear and standards of conduct are set largely by group membership and partisan loyalties, lies at the other. But the actions of those who blow the whistle on others are intelligible not on the basis of external standards brought to bear on the exercise of office, but in terms of standards internal to the office and to the practice of politics.

There are, however, numerous other instances in which resistance to orders, or challenging orders, is motivated by something other than internal standards—cases where loyalty and commitment to office in the practice and activity of public service are being trumped by independent standards. The group of ethical resisters I identified earlier take some standard external to the role they occupy as providing appropriate criteria for the assessment of the reasonableness of the demands made within that role. These external standards may be professional in character, or they may be personal, ideological, political, or moral commitments; but when acting on such commitments, they are not acting from loyalty to their office, and they are essentially repudiating the claims of office in favor of some alternative set of standards. Those who approve such action need to consider how reasonable it is to expect convergence on such standards and how robust the aura of legitimacy for such actions is. Do they represent a consensus, or do they threaten to introduce into the order of political rule a set of competing and conflicting claims about moral standards that, in effect, weaken or challenge the order that politics attempts to impose? Those who support such ethical resistance are, in general, confident of the universalism of the moral values to which they appeal. Those who are suspicious of it do not deny that there may be occasions on which moral principles should trump political and institutional loyalties, and should do so in ways that result not simply in the individual's withdrawal but also in an attempt to challenge some aspect of the political system, yet they tend to be more conscious of the extent to which the political order is a pre-condition for the development of certain standards. They are conscious too that an appeal to the public from purportedly moral high ground is essentially a political claim. Those concerned with the loyalty of those in public service will also be concerned that the instruments and practices developed to administer the political order do not themselves fall prey to the moral and ideological conflicts that the order itself was initially designed to resolve for the broader society.

In their capacity as subordinates and loyal servants of such a state, questions about whether the orders office holders receive and the conduct they observe are in keeping with the functions that their office serves within the state are naturally asked, even if they are simultaneously painful. They are so because the answers are not self-evident but require a sophisticated understanding of, and an identification with, one's office and the order of which it is a part, and a judgment about how one should act that plumbs the depth of this identification and of one's loyalties. Whistle-blowing is a prime example of the difficulty of identifying in advance how someone in public service should act, as well as demonstrating the importance of a deeply contextual understanding of the duties owed in office. Moral protest is part of a broad pattern of behavior that seeks to make public office directly answerable to an imagined public discourse. That process, I have suggested, is often part of a more general project of establishing popular political control over the state, but it is one that is potentially destructive of much that is essential to public office.

The next question to be addressed is whether those subject to political authority, who lack the institutional loyalties of those in office, can nonetheless recognize its exercise as fair and reasonable. It is to this task that I now turn.

PART III

Subjects, Citizens, and Institutions

CHAPTER 8

Resistance and Protest

In January 1963, in preparation for a meeting with leading members of the Southern Christian Leadership Conference (SCLC), Wyatt Tee Walker drew up a document of fewer than ten pages referred to as "Project C." The C stood for confrontation. The document targeted a number of downtown stores in Birmingham, Alabama, with fall-back targets of federal buildings, and, finally, a tertiary group of suburban variety stores in shopping centers. The plan had four stages: small-scale sit-ins to attract attention to Birmingham's segregation, coupled with nightly mass meetings; a boycott of downtown businesses linked to larger demonstrations; mass marches to enforce the boycott and fill the jails; and finally, calling in outsiders for help. The aim was to "cripple the city under the combined pressure of publicity, economic boycott, and the burden of overflowing jails."[1]

The plan was presented at a secret meeting of the SCLC chaired by Dr. Martin Luther King Jr. in Dorchester. It was accepted without correction by the eleven men there and after a delay of three months was put into operation on April 3. On April 12, after a disappointing start to the campaign, King was jailed. The day he was jailed, James Bevel arrived in the city to support the protests and to lead workshops on nonviolent protests, which attracted an increasingly large and young audience. Responding to this development, King agreed that Bevel could organize a march of high school students on May 2. Bevel and Walker called it "D-day." Some 600 children were in jail at the end of the day. The following day, more students marched, to be met with water cannons and attack dogs. On May 4 the police sealed off some of the local churches where the students were assembled and an increasingly angry crowd of onlookers, not schooled in nonvio-

lence, "began to organize their guns and knives and bricks." Bevel crossed
to the police lines, seized a bullhorn, and addressed the crowd:

> I took the bullhorn and I said, "Okay, get off the streets now, we're not
> going to have violence. If you're not going to respect people you're not
> going to be in the movement." It's strange, I guess, for them: I'm with the
> police talking through the bullhorn and giving orders and everybody was
> obeying the orders. It was like, wow. But what was at stake was the possi-
> bility of a riot. In the movement, once a riot breaks out, you have to stop,
> and it takes four, five days to get re-established. I was trying to avoid that
> kind of situation.[2]

Bevel's action was, undoubtedly, a judicious piece of political leadership.
For many, what is most striking is that it testifies to the movement's commitment to nonviolence. Time and again in the civil rights movement in the
United States, black leaders achieved an extraordinary degree of restraint
among their supporters.[3] Despite the lynchings; the cold-blooded murders
of activists; and the brutality, intimidation, and terrorism directed against
ordinary black people, the movement largely sustained its stance on nonviolent civil disobedience until late in the 1960s. The emergence of the Black
Power Movement, and the Black Panthers, and their willingness to subscribe to armed resistance, is surprising only because it took so long—"there
is a point at which caution can become cowardice."[4]

Although Bevel's intervention with the crowd is linked to his commitment to nonviolence, it is clear that this commitment was tactical. A riot
would reduce support for the movement from the moderate black community and sympathetic whites, it would legitimate Bull Connor's brutality, attract huge adverse publicity, and increase the reluctance of marchers to risk
confrontation and imprisonment. For many involved in the debates prior to
May 2, a different issue of political responsibility was raised concerning the
use of schoolchildren, some as young as six, in the marches on the city.
Bevel apparently won the argument by pointing out that if the children
were old enough to be members of a church and to be treated as if they had
responsibility for their immortal souls, then they were old enough to get arrested in the name of desegregation.

Whichever way one looks at the decision, it is clear that we are dealing
with political judgments that have a number of features in common with
those made by politicians who direct the actions of others and expose them
to risks. The civil rights movement involved clear decision making, a long-

term strategy, and a range of tactical judgments. Its leadership was complex and several organizations, following different paths and with different agendas, were involved. Most of the time there were leaders who were planning campaigns, mobilizing support, and taking risks. Registration and antisegregation campaigns led to black workers losing their jobs, and sometimes their homes; people were intimidated, spat upon, assaulted, and in some cases beaten to death, shot, or bombed. Some of these people were prominent members of the movement, such as Medgar Evans, Jonathan Daniels, Viola Liuzzo, Jim Reeb, and later King himself, but many were ordinary working people, with little political experience. Some of those most out of their depth were white college students from the North who came to the movement out of youthful idealism and curiosity and found that they were in another country entirely. Bob Zellner, a Student Non-Violent Coordinating Committee (SNCC) activist, newly arrived in the South to work on white campuses, turned up in McComb shortly after the killing of Herbert Lee and joined a crowd of predominantly black demonstrators outside of City Hall. Some hours later, having narrowly escaped being beaten to death and having managed to reinsert an eyeball that a member of the local mob had gouged out, he wound up in jail. He was lucky. Mickey Schwerner and Andrew Goodman, and their black colleague James Chaney, were not. Nor were many others.

The violence to which activists were exposed, and that their nonviolence was tactically designed to minimize, is integral to our understanding of the movement. When Fred Shuttleworth asked President John Kennedy to explain why four little girls were killed by a bomb in the basement of the Sixteenth Street Baptist Church in Birmingham, Kennedy apparently replied that, "as tragic as it is, in every war, some people have to die."[5] Many in the movement plainly recognized this. In Lowndes County, Alabama, in 1965, a white Roman Catholic priest, Richard Morrisroe, and a white Episcopal divinity student, Jonathan Daniels, were shot by a part-time deputy sheriff, outside a soda store, having just been released by police alongside two black female activists, Joyce Bailey and Ruby Sales. Daniels was killed.

He was not the first I had seen die. I had seen those much closer to me die. Certainly I knew that in no way was it to stop or slow down my work. So I was deeply sorry about his death, but only sorry he was the one who had to go. Then I had to analyze it: someone had to go, and unfortunately it was him. It was one of those things which came to affect those of us in

> SNCC on the Alabama staff so strongly that our position was correct, that to
> bring white workers in was just, in fact, to court their death.[6]

If we see the civil rights movement as involved in a war, the terms of discussion that are normally applied to protest movements no longer make much sense. Those who instigate and lead such movements cannot be judged as acting wholly within an established framework of political and legal rights and responsibilities, to which they are accountable for the choices and decisions they make, any more than one side in a war can be regarded as wholly accountable within the legal and political framework of their opponents.

Even if the metaphor of a war is an extreme one, we are clearly dealing with people acting in ways that raise serious questions about the legitimacy of the state, which set them outside the law and give to those who direct the movement a special responsibility toward those who follow their leadership and who may suffer in consequence. We cannot handle these issues by referring to the rights and responsibilities of citizens, since these protesters stand in part outside that framework. In standing outside it, they assume special responsibilities: They act, not simply as subjects under the law, but as leaders and lawmakers in their own right. This role raises additional questions about their wider responsibility for those who become touched by or identified as part of or as symptomatic of their campaign (for example, Addie Mae Collins, Carole Robertson, Cynthia Wesley, and Denise McNair, the victims of the Baptist Church bombing; Herbert Lee, William Moore, Jimmy Lee Jackson, and numerous others killed in protest efforts). In the midst of the Montgomery bus boycott, E. D. Nixon attacked Montgomery church leaders for getting cold feet about participating in a meeting because press photographers would be there:

> Somebody in this thing has got to get faith. I am just ashamed of you. You
> said that God has called you to lead the people and now you are afraid and
> gone to pieces because the man tells you that the newspaper men will be
> here and your pictures might come out in the newspaper. Somebody has
> got to get hurt in this thing and if you preachers are not the leaders, then
> we have to pray that God will send us some more leaders.[7]

The civil rights movement is one of many cases of such political action, albeit it is the one that provided the inspiration for a good deal of the literature on civil disobedience in the 1960s and 1970s. Unfortunately, that literature tends to mischaracterize the movement, which is better understood as part of a much larger set of popular movements of protest, resistance, and contention directed against the state and its policies over the last two hundred or so years. We can follow Sidney Tarrow in recognizing these movements as sharing four basic components: (1) collective "contentious" challenges (i.e., using disruptive direct action) (2) based on common purposes and value commitments and (3) social solidarities and collective identities (4) in sustained interaction with elites, opponents, and authorities.[8]

Protest movements need to be distinguished from normal civil activity. In most Western democracies the majority of ordinary people have relatively little contact with the formal political system: they may vote in elections, serve on juries, be members or supporters of political parties, or be associated with petitioning or lobbying on certain issues. Some political theorists enjoin more active forms of participation and civic virtue but few find that Western states demonstrate many examples of this. Rather than there being a high level of participation among citizens, there tends to be a generally low level, punctuated with periods of political activism—a significant proportion of which involves contentious or abnormal politics, rather than more standard forms of participation. That is, these active periods do not reflect routine participation in the established systems for communicating interests and aims to the political system but involve challenging the political system on some aspect of its activity and by going outside the formal routes of political access. The characteristic methods are those of protest, demonstration, disobedience, and resistance. The activity is often strongly value-based: for the rights of women and the equal treatment of minorities; against the development of nuclear weapons, and two decades later against the deployment of tactical nuclear weaponry on European soil; against the growth of the nuclear power industry; against animal experimentation; for or against abortion; against activities that damage the environment; against the institutions of global capitalism; and so on. It is difficult to be certain that the scale of such activities has increased in the post–World War II period, although what evidence there is suggests that it has. The development of the concept of *new social movements* together with a burgeoning literature testifies to political scientists' perception that they are dealing with something new, although the premium attached to identifying something new can be rather seductive.[9] Certainly, there are elements in these organizations that seem new—their ability to exploit new technologies, their large middle-class involvement, their relative youth, and their relatively nonhierarchical organization—but their activities remain similar to political and labor movements of the inter-war period and before. Across the board, such groups have stood outside the political system and sought to challenge the activity of the state or its support for other organizations and interests in the community. Moreover, their challenges have often been based on their belief that their commitments are in a zero-sum relationship to the state. Labor movements that see an elemental incompatibility between the interests of labor and those of the capitalist system take such a view, as do movements asking for a dramatically different ecological policy, or a rejection of the nuclear arms race, or the recognition of full equality for women and/or minorities.[10] Confrontation and resistance is fuelled by the belief that the state can only back one policy and that it is backing the wrong one, and by an accompanying sense that the issues concerned go to the heart of the state's responsibilities toward its citizens. For the state to side with the interests of capital is for it to deny its fundamental responsibilities to the welfare of ordinary people; for it to commit itself to the nuclear arms race is to put at risk the citizenry it is instituted to defend; to adopt a noninterventionist policy toward discrimination against women or minority groups is to endorse patriarchy, to compound a historical injustice, and to fail to ensure substantively equal treatment for all citizens; and to adopt a laissez-faire attitude toward the environment is to sacrifice the interests of subsequent generations. In each case, the state acts more in some interests than in others, and it fails (in the view of those attacking it) to recognize its fundamental responsibilities toward its citizenry as a whole or to give equal weight and equal concern and respect to certain groups whose standing is, as a result, demeaned or downgraded. In such instances, the case against the state is always partly a moral and principled one, even if there are also elements of class or group interests, and people take to the streets in such situations to raise the issue in a highly visible manner and to challenge the state to answer the moral issues, rather than attempting to overthrow state power by populist action.

Political action of this form, although (in Western liberal democracies) rarely designedly revolutionary, often involves confrontation with the police, the law, and established authorities. In terms of "normal" politics, it is a case of citizens behaving badly. Such behavior is responsible for the majority of most Western states' annual consumption of tear gas, and has prompted the development of increasingly sophisticated riot equipment and methods of surveillance for their police forces. For those in government, the threat to law and order, and persons and property, legitimates the exercise of the full authority of the law, although there is often an awareness that doing so can escalate the confrontation, not least by denying the seriousness of the issues that drive the protest. Moreover, in the nature of their commitment to their cause, those who protest are often uncompromising. Their conviction of the principles at stake, and their nonnegotiable character, means that it is difficult for them to see how an accommodation can be reached—a view inevitably shared by those in power. Along with Hume, we can recognize the incommensurability of disputes enjoined by "parties of principle" and the associated fervor with which they are engaged; with Burke, we can see that when faced with such parties the state may opt to preserve its rule at all costs: "Kings will be tyrants from policy when men are rebels from principle."[11] One safeguard in liberal-democratic states is that tyranny is not an attractive option in the medium- to long-term (or sooner depending on the electoral timetable), which means that they must attempt to negotiate this difficult territory beyond normal politics. The challenge for political theory is to identify the distinctive character and normative structure of this type of political conduct.

The literature on resistance in liberal democratic societies is predominantly focused on civil disobedience. It is concerned with occasions when individuals break the law or challenge authority in some way because of the strength of their convictions or because they believe that the government has overstepped its bounds or failed to ensure adequate consultation or sufficient protection for groups or communities within the state. In this view, civil disobedience arises not because we reject civil authority as such, but because we recognize a clash between what the state is asking of us and what we believe the state has a right to ask of us.[12] Moreover, the majority of the literature emphasizes that one of the distinctive characteristics of civil disobedience is the participants' acknowledgment of the legal right of the state to punish them for breaking the law, and their largely nonviolent conduct in breaking the law. Sit-ins, people chaining themselves to the railings of public buildings, or engaging in acts that are disruptive to public order do not necessarily have a direct link to the issues for which protesters fight (such as votes for women, votes for ethnic minorities, antinuclear weapons protests, antiwar demonstrations, and so on); their aim is to draw attention to their cause. These accounts see the liberal democratic state as distinctive in its tolerance toward such actions, which depends on its ability to distinguish between an attack on its authority and an attack on the validity of a particular piece of legislation or policy, and to see there are public ways of questioning the latter that do not amount to the former.

The literature on civil disobedience is barely concerned with resistance more broadly. Indeed, its objective is, for the most part, to separate off civil disobedience from types of resistance that deny the authority of the state more widely and that seek a change not only in a particular area of legislation but in the fundamental order of the state. But even those who defend the concept of civil disobedience recognize that some cases are borderline. In Britain, the animal liberation movement has a number of wings, some of which lobby, some engage in civil disobedience, and some resort to terrorism. These latter activists clearly believe that they have a right and duty to challenge the state-sanctioned experimentation on and killing of sentient beings. Just as we would regard the systematic killing of ethnic groups as indicative of the wholesale illegitimacy of the state, so some members of these groups may on similar grounds see themselves as at war with the state, not just with its stance on a single policy issue. Other social movements whose value-orientation is not open to compromise may take a similar view. In doing so, the literature concurs that they can no longer be considered as engaging in civil disobedience.

But drawing the line between civil disobedience and broader resistance is not easy. Many definitions, for example, insist that "to engage in violent acts likely to injure or hurt is incompatible with civil disobedience as a mode of address."[13] Others invoke the sanctity of personal or property rights. Similarly, the criterion of conscientiousness, that those who participate should do so avowedly and should accept responsibility for their acts, captures one feature often associated with such disobedience. So does the stipulation that action must be intentional, goal-orientated, measured in its means, and should aim to stimulate a broader public awareness and discussion of a particular issue, within the bounds of the state. These conditions respond tactically to a legal order: it is not outright rebellion, and it should not be confused with outbreaks of mass unrest and political refusal; it is not burning and looting. It is essentially a form of tactical campaigning within a state that we regard as essentially just. The consequence of such restrictions, however, is simply to draw attention to how narrowly defined is the scope for civil disobedience, and should alert us to its relative rarity as a form of political action and protest in comparison with more contentious forms of political action.

The political theory of liberal democracy works largely from a position that takes as given the state's role in guaranteeing the protection of certain fundamental rights and the meeting of certain basic claims for citizens. This role is complemented by a moral obligation on the part of citizens to obey the law. Civil disobedience has a place only because the state may act by majority decisions, happenstance, or poor judgment in ways that do not, in the view of some of its citizens, adequately respect those fundamental rights and claims. The theory of civil disobedience takes as its presumption a commitment on the part of the state to protect these rights and it presents itself as a mechanism to convince the state to recognize such primary obligations. If the state had no such commitment, or if it categorically refused to recognize its obligation in such areas, civil disobedience would not be possible, since the challenge to a particular law would be indistinguishable from a challenge to the state's authority more generally. The range of acceptable political activity open to ordinary people in a liberal democratic state, understood in this way, is, then, both wider and much more sharply defined than in nonliberal states. Although disobedience becomes possible and is partly tolerated, it is premised on the fundamental rights and protections owed to the citizen. In contrast, where there are no such rights or protections, fighting for them, even if this means violence, can be an understandable and morally legitimate option, although it is often romanticized and is sometimes unjustifiably costly. The difficulty with such a distinction, however, is that it is unclear that the activities of many contentious social movements readily fall in the category of civil disobedience thus defined.

We ascribe a greater moral value to civil disobedience than to rebellion and resistance in liberal democratic orders because it appeals to the reasonableness of the order, rather than to force or simply the weight of numbers. The strategy is reasonable because it has some chance of success (at least to the extent of airing legitimate concerns), because it can be seen to appeal to a basic idea of the constitutional order as a fair compromise between the different interests within the state, and because we take those in authority to be receptive to the same understanding of the order and the character of their responsibilities. In acting disobediently, but conscientiously, people are appealing to the idea of a deeper set of shared moral and political values. However, the more insecure an order is, the more heroic or foolhardy does action that trusts the state to abide by its basic rules and procedures become, and the more reasonable it is for us to act in ways that we believe will maximally protect those things we most value. Many of the protest movements of the post-war period have lacked grounds for confidence in the stability of the liberal constitutional character of their regime that civil disobedience requires.

Civil rights activists, for example, could plainly see that the bastion of U.S. liberty, the American constitution, could not prevent them being beaten or murdered not just by other citizens but by those formally responsible for implementing the law. In the same period in Europe, the behavior of French riot police, the willingness in Britain to invoke the Official Secrets Act to silence journalists, the persecution of communists in West Germany, the Italian handling of terrorism, the generalized racism common to most police forces, and so on, all gave protesters grounds for having less than full confidence in the liberal credentials of their state and its law enforcement agencies. Liberal-democratic constitutional regimes are, in almost all cases, a phenomenon of the twentieth century, and in the vast majority of cases they are achievements of the second half of that century. Even in long-standing democratic states, such as the United States, the fundamental civil rights of some minority groups have only recently been secured. On these grounds alone there is justification for a certain tentativeness about protesters' belief that the state will respond with due proportion. Indeed, a great deal of the literature on civil disobedience that grew out of the era of protest in the West might best be understood in performative terms. To activists, and to many theorists of civil disobedience, it could not have been clear that these states would place fundamental constitutional protections over immediate policy objectives (such as in the Vietnam War) or entrenched interests (such as over segregation), but civil disobedience theory was in part an attempt to clarify the nature of the choices open to activists and in part an attempt to frame the issues in a way that would persuade the government and the legal system to make the right, constitutional response. For these protesters, the intuitive contrast between civilly disobedient non-violent action and fighting back required a judgment over which way the political order would go in the intermediate and long term—whether, that is, it would live up to its liberal constitutionalist rhetoric or continue to tolerate the systematic violation of minority rights in the name of the status quo. It also required that they should take substantial short-term risks and incur substantial costs for uncertain long-term gains. To young black men and women living in urban ghettos or Southern segregationist states it might be difficult knowing quite where to place one's bets; and, in the absence of any secure sense that the constitutional order would win through, while looking up at the wrong end of a city policeman's billy-club, civil disobedience might seem a mistake as an option, especially compared to more militant strategies that allowed a greater degree of self-defense. Above all, as Lyons has recently insisted,[14] it is difficult to see that, given the fundamental injustice of segregation, there could have been a prior moral obligation to obey the law. If there was no moral obligation to obey, then we are better off understanding people's behavior in terms of resistance rather than civil disobedience.

The line between civil disobedience and resistance is further complicated by the fact that some of the features of civil disobedience that political theorists have particularly stressed (such as conscientiousness, publicity, and a willingness to accept punishment) rely on an assumption that the costs of engaging in this type of collective action will be somewhat diminished (although they are still borne individually). Each participant, then, needs considerable confidence in the capacity of the political system to recognize the conscientiousness of the act if disobedience is to be an option. Moreover, protesters need confidence in those who judge them and in all those with whom their actions bring them into conflict. To know (or even reasonably to fear) that one will be beaten or abused in police custody, to know that one's family and friends will be implicated and interrogated, to face certain imprisonment or time in a work camp, all serve to increase the cost of one's actions. In doing so, collective civil disobedience becomes an empty category, and those who continue to act do so more and more as an expression of conscientious refusal.[15] Insofar as this occurs, the choice becomes one between individual conformity and resistance to the order, or compliance through fear as against hopes of successful rebellion. The space for civil disobedience disappears.

Something similar might be said for the position of many groups in liberal democratic regimes. We have to ask both whether the law that the state enforces is just, and whether, even if it is just, the state enforces it in a way that ensures the protection of those subject to it. For example, immigrant and refugee communities in many European states experience their physical safety and civil rights as inadequately secured by the activities of their adopted state (in many cases this is simply a matter of fact), which is grounds for denying that one has a moral obligation to conform to the law since, whatever its intent, its effect is unjust. It may be unclear at what point such groups will cease to trust the state for protection and come to rely on their own resources, accepting as inevitable the associated confrontation with the police but, at present, in many such communities it would not be unreasonable to take this option. Nor is it surprising to find in these communities alienated young men and women attracted to more radical methods and objectives—resulting in further deterioration of their relationship with the dominant culture.

Time also complicates the relationship between power and resistance. Those who are currently excluded and exploited have little ground for confidence that the state will live up to its liberal democratic rhetoric; similarly, those whose current standing within their society has roots in their past ill-treatment have no reason for confidence in the reasonableness of their political order. The events of the past remain alive in the memories of the present generation and can be rekindled, and collective identities that carry collective memories can also be invoked in responding to challenges in the present. The oppressed may continue to fight battles today that are essentially those of yesterday. The constitutional orders of America and Australia may be keen to move on in finally recognizing the equal rights of all their citizens, but these include indigenous people disinherited by colonialism and decimated by disease, racial violence, and brutal political rule. In both countries, that past is seen by its remaining indigenous inheritors as the basis for claims in and against the present, although the existing political orders had assumed, until recently, that this past was largely laid to rest. Under such conditions, the idea that the liberal state can be thought to be essentially just, and the associated idea that those in the state have a moral obligation to obey the law of that state, must seem pretty rich to the descendants of the original indigenous peoples. Clearly, attempting to eradicate a population is not a good foundation for a claim that one's rule is just, and the potential for such historical memories to resurface as the basis for challenges to the state remains extremely strong.

Those who rule have strong incentives to transform power into authority and to institutionalize and regularize political rule—to turn from particular confrontations and acts of domination, to general systems of rules and principles for the ordering of populations. Both sides gain: masters become rulers, servants become subjects; rulers become constitutionally accountable holders of office, and subjects become citizens. But, relatively speaking, the subordinated often gain less. It may be a huge improvement to be a citizen in a modern democratic state than a slave to a Roman conqueror, but the fact that the rights and welfare baseline for those at the bottom of the political and social system may have improved dramatically does not change the fact that it is still the bottom. Those in politics have to be able to manage this sense of relative disadvantage that people experience, together with intertwined historical memories of absolute injustices; acts of oppression or callousness; or systematic indifference to racial, religious, or cultural identities and experiences. Progress over time does not necessarily mollify those whose present position remains relatively disadvantaged and the past provides a potential arsenal for grievances with which to attack the status quo. As a result, trust in the current political order in the light of its historical past may be extremely attenuated, leading to demands for self-rule that even liberal democratic states find difficult to meet. Moreover, states whose liberal democratic record has yet to be established, those where it is of very recent provenance and of uncertain stability, and those whose record has been good but that suddenly looks fragile, will generate these conflicts still more acutely. If those who protest do so in ways that challenge the state more widely, then the state's reaction may further exacerbate the conflicts.[16] This is not merely a plausible causal story of the origin of civil disorder, it also suggests that a credible case can be made for people behaving in ways that are individually reasonable and justifiable, but which may be cumulatively destructive to the authority of the state.

On these several grounds, then, the classical theory of civil disobedience is of limited assistance in understanding the issues raised by, and the responsibilities of participants in, contentious political action. The category of disobedience is too tightly drawn, and applies in too narrow a range of cases. Above all, the nearly just state, whose commands are such as to impose a moral obligation to obey, is one that most contentious protesters do not recognize. Their value commitments and the accompanying sense of their nonnegotiable character entail that the state is already failing to do them justice. Moreover, many of the most famous cases of civil disobedience are inappropriately classified. For Southern blacks the United States was not a nearly just state to which they had a moral obligation—the law was racist in character and imposed in a thoroughly partisan manner (witness the ability of whites to murder with relative impunity). Nor did the role played by the federal government indicate the appropriate degree of moral leadership on the race issue, exemplified by the FBI's decision that King was unfit for mediation or negotiation.[17] That the movement chose tactically to appeal to values that they hoped the federal government would recognize as central to the Constitution does not mean that they knew that the appeal would work, nor does it mean that a more confrontational strategy would have been illegitimate. In such cases civil disobedience describes a tactic toward the state, not a special kind of civic agency, let alone a moral responsibility.

More recent movements—against nuclear weaponry and power, against environmental destruction, for women's and minority rights, and against the domination of global capitalism—have a similar moral standing for those involved. Whether or not we share their values, we can understand their view that the state is acting in a deeply irresponsible manner. An irresponsible state cannot be a just state, and an unjust state confers no obligations to obey the law. In such a state, civil disobedience might be a good tactical option, but we cannot justifiably conclude, as much literature on civil disobedience does, that such behavior implies or acknowledges the essential justice of the state and must be restricted to conscientious, nonviolent, and civically responsible conduct.

A still more difficult question prompted by recent social movements is whether there is an inevitable process of substantive moral disagreement in modern states that means they will always be potentially open to such challenges. That is, that *just* or *nearly just* are simply not stable states of affairs over the long run, and that convergence in politics is inevitably open to being unsettled, leading to the reemergence of conflict. The sources for such conflict (as we have seen in Chapter 3) can be many and varied, from the fragmentation of value, through the re-eruption of conflicts thought to be authoritatively ordered by the state, to those areas of contention that arise as a result of the state's own conduct or to those linked to international rivalries. If, as I have argued, politics involves the authoritative allocation of values and ordering of conflict, such allocation is often fragile and the means used to solve problems in one domain can become the source of problems in other domains.

That we experience the state as unjust does not thereby legitimate every type of behavior. Even if we lack a general obligation to obey the law, or a particular law, we may have independent grounds for obeying parts of the law. This is because often there are subsets of the state's authority that remain intact even when it has damaged its general claim, or because of general injunctions against the harming of innocents or needless violence or damage to property. Those involved in the leadership of protest movements have responsibilities to those in, and out, of their organization. They make decisions that have a profound effect on other people's lives, and some of those decisions involve making tactical judgments in which people are intentionally exposed to a higher risk of harm. In some respects, the leaderships of contentious political movements, in part by the very challenge that they issue to the legitimacy of the state, constitute themselves as an alternative political order—perhaps less hierarchical, less authoritative, but nonetheless capable of giving orders, coordinating activity, making decisions, and setting the pattern of action for others in ways that will have profound consequences for members of the movement and those linked to it. Most claim such authority implicitly, and many do so explicitly to gain ascendancy and direction over forms of protest that they then shape to their own, more specific, ends. "When in an action project, a CORE member will obey the order issued by the authorized leader or spokesman of the project, whether these orders please him or not. If he does not approve of such orders, he shall later refer the criticism back to the group or to the committee which was the source of the project plan."[18]

While this kind of authority exists widely in civil society, for oppositional organizations such authority can launch individuals into direct conflict with the law and can expose them to substantial risk of harm. Of course, members of these movements sign up for these activities, but they also act on the basis of trust in and loyalty to those who lead them. It was Bevel's judgment that teenage children were not going to be killed or maimed on the streets or violated by those who arrested them or by their jailors, yet June Johnson, Annell Ponder, and Fannie Lou Hamer were beaten by Winona police in June 1963. Many of those who joined Bevel did so with a certain understanding of the consequences of doing so, and with an understanding of the consequences of their actions; the lessons in nonviolence gave them an indication of what they could expect (although how far eight-year-old children grasped the risks is unclear). But it was a judgment about acceptable risk—one that was out of line for Johnson, Ponder, and Hamer, and way out of line for Chaney, Schwerner, and Goodman. Politicians who declare war usually entrust the conduct of the war to trained professionals who have some awareness of the consequences of their profession, but those who play leading roles in contentious politics rarely have the same awareness or the professional training and experience in making decisions that can result in the killing or maiming of those who follow them. Yet such people lead, and make decisions, and are followed and obeyed. And sometimes people die.

The existence of such authority distances contentious political action from mere riot or other overt demonstrations of anger and frustration at the existing political order. In the latter cases, behavior is extremely difficult to control except perhaps in rather special circumstances, such as the "moral economy" rioting in eighteenth century Britain.[19] Otherwise, rioting often provides cover for a lawless empowerment of individuals the effects of which can be simultaneously intoxicating and appallingly violent. Few political organizations wish for such an outcome, and most organizers seek, like Bevel, actively to forestall it. Even if revolutionary movements aspire to generating the collapse of state authority, they are also assiduous in their attempts to convert people's anger into a more organized and disciplined movement against the established order. In line with Kennedy's remark, they are more interested in a war that they will win than in the creation of a maelstrom of violence in which everything they stand for might perish.

Contentious political action, then, charts a path that can embrace the use of tactical civil disobedience without accepting the state's legitimacy or its right to punish. It seeks to challenge the state politically in the field of public legitimacy, rather than through military means, but it regards as legitimate a range of actions that sit uncomfortably with civil disobedience as traditionally defined. However, unlike rioting, contentious politics does allow us to identify those who formulate strategy and make tactical decisions and to regard them as having a special political and moral responsibility for the outcomes of those plans, which does not thereby diminish the moral responsibilities of others for their actions. Whites who systematically intimidated, brutalized, and murdered civil rights workers have full responsibility for their actions, even if civil rights leaders had responsibilities to weigh the probability of white retaliation against the long-term gains that the movement sought and a duty to be clear to their fellow activists about the risks they faced.

The calculations of those who lead such protests are complex, which accounts for the extent to which such groups pursue multiple strategies and often engage in an array of symbolic confrontations to test the level of public support and the depth of state resistance. The politics of carnival (combining protest and celebration) in its many forms is often an essential mechanism for testing the state's commitment to a tolerant and constitutionalist response. Sidney Tarrow cites the behavior of Serbs in Belgrade following the refusal of the state to acknowledge the Zajedno party victories in the 1996 elections. Night after night Zajedno activists and students organized peaceful nightly marches in the city, and when the police demanded that only ordinary pedestrians use the streets of downtown Belgrade the city became transformed into a mass of dogwalkers! On New Year's Eve, some 300,000 people took to the streets in a carnival atmosphere. After three months, the Zajedno election results were finally acknowledged. Such methods are neither idiosyncratic nor new. Protest songs that dominate the memories of those associated with civil rights movements can be found in similar form in mid-eighteenth-century absolutist France and in the popular movement in Britain against the war with revolutionary France at the end of the eighteenth century; political caricature and symbolic representation of the weaknesses of political leaders is as old as politics itself (Caesar was extensively caricatured and mimicked by Roman crowds, and many Greek comedies did much the same to their élites). Carnival is a centuries old tradition, and, while every generation of protesters has its originality and inventiveness, there are earlier models and patterns to draw upon.

Throughout history there have been many ways in which subordinates test the resolution of their rulers and negotiate the conditions of their subjection, and these mechanisms continue to inform the repertoire of those who seek to influence the way that the state rules. Such protest characteristically emanates from multiple sources and is rarely centrally controlled and directed. One consequence of this is that, as the result of many small actions, the state is sometimes goaded into a repressive response that can be extremely costly to participants. Unfortunately, this makes it still more difficult for protest groups to act responsibly toward their members, not least because that sense of snowballing pressure from many sources plays a central part in their tactics of protest and persuasion.

Three other dimensions of responsibility for those orchestrating protests concern the impact of confrontation on their own members' behavior toward nonmembers and representatives of the state, their behavior toward law enforcement agents, and their impact on bystanders. Wyatt Tee Walker, the originator of Project C, whose wife escaped without injury when she and two of their children were caught up in a bomb attack on a Birmingham motel in 1963 only subsequently to have her head split open by a state trooper, asked Bob Gordon, a UPI reporter, which trooper had hit his wife and then went for him. Gordon's tackle probably saved his life, but Walker's reaction is entirely understandable, even for someone schooled in nonviolence. After the Birmingham Baptist Church bombing Bevel and his wife considered abandoning the movement so as to identify the bombers and have them killed.[20] Many activists ended up in positions where nonviolence seemed no longer appropriate. Leaders of such protests have to take account of this propensity for human emotions to get out of hand. The more serious the confrontation, the more it behoves those orchestrating the action to ensure that those they command have some understanding of how they are to act if the confrontation becomes violent, and what is considered legitimate as a form of self-defense.

It must also be emphasized that the legacy of repression and violence is not easily expunged. Suddenly to remove the controls that have subordinated and humiliated people for most of their lives, and simultaneously to place those who symbolize that system of subjugation at the mercy of an exhilarated and riotous crowd, is usually to sign their death warrants. Moreover, human susceptibility to finding in others signs either of their sameness or their otherness gives a ruthlessness to our revenge. That is, the man who has scorned me is taken to justify my acting against his community, his race, or his faith; humiliations are avenged by acting against people whom we identify with our enemies and oppressors. Injustice breeds injustice, and while some theorists, like Burke, tend to romanticize and excuse past injustice for the sake of order, others, such as Marx or Fanon, romanticize revolutionary violence as the precondition for a utopian future. These situations are most common when we are dealing with full-scale rebellion or a dramatic change in the whole political and social order, but political movements must be alert to the potential for such chaos, and they must recognize their own agency and responsibility in bringing it about.

The tactics of nonviolence in the civil rights movement meant that white mobs and the police risked little in their confrontation with black protesters, unless a riot developed. Few contemporary protest movements are as restrained on the principle of nonviolence. Of course, in any movement there are factions with more revolutionary or anarchic ambitions who have an interest in escalating conflict and who may well inaugurate violence against the police, resulting in a violent reaction that is rarely discriminating between types of protesters. But this is a risk that protest movements run and against which it is difficult to guard—as is the associated damage to property or injury to bystanders by both protesters and police. In each case, those concerned have to judge whether their means of protest is likely to achieve its ends, and how far it is likely to be harmed by the eruption of violence between those under its banners and the police. They have to pursue their cause, but with a sense of proportion and responsibility and yet, unlike Weber's elite, they are not for the most part leading well-ordered bureaucratic machines that translate their policies and aspirations relatively undiluted into action. Many of those who become leaders have not been schooled extensively in the practices and virtues of politics, but come to it new and often from a position of exclusion, which makes them distrustful of political negotiation and compromise. The realities of political contention and the disorder it generates renders leadership more fragile and makes it harder to produce disciplined action that sees through the commitment to responsibility and proportion. Moreover, the existence of a more militant and potentially violent dimension to a movement may be something that is difficult or impossible for those leading the movement to control or wholly to disown since it can be a considerable asset, providing an incentive for the state to make concessions for fear of something worse. This uncertainty about the degree of control over one's followers becomes, then, an integral part of the tense dynamic within such movements and in the relationship between protesters and the law.

In addition to its dissent with the federal government, the civil rights movement faced white supremacist organizations that also used tactics of protest. But there were important differences. White supremacist organizations lined up with, were systematically linked to, and were sometimes identical with, the local forces of law and order. They were political organizations within the local state seeking to sustain their position of privilege against black members of their communities. That degree of segregration could not meet even elementary standards of fair play and justice, nor could it be defended within the Constitution of the United States. These organizations denied the black community the most basic forms of civil and social equality, they orchestrated campaigns that violated their rights as citizens, and they used racial violence as a form of terror. Their respect for local and federal law was wholly opportunist—limited to areas where it delivered judgments that supported their position. Clearly, such groups believed that a way of life that they valued was being destroyed (of course, that way of life rested on the social, political, and often physical exclusion of men and women who had every just claim to citizenship and equal treatment), but there was no attempt to persuade their opponents of the justice of their case, doing so would have accorded them an equality they wished to deny, instead they relied upon intimidation and coercion.

I doubt this really needs spelling out. However, not all protest movements have the same sense of justice and clarity of vision as the civil rights movement, and not all forms of opposition to such movements are similarly oppressive. But the more ambiguous cases, such as the pro- and anti-abortion movements, or certain sectors of the animal rights movement, serve to highlight the distinctive character of protest movements. They use a variety of tactics to create a groundswell of feeling within the state for a change in the policies pursued by the state; they may become involved in violence, but largely because of the complex dynamic of their relationship with their own followers and with law enforcement agencies and the state. They remain protest movements insofar as they do not set themselves up as judge, jury, and executioner for particular individuals and insofar as they challenge the law rather than taking it into their own hands. They challenge the state to do what they believe is right; and they confront the police and use attacks on property to make their political purposes clear and highly visible, not to force a particular outcome on others. When people take up arms against abortion clinic workers or research scientists working with animals, they step over the line demarcating protest from rebellion or terrorism. In doing so they arrogate to themselves the right to the ultimate judgment of state sovereignty—the power of life and death with respect to others.

The assumption behind the classical doctrine of civil disobedience is that we need a special reason not to fulfil our obligation to obey the law, and that it is rarely the case that there is no justice at all in the state. Laws protecting individual liberty demand our compliance because (or insofar as) they are just; they must therefore act as *prima facie* (i.e., not necessarily overriding) constraints on our conduct even when we protest against other laws that we regard as fundamentally unjust. Lacking a general political obligation to obey the law does not entail lacking an obligation to act in ways that treat others with concern and respect and that respect their liberty and their right to life. If we are destined to be at loggerheads with each other over what it is legal for researchers to do to animals or fetuses, then our choices are to agree to the binding authority of the state but attempt to use all possible means to ensure that it is exercised in the way we think fit, or to deny the authority of the state and the rights and protections it accords to existing individuals (including ourselves). This latter course involves a rebellion against the state, not just an act of protest.

Most participatory forms of political action in democratic orders will be driven either by the pursuit of individual or sectional interests operating within the framework of normal politics, where the state provides the coercive resources and other incentives to ensure compliance with rules, or by challenges to the legitimacy of the established procedures of the state through protest at its failure to meet certain fundamental values and demands. Where the object of the protest is itself the outcome of the democratic process, the protest involves (implicitly or explicitly) the claim that these outcomes cannot be justified by that process—that certain more basic claims or rights or principles have to be met as a threshold (and are not being met) for the democratic procedure to be legitimate. What such movements often demonstrate, however, is that consensus on such a threshold is substantially more difficult to achieve than the founding fathers of liberalism acknowledged, and that conflicts over this threshold are likely to continue to erupt in ways that challenge the authority of the liberal democratic state. They will persist because the beliefs and attachments that drive people often engender conflict between them and, in the complex and heterogeneous social orders that mark modern societies, it is not possible to eliminate or resolve all conflict through socialization, education, and other methods of normative integration. Democratic procedures do solve some problems, and in that sense we might acknowledge an advance over more traditional states where decision making is dramatically more hierarchical and less open-ended. But there remain many issues on which modern liberal states must simply rule, backing their decisions with the necessary coercion. Such issues might include determining the criteria for admission to citizenship (a decision that must be imposed at least on those excluded by it) and the standing to be accorded to noncitizens in the public domain; or, the range of rights that are to be treated as inviolable by the state or democratic decision-making mechanisms. Moreover, on some issues, such as abortion, euthanasia, animal rights, and environmental issues, the refusal of groups to accept that the ruling of the state trumps all considerations of right or wrong is certainly intelligible, even if we do need an authoritative decision backed by power—when someone insists that abortion is always wrong and denies that others have a right to decide for themselves, the state must rule authoritatively. Indeed, any instance where people believe they have a right to require something of others and seek to enforce that right creates a need for an authoritative judgment, either to support that claim or to defend others from it. Finally, there are cases where rights of association come into fundamental conflict with issues of equality and citizenship, such as where the state supports the right of social, ethnic, or religious groupings that practise forms of exclusion against groups on the basis of color, sexuality, or ethnicity, such that the absence of state interference can form the basis for protest as deeply felt as that generated by the state's decision to intervene. In the course of time and with changes in legislation some issues do become increasingly uncontentious, such as according democratic rights to women. But even here the consequences of those changes can have extremely problematic knock-on consequences: it is difficult to believe that abortion could have become the issue it has in the United States without the prior recognition of women's rights, and negotiating the application of these rights in, for example, religious communities that do not accord women equality with men, is likely to generate further controversies in the future.

Every democratic state has to provide authoritative allocations of value or rulings that create a framework within which democratic procedures then operate, but in doing so the potential for protest against such rulings is also created. As discussed in Chapter 3, most liberal political theory takes the position that pluralism can be rendered into reasonable pluralism and that the sphere of politics can become a forum in which those who hold competing but reasonable comprehensive doctrines can agree to abide by rules and decision procedures which can be justified to all.[21] The difficulties with this view are three-fold. First, it is an ideal picture based on certain restrictive assumptions that are belied in the histories of particular states, and histories of oppression and disadvantage cannot but color citizens' sense of what minimum they must demand from the state, yet those prepared to admit them as equals may nonetheless reject that minimum. The second problem is that, rather than pluralism being a feature of societies that stands prior to and independent of the state, we have to recognize that, whatever the ideal, the state is nowhere a purely neutral actor, and its past actions inevitably contribute to the generation of both plural and antagonistic doctrines and commitments among its citizens and subjects. This is not just a point about the state's failure to achieve neutrality of effect (which is inevitable), it also involves the recognition that, when acting against the background of their particular state's history, neutrality of aim or justification is rarely experienced as such by those whose interests are disadvantaged by such decisions. For people to accept the state's claim to neutrality of aim they need to accept that their basic commitments can legitimately be trumped by considerations of fairness and reasonableness to others. But the depth of identification that people have with their values, and the fact that this is intensified when those values are experienced as threatened, militates against recognition of the demands of impartiality. Third, the very processes of politics that we have examined in this book—the importance of leadership, the char-

acter of political ambition, the dynamics of loyalty—tend to generate challenges to political consensus. Indeed, they do so not simply in the hands of
irresponsible leaders (who are not in short supply) whose convictions or
predilection for violence leads them to ride roughshod over the rights and
claims of others, but also with leaders who act with a sense of proportion
and responsibility, as the vast majority of those in the civil rights movement
did. Responsible leadership does not mean accepting injustice or shying
away from a confrontation with the state. Indeed, it can be exemplified in
contentious politics, and, on occasion, can take the form of rebellion and
resistance. Of course, this is less likely in liberal democratic states, but
largely by definition: what it is for a state to be liberal democratic is that it
respects the rights of its citizens and provides adequate avenues for the representation of interests. What weakens this claim, however, is that it is precisely disagreement over what counts as respect for rights and adequate representation of interests that marks such contention. Moreover, it is not
difficult to see, for example, that when liberal democracy is taken to mean a
system that protects the interests of capital, sustains systematic inequality,
and limits representation of minorities and the working class, then an alternative set of values revolving around equality, the meeting of needs, and
the emancipation of the underclass could form the basis for a movement
which systematically downgrades concerns with rights and individual liberty. Whether we assess leaders of revolutionary working-class movements
in the nineteenth and early twentieth centuries as acting responsibly depends on whether we think that the states against which they fought were
ones that adequately protected their rights and interests. Equally—indeed,
uniquely—troubling for many liberals is Nagel's suggestion that some forms
of inequality between states (and inequalities within states) are such that
"the degree of sacrifice by the rich that it would be reasonable for the poor
countries to insist on in some hypothetical collective arrangement is one
which it would not be unreasonable for the rich to refuse," since this suggests that there is no ground for a wholly rational consensus, and that resolution depends on the political process generating an answer that will stick,
while the lack of a reasoned basis renders any such solution essentially
fragile.[22]

On these several grounds, we have good reason to believe that liberal
democratic states cannot preclude challenges to their legitimacy from
groups whose commitments put into question the basic fairness with which
the state treats those within its borders (or indeed, outside). In responding

to these challenges the state cannot simply increase the scope of its tolerance since, in many areas, value conflicts are zero-sum: to meet one set of
concerns is to deny another set. Stable solutions to these problems cannot
be guaranteed. Those who lead such movements, and those who head the
state, can sometimes render viable solutions that less able negotiators could
not approximate. Sometimes luck and judgment coalesce, sometimes they
part company. If there are stable solutions, they are political—in the narrower sense of forged in the process of bargaining and negotiation—rather
than being simply a function of reasonableness or the need to consider matters impartially. Furthermore, the stability of the solution will also be a
function of ongoing political work, rather than a matter of a once-and-for-
all agreement.

CHAPTER **9**

Democratic Citizenship

Those who engage in contentious political action are clearly only a small minority of the citizenry of liberal democratic states. What about the political responsibilities and virtues of other citizens of such states? In this chapter I discuss three central features of modern democratic citizenship that must frame any discussion of the virtues we should expect of citizens in liberal democratic states. The first concerns the recognition that, while the process of democracy allows the representation of interests and preferences, support for the political process through which these are expressed cannot be conditional on the extent to which its outcomes meet our interests and preferences. There needs to be a degree of commitment to the procedures and practices that frame our participation, independent of their outcome for us in any particular case and, insofar as we talk about citizen virtues, it is partly in relation to their role in securing the acceptance and support of procedural constraints on the pursuit of individual or sectional interests. Second, while participation in politics is vital to safeguard the rights and liberties of citizens, the exercise of these individual rights and liberties may undermine the motivation for such participation. Theorists of liberal democratic citizenship have consistently wrestled with the tensions between the individualistic and atomized culture of advanced capitalist societies associated with the culture of individual rights, and the need to motivate citizens to participate in the political institutions of their states so that their rights and liberties remain secure and free from state interference.[1] These two cross-cutting insights, that democratic institutions must be able to motivate compliance with their procedures even when these deliver outcomes contrary to our individual interests, and the acknowledgment of the tension between the private lives we want the state to protect and the need to motivate public participation in politics so as to guarantee that protection,

provide an essential starting point for an account of the virtues of democratic citizenship. They encourage us to start without expansive assumptions about individual reasonableness or civic virtue and to begin by asking
two questions: What level of citizen participation is required to sustain
stable, orderly, and legitimate rule in democratic states and to prevent authoritarian or arbitrary government? and What types of motivation for political participation exist, and how far can these motivate the minimum
levels of participation and of compliance that are required for democratic
political rule?[2]

The third issue central to modern democratic citizenship remains. Many
political philosophers have referred to the need for citizen virtue in liberal
democratic states; however, as I have argued, virtues must be set in the context of practices and roles that are sufficiently deep and engaging in character. One of the central problems for theories of citizen virtue is identifying
practices and roles that go deep enough in their demands, engage citizens
enough, and contribute to the exercise of authority and the resolution of
conflict sufficiently for us to talk intelligibly about virtues, rather than
simply postulating the requirements as ideals that individual citizens ought
to meet (but where the word *ought* captures the disjunction between the
motives we want citizens to have, and those that can actually be relied
upon). To claim these as citizen virtues is to assume that there is sufficient
frequency and depth to the citizen's relationship with the political process
for the demands of that process to frame his or her conduct in a way that
engages his or her most fundamental commitments. It is certainly plausible
to think that some citizens in ancient Athens were so engaged (in some periods), and Machiavelli certainly tries to persuade us of the same for those
of ancient Rome. But modern citizenship is less encompassing, and less engaging—it makes fewer and less frequent demands, and it faces stiff competition from other value systems and commitments (for example, personal,
social, and economic relations). If this is the case, in what sense are the
practices of liberal democracy sufficiently inclusive, engaging, and, in an
important sense, quotidian enough to shape our commitments and allow
the development of excellences of character that warrant the term *virtue*?
Even if we recognize that liberal democracies would be dramatically improved if citizens regularly demonstrated the range of virtues proposed for
them, the more basic concern is with the extent to which the actual practices of civic engagement warrant the term *virtue*.[3] This last question is

tackled in the final section of the chapter, following a discussion of the nature of citizens' duties.

Citizenship describes a form of standing in politics—one that accords the individual the right to be ruled politically; that is, in accordance with the legitimated procedures or principles of the political domain.[4] People can have civil and personal rights without being accorded citizenship, but certain citizenship rights and liberties (i.e., rights in politics) do seem necessary to secure and protect civil and personal rights. At the heart of citizenship lie the rights of individuals and/or groups to make demands on their political institutions and, in some form, to hold their rulers accountable for their actions in office. To deny these rights is to deny people the political rank of citizenship; it is to rule people coercively or paternalistically, not democratically.[5] States ruled this way can be orderly and (sometimes) stable, but they achieve this by means they do not legitimate to those they rule.[6] Democratic politics rests on its citizen's distinctive "standing;" that status entails certain basic rights against those who rule coupled with rights of representation and certain responsibilities in the political domain. Different democratic states operate with differing conceptions of this standing and its associated duties, but the role that politics plays in the authoritative resolution of conflict ensures that the expectations of citizens are broadly similar.

Democratic political rights come with a number of associated procedural responsibilities: if a citizen makes representation or otherwise seeks to influence the political process and its outcomes, implicit in the right to do so is the responsibility to abide by that process, its spirit, and its outcomes. But democratic rights and responsibilities are not exhausted by these procedural requirements; even relatively parsimonious theories of citizenship, like Benjamin Constant's, also stress the responsibilities that citizens have to exercise their rights of participation so as to sustain a culture of accountability for those occupying positions of political power and trust. If we do not exercise these participatory rights they will increasingly be eroded, as will our personal and civil rights. We have a duty to participate in addition to the duties that arise in association with our participation. *Procedural duties* are generally acknowledged as entailed by the exercise of political rights, but participatory duties are not equally recognized (compounding the fact that they are subject to a major free-rider problem). "*Participatory duties* cover the engagement of citizens in the formal institutions of the system, such as elections, sitting on juries, and broader engagement in the civic and political culture that sustains links between the citizen on the street and those in public office.[7]

Procedural duties include both duties to support the procedures of the political process and duties to support and accept the outcomes of that process. States that permit citizens to make representation to those in office without acknowledging the rules and norms of the political process create the conditions for extensive corruption and maladministration. Corruption can stem from individuals seeking to use illegitimate means to achieve desired outcomes (such as threats, bribes, and so on), and from élites seeking to secure and sustain their hold on power by gaining the support and compliance of groups through illegitimate means—as through patron-client relations or by violating norms for the appointment of public officials to build political machines. The phrase *output-abidingness* relates to the concern that groups and communities should acknowledge the legitimacy of the political procedures and comply with the letter and spirit of the agreements negotiated through these procedures. Where most people abide by the spirit of their agreements it becomes possible for some to free-ride—to accept the benefits of this general compliance without themselves bearing any of its costs (or accepting any of its restraints). If free-riding becomes widespread, general compliance collapses. Keeping to the spirit of one's agreements involves not free-riding on others' willingness to do so, for example by raising questions about the legitimacy of the process as a tactical move to gain advantage over those who comply without complaint. We may call these *horizontal* responsibilities because the benefit we forgo by complying is one that we could have gained only by free-riding on other citizens' procedural restraint;[8] whereas *vertical* responsibilities concern relations directly with those in public office. People fail to fulfil these responsibilities when they seek illicit preferential access to resources or influence over decisions by in some way suborning those whose political office gives them control of these resources or decisions.

In contrast, participatory duties include vertical participation in activities to which one has a right by virtue of one's citizenship, such as in voting, making representation, involvement in interest group activities, joining and acting in political parties, writing letters to newspapers and representatives, performing jury service, and so on. But such duties also involve the more nebulous horizontal responsibility to engage with and sustain the civic culture that links citizens to those who exercise political rule. We might think of this as a form of "social capital"[9] among citizens outside the directly political arena that provides a background of trust, shared information, and political intelligence. That culture informs and motivates more formal participation in the system, and sustains a culture of accountability for politicians. Both types of participation play a central role in Tocqueville's writing. The first is evident in his eulogy to American townships in volume 1 of *Democracy in America*, where it is seen as central to the preservation of a spirit of liberty—by which he means the ability to resist encroachment on liberty by political authorities. Participatory duties animate the second volume, which dwells on the corrosive effects of individualism on the political system and on the willingness of citizens to cede ever greater areas of responsibility to an increasingly centralized and bureaucratic state.[10]

Tocqueville's discussion in his second volume, in which he sees secondary associations as central to the exercise of individual liberty and to the formation of a public identity and a civic spirit among citizens, defends one side in a long-standing argument concerning civic culture.[11] The other side, the Spartan variant espoused by Rousseau, takes the sole unit of participation and identification to be one's *patrie*, with secondary associations being seen as wholly inimical to the formation of the general will. The division between Tocqueville, who emphasizes the benefits of associations with respect to the state, and Rousseau, who emphasizes the costs, revolves around the issue of how far membership of civil society and its various associations produces a consistent identification with the norms of the political domain, either directly (because of the way that participation enlarges the scope of one's interests), or by default (through the sheer proliferation of interests and the inability of any particular interest to gain ascendancy over all others),[12] rather than threatening to make the political process hostage to the strongest societal interests—as in Adam Smith's comment that "People of the same trade seldom meet together, even for merriment and diversion, but the conversation ends in a conspiracy against the publick."[13] While horizontal participation is crucial, loyalties to a group do not necessarily lead to a more general form of civic spirit.

This fundamental point of disagreement has recently taken a new form, generated by the presence of different systems of communal value and cultural life coexisting within liberal democratic states. When communities demand collective rights to protect their distinctive cultural values and practices, they effectively deny that their standing as citizens within the modern "procedural republic" adequately protects their concerns.[14] Indeed, one feature of these debates has been the insistence that such cultural differences pose a different order of problem than do individualism or interest-group conflict. In this view, whereas conflict over distributive issues is in principle positive-sum, negotiable, and can be organized within a common framework of rules, conflicts involving a politics of identity are zero-sum, non-negotiable, and resistant to shared political procedures and practices. Communal identity becomes the constitutive feature of individual identity, framing the person's deepest dispositions and motives, and profoundly affecting whether group members can recognize the legitimacy of the procedures and rules of the extra-communal political order. Under such conditions, identity trumps citizenship, and is likely to fuel the type of contentious politics discussed in the previous chapter.

The literature on citizenship allows us to distinguish three distinct motives for citizens' compliance (modus vivendi, civic virtue, and procedural norms). each of which has different implications for how far citizens can meet the procedural and participatory demands of the modern democratic state.

Modus vivendi compliance occurs where conformity to political norms is conditional on those norms offering an interest-maximizing strategy for the individual or group.[15] This need not mean narrow self-interest maximizing, since the ends an individual pursues may involve group, or even global, altruism.[16] But it does imply that the interests or values that are maximized are identified independently of the norms and values that structure the rules of the political domain. Without that condition we would be solving the problem of motivation by definition. Nor need the modus vivendi account insist that citizens comply only when they judge that a specific act of compliance is directly optimal. Acknowledgment of the role played by threshold judgments and coordination problems helps us see that compliance may be forthcoming, not because the norms of the political system are accepted, nor because conformity with them maximally serves group interests, but because a certain threshold for collective action would need to be crossed for nonconformity to be a viable strategy.[17] In each case, however, the motive for compliance in politics is given by these interests and values and my standing as a citizen plays no role in my willingness to meet its demands—I accept or reject such demands wholly on the basis of their compatibility with my existing values or commitments. This may not pose a problem where a society is marked by a high degree of consensus on values and where the state's institutions and procedures are wholly congruent with such values. But state-building, the development of capitalist economies, democratization, and modernization have combined to ensure that most modern nation-states are marked to varying degrees by atomism,[18] value pluralism, and group and/or ethnic conflict, and under such conditions we cannot assume that individuals or group interests will find any fit with the procedural constraints they must submit to in the pursuit of their ends. This does necessarily lead to widespread noncompliance, since compliance can be produced simply by threats and effective sanctions. Citizens are often procedure-abiding because the state punishes those who violate procedural norms.[19] Similarly, horizontal—or outcome—compliance can be generated by the imposition of costs on defectors. Indeed, individuals and groups may find it in their interests to support such activity on the part of the state (because it is cheaper than suffering the noncompliance of others), even if it makes it more likely that their own defection will be successfully punished.

Where there is extensive group conflict, however, procedural compliance is much more difficult to motivate, not least because communities can offer individual members some insulation from sanctions by the state, especially when the state is perceived as hostile to the group. Despite the tendency among political theorists to treat ethnic conflict as fundamentally different from class conflict, it seems likely that, whenever the individual's identity (whether class or ethnic) is rooted in a solidaristic community and is coupled with an antagonistic relationship to the state, we will find something very like a politics of identity—and a similar ability (because communal solidarity facilitates collective action)[20] to mobilize to evade state sanctions. At the other extreme, élite groups with close relationships to the state will also be able to avoid sanctions, and have few incentives not to exploit their position to their advantage.

While procedural compliance may be differentially elicited under modus vivendi depending on whether the social order tends more to atomism and individualism than to group conflict, in neither case is participation easily motivated. In cases of group conflict, if participation is elicited only when it is interest-maximizing, and if it is procedure-abiding only when *that* is also interest-maximizing, it is probable that participation will be destabilizing. Under atomism it is unclear what the incentives for voluntary participation could be, hence the adoption in some states of enforcement mechanisms, such as penalties for nonvoting or sanctions against those resisting jury service. Moreover, there seem to be no incentives for the broader, horizontal forms of participation we have identified, not least because there are (by hypothesis) few group structures or associations to support such participation.

This conclusion needs some qualification: the concern with protecting and promoting one's interests does not necessarily militate against political participation. There may be less participation under a stable political order, since free-riding really does look costless; and for different reasons, participation will be perceived as unproductive where there is a highly coercive, authoritarian state. But acts of protest against, for example, blatant cases of corruption, fraud, or insouciance toward civil rights by some section of the political élite, might be generated by modus vivendi motives if the potential gains are large and the threshold for collective action is shown to be securely crossed—perhaps by the example set by some other group, not similarly motivated, such as the judiciary or the police. Getting out from under corrupt patrons may be in our interests, and acting to do so may also be an interest-maximizing strategy if doing so can be shown to be relatively safe (the incentives increase if remaining under such patrons can be seen to have escalating costs). Thus, collective acts of resistance to derelictions of public duty may be motivated wholly or largely by self-interest; that is, if the behavior of others signals that such behavior is both low cost and has a high potential return. Individual acts of resistance to authoritarian regimes, if rigorously penalized, will prompt few imitators, but examples of unpenalized opposition may prompt others to add their voice; and once there are a few, then many more may treat this as a sign that they can oppose without penalty. The diverse thresholds for collective action in a population may allow a rapid snowballing effect to follow from a relatively minor incident. The downside is that virtuous compliance can unravel into self-interested noncompliance and free-riding in a similar type of spiral.[21]

Therefore, when citizens are motivated by nothing more than a modus vivendi, the greatest danger to political stability arises when lip-service to participatory demands masks group or identity conflicts. In cases of atomism, modus vivendi may motivate procedural compliance but is unlikely to motivate participation, thereby diminishing the restraints on those in power.

Civic virtue is a central concept within the classical republican tradition. It refers to the citizen's desire to further the public good, with "virtue" being understood as an ingrained disposition to serve the polity, and to recognize the demands of citizenship as delimiting their other concerns.[22] Because private (or even global) interests are admitted only when compatible with or actively shaped by one's civic concerns, it is sometimes difficult to establish that the agent is acting from civic virtue rather than from compatible private-regarding motives.[23] As a result, civic virtue is most easily recognized in situations where the individual's independent interest in conformity is weak—because of the costs imposed on the agent. Analytically, civic virtue requires that it be the person's commitment as a citizen that motivates his or her compliance in the face of individual incentives not to comply. This does not require that citizens act wholly without concern for how others act: civic virtue is not the same as unthinking self-sacrifice, but it does require that the virtuous citizen does not set the threshold for others' compliance entirely by prudential criteria. Citizens cannot rationally be indifferent to outcomes and must assess the costs of complying where others do not (they might, for example, face certain death, financial ruin or reprisals against their families, and it is implausible to think that the virtuous citizen must regard these costs as negligible or to hold that they cannot sometimes outweigh the benefit to the public good that the citizen is likely to bring about—which in some cases may be very small indeed). Individual interests can, then, have some weight, but virtuous citizens are those whose commitment to their citizenship and to political norms takes them beyond an immediate calculation of their interests, and where it is that commitment that motivates them to act in support of those norms—so that it is their commitment to their values and principles *as citizens* that motivates their compliance.

In cases where general compliance is not going to be forthcoming or where it is extremely improbable that it will be, where the potential costs of compliance are exorbitant, and where the contribution we can hope to make is small, then we may have to decide that civic virtue has become disproportionately costly and that citizenship has become impossible (since the demands it makes can be reasonably refused). In such circumstances we might get acts of heroism or instances of great personal courage but the need for this—in cases of domestic politics—is often an indication that the political order is too weak to be independently effective, which then makes it difficult for us to think of those acts as instances of civic virtue.[24]

Civic virtue can motivate both compliance and participation across the full range of citizenship demands. But, within the republican tradition, it tends to do so by giving overriding weight to the person's political standing over all other identities, by suggesting an inevitable tension between private interests and the demands of the common good, and by believing that a process of political education is essential to ensure that the appropriate degree of identification with the polis and the common good is achieved.

The tradition draws on an understanding of politics as a fragile achievement for which the highest personal sacrifice can be asked, and in which the citizen's other interests and commitments are accorded relatively little weight (since the sustaining of the republic is seen as a necessary condition for achieving all other ends). However, writers as early as Montesquieu recognized that in the more plural and complex world of the modern state, in which the unity and face-to-face character of the classical republic has been lost, it is not easy to see how to motivate this degree of commitment.[25] Indeed, on Marx and Engels' account, it is wholly irrational to believe that we could do so:

> What a terrible illusion it is to have to recognise and sanction in the rights of man, modern bourgeois society, the society of industry, of universal competition, of private interest freely pursuing its aims of anarchy, of self estranged natural and spiritual individuality, and at the same time to want to annul the manifestations of the life of this society in particular individuals and simultaneously to want to model the political head of that society in the manner of antiquity.[26]

It seems that we would have to reject many relatively standard features of the modern state, such as pluralism, a flourishing civil society and economy, and the right to pursue one's own conception of the good as one sees fit, to secure the appropriate levels of civic virtue. This is not to say that it is never possible to generate such republican virtue. During wars or in situations of high international tension, for example, nationalism or patriotism may result in high levels of public participation and commitment; but this is neither a common situation, nor an ideal one. State-led nationalism, and state-led forms of cultural unity more generally, threaten to increase political solidarity and conformity only by decreasing the extent to which citizenship remains the basis for claims *against* the political order (as indeed Marx and Engels suggest). The problem of citizenship in liberal democratic orders is one of ensuring that there is compliance with political procedures while sustaining some sort of civic control on the institutions and officials of the state, and defending the sanctity and security of the private concerns and interests of citizens. Small-scale, homogenous, face-to-face communities might have enough solidarity to ensure that citizens are committed to the common good in a way that sustains compliance, critical distance, and individual security, but modern states, for the most part, do not.[27]

This was broadly the basis on which Constant repudiated the tradition of ancient liberty, and if there is a case to be made for civic virtue (and against Constant), it must be one that shows that modern liberal democratic states cannot remain resiliently stable without this degree of mobilization. But the strength of Constant's characterization of the problem of citizenship is his suggestion that if liberal democratic states cannot survive without civic virtue, it is also the case that they cannot remain both democratic *and* liberal if they have to rely on its generation.[28] For civic virtue theorists, the argument must move from showing that liberal democracies as we know them need civic virtue, to acknowledging that the very ideal of a liberal democracy is flawed. Rather than embracing this course we might do better to look elsewhere for an understanding of the character of compliance required by modern democratic states.

One alternative to civic virtue is the idea of overdetermined compliance, which arises when the interests or values of the individual and the group endorse compliance in broad terms (while also providing limits to that endorsement), supported by some degree of independent commitment to the norms of the political domain so that, within limits, compliance is not dependent on securing the optimal advantage.[29] Something along these lines can be recognized in the later work of John Rawls, under the term "overlapping consensus." In contrast to the particularist and irrationalist approach to political unity adopted by nationalists and patriots (including some republicans), Rawls's account looks for a grounding in political values and the values of public reason. His approach is attractive because he recognizes that the values of public reason need not be treated as wholly freestanding universals (which would imply the irrelevance of one's particular citizenship), but can be recognized as emerging through the particular practices and shared experiences of a political community, and thereby as sharing some of the features of the practices within which virtues are embedded. Consequently, what public reason demands is a local question, albeit one informed by the desire to ensure the highest and most general standard of justification; it is not simply an empirical issue of what passes muster for public reason around here but also involves a judgment that what counts as public reason does so for the right reasons. Our citizenship, then, gives us access to institutions, shared practices, and deliberative arenas; it requires us to act in these spheres in accordance with a common set of political values and standards of public reason; and we develop our understanding of our responsibilities as citizens through our participation in institutions and practices regulated by public reason that enable us to recognize our obligations to other citizens and to accept the necessity for procedural rules to govern the formation of law and public policy.

There is something of a concern here about bootstrapping: how do we get from a default position of modus vivendi to one of self-restraint in line with public reason without implicitly presupposing the presence of the latter in the former? Rawls believes that the connection between the two motives (our personal and/or communal values and our commitment to public reason) will tend to be positive, and increasingly so, unless disrupted by external factors (such as war, natural disasters, etc.). For example, he sketches a story of the transformation from a modus vivendi through a constitutional consensus to an overlapping consensus.[30] In a constitutional consensus, the constitution satisfies certain liberal principles, but these principles are not deeply grounded in a shared public conception of society and the person, although they are affirmed as substantive principles. Rawls believes that, over time, "liberal principles of justice, initially accepted reluctantly as a modus vivendi and adopted into a constitution, tend to shift citizens' comprehensive doctrines so that they at least accept the principles of a liberal constitution . . . Simple pluralism moves towards reasonable pluralism and constitutional consensus is achieved."[31] However, in part because a constitutional consensus is "a consensus taken literally," it lacks the conceptual resources to guide the interpretation and amendment of the constitution.[32] The search for such resources drives us from a constitutional consensus to a deeper and broader consensus on the principles that should structure the political domain.

This is an optimistic picture built on a number of very restrictive assumptions, but it is not without foundation. As we have seen, where compliance is widespread, continued compliance becomes relatively frictionless, and we can follow Hume in thinking that it can become increasingly so.[33] Moreover, we may draw on a range of accounts of virtuous mechanisms in social institutions to understand how people who come to an institution with one set of interests can develop a different set through their participation—or can come to make war and stay to make peace.[34] However, we need to recognize that such arguments might not apply with equal force to the different types of citizen responsibilities we have identified.

The strongest case for participation leading to the inculcation of a sense of obligation to other participants and to conduct that conforms to procedural rules and public reason is one that focuses on procedural norms. In this case no assumption needs to be made about virtuous motives prompting participation, since self-interest can motivate participation in the procedures. Instead, we can focus on the mechanisms by which this self-interest is gradually transformed through participation so that those involved come to recognize the legitimacy of a range of rules and procedures and come increasingly to justify their demands with reference to public reason, thereby engaging in a self-laundering of preferences. Where the weight of this explanation rests is a matter of judgment: we might emphasize the inherent rationality of communicative action or the transformative effects of free public reason; we might recognize that the capacity of the state to enforce its procedural rules creates incentives for a degree of conformity that eventually becomes habitual; or we might run some combination of these accounts. We need not insist that such effects are guaranteed: in some conditions the absence of trust between parties will ensure that the incentives to defect from a procedure will be far greater than those to conform, so that the suasive effects of the procedure never have a chance to operate. That these mechanisms do not always operate does not detract from the fact that they sometimes do, sometimes very powerfully, and they tend to operate most powerfully in polities where social and political conflict is not extreme and where there is stability in institutions and trust and transparency in decision procedures.[35]

Procedural compliance might be self-reinforcing in the way Hume implies, but does such compliance necessarily encourage virtuous participation in other areas of the system? Because procedural compliance supervenes on attempts to get the political system to respond to our interests and concerns (so that we become guided by procedures and public reason in the pursuit of these specific concerns), it does not follow that we are further motivated to bear responsibilities that we have no independent interest in bearing, nor that our involvement in the groups, subcultures, and associations of civil society will necessarily have positive implications for our attitudes toward or involvement in the political arena. One linking element may be that horizontal participation might stimulate groups to try to influence the political system, thereby drawing them into the virtuous cycle of procedural compliance. But a great deal depends on how these groups and associations define themselves with respect to the state and the political process. Groups that define themselves in zero-sum terms will simply lack the basic trust required for positive identification with political norms to get off the ground, as may others in conflict with the state. It is difficult to identify the range of factors within a community or subculture that may result in high, rather than low, levels of identification with the norms and procedures of the political process, but it is certain that horizontal participation does not necessarily encourage either vertical political participation or virtuous identification. Indeed, there are clearly possibilities for perverse disjunctions between the two dimensions of civic duty. For example, if conformity to procedural norms becomes increasingly habitual and unreflective it may become less firmly and independently motivated, and when participation in one's local community and culture is working to reinforce one's more local value system we may see a covert slide to modus vivendi compliance.[36] When the motives that underpin conformity become increasingly fragile, others' expectations about the resilience of conformity become correspondingly unfounded, with the result that observers can come dramatically to overstate the stability of an order only to find that relatively minor conflicts throw it into question.

It seems clear that a virtuous cycle that delivers an overlapping consensus may be quite narrow in its effects, applying to areas where we have an independent interest in influencing the state but having no necessary knock-on effects for participation or compliance in other areas of the political system: Horizontal participation does not necessarily issue in vertical participation. Moreover, even when procedural compliance is high, more extensive participation can be difficult to motivate—not least, prosaically enough, because for most citizens the costs of vertical participation are high relative to the rewards.[37]

There remains, then, a nagging doubt about whether we can resolve Constant's and Tocqueville's anxieties that liberal democratic systems need a level of participation from their citizenship that they find extremely difficult to motivate even when they achieve high levels of procedural compliance and a reasonably wide agreement on political principles. Based on their accounts, there will remain problems, even in the most auspicious of circumstances, in resiliently motivating the type of participation necessary for sustaining liberal civic cultures within modern, pluralist states. There is still more of a problem where circumstances are not so auspicious. The attempt to recruit Rawls to solve this difficulty cannot be counted as a success—he too has problems motivating participation. This leaves us with the question of whether liberal democracies are inherently flawed, or whether the difficulty lies in the expectation that democratic states must rely in some way on the procedural compliance and participation of all citizens. Constant's view, that surrendering our political liberty to those who rule is also to surrender our civil liberty, seems indisputable, but it is less clear that civil liberty is necessarily at stake when political participation is not citizenwide. Clearly, there are areas in the political system that require participation if those who rule are not to ride roughshod over the civil liberties and rights of some of its citizens. While most modern theories of citizenship assume that this means full citizen participation, I shall suggest, in the final chapter, that this is not necessarily so. Before doing so, however, we need to consider the third issue raised in the introduction to this chapter; namely, whether the kinds of participation and compliance that we have been discussing warrant the language of virtue, given the relative infrequency with which they engage in these roles and the competing claims on their commitments.

Most people's involvement in politics is likely to be too occasional and superficial to justify the term *virtue*. That pessimistic conclusion, however, does not entirely do justice to the way in which those who defend democratic institutions see these institutions as developing the virtues necessary for their reproduction. A brief exploration of this more ideal picture will give us a stronger sense of when the term is justifiably applied to citizens of modern democratic states, while suggesting the distance such states have to travel to allow that move. Moreover, it helps set the scene for the discussion in the concluding chapter about alternative ways in which institutional arrangements can help ensure that the political conduct of those in power remains free of the abuses that modern democratic states seem to invite.

I start from a slightly unusual position for those enthusiastic about the potential of democracy by advancing the case on the basis of a procedural understanding of democracy, rather than relying on the more ideal and deliberative pictures available in the literature. A procedural definition of *democracy* identifies it with the presence of certain procedures for popular decision making: what makes a democracy a democracy is that there are regular elections which determine access to political office, wide rights to vote in elections, recognized procedures for determining citizenship and the scope of public decision making, and recognized protections for democratic participation in the formation of political agendas, such as freedom of association, freedom of expression, and freedom of the press. To take this as an adequate characterization of what it is for something to be a democracy is to adopt a procedural definition. The attractions of focusing on procedures as central to understanding democracy can be seen if we look at the way in which procedures and outcomes are related, and at how far the former serve to justify the latter.

Consider the contrasts among perfect, imperfect, and pure procedures.[38] A perfect procedure is one for which there is an independently defined right outcome, such as the equal division of a cake, and where we have a procedure that always delivers that outcome.[39] In cases where there is a right answer but where our procedures cannot guarantee delivering it, we have an imperfect procedure. The jury system is one example: either Ms. Smith committed a crime, or she did not, but the jury system is the best (but certainly not perfect) procedure we have for determining which is the case. In a pure procedure, there is no independently specifiable right result beyond that which the procedure delivers. A lottery determines results entirely through the play of chance, so that the result is the right one, whatever that may be. Similarly, the race goes to the person who crosses the line first (even though they may not in fact be the fastest runner). Exactly what type of procedure is involved can sometimes be obscure: in the case of cake dividing it is moot whether the mechanism (in the two-person case) of A cuts/B chooses is an imperfect procedure to produce equal shares (an antecedently defined right outcome), or a pure procedure in which each person's gets only what he or she chooses or cuts.

If we understand democracy as an imperfect or perfect procedure, we would see it as producing decisions that approximate to some externally specifiable standard. Analogs to guilt and innocence in the jury case might be the general will, the common good, maximum aggregate utility, or the interests of the people. Each is an end or state that the specified procedures perfectly or imperfectly secure. In each case, the value of the procedures (whether perfect or imperfect) derives from their output.[40] If the choice is between regarding democracy as a perfect or as an imperfect procedure it is clear it would be the latter, although the imperfect account may take more or less complex forms. For example, rather than specifying the outcome in terms of some positive value (such as the common good), an imperfect account might do so either negatively or by a "satisficing" requirement (i.e., one that sets out the minimum requirements necessary for attaining a particular goal). A negative account might deny that there is an independently specifiable right answer that democratic procedures track, but argue that there are certain outcomes that it should exclude, and that it is more likely to do so than other political decision-making procedures.[41] A satisficing account takes the view that rather than judging democratic procedures by whether their output optimizes the output of a good, we should accept their results if they meet certain minimum standards.

The alternative to seeing democracy as a good but imperfect procedure is to see it as a pure procedure where the outcomes of the procedures are valid so long as they flow from and respect the procedures themselves. Of course, we have to guard against distortions in the procedure, just as in a lottery we have to specify the procedure so the outcome is wholly a function of chance. Similarly, the pure procedural account might invoke the principle of each to count for one, and accordingly propose a way of ensuring that all binding decisions are the result of a majoritarian choice between two options. Or, if we take something like *isegoria* to be central—the equal right to be heard in the sovereign assembly of the state before public decisions are taken—then a procedure that entrenches voice would be essential.[42] Furthermore, if we understand democracy as a collective process of negotiation, deliberation, and compromise, then we need the decision procedure to enable those processes. In each case, however, while the procedure is set up to meet certain basic commitments, the output of the procedure is justified by being the output of that procedure, rather than because it directly expresses those input values. There are thicker and thinner versions of such positions: the more we stipulate in detail the values the procedure must embody, the more the output is determined wholly by those values—and thereby also justified by them, eclipsing the pure procedural by an imperfect procedural account. The more thinly we sketch the components of the procedure, the more the answer the procedure gives is derived from and justified by the procedure, not by the principles or ideals that the procedure embodies.

One reason for understanding democracy as a pure procedure is the fact that, as a preference aggregating mechanism, it is subject to various public and social choice problems, such as Arrow's General Impossibility Theorem or Condorcet's cycling problem, that preclude standards of maximum aggregate welfare or the common good. Similarly, the arguments advanced in this book about the character of politics support the view that we have to recognize the open character of the political process, the complexity of the cross-cutting interests and conflicts that politics attempts to order, the crucial role for interpretation in the concretizing and realization of abstract values and commitments, and the element of decisionism in the way that political decisions and policies are to some extent made right by the way that they are delivered and seen through in the political process. A perspective on democratic politics that recognizes that there are no prior external standards against which to measure the outcomes of the democratic process is grist to the mill of the account that I have been proposing here of the character of politics. We might complement this perspective by holding that there are some outcomes that are unacceptable and that these should constrain the democratic procedure where they clash, but that the procedure is appropriately used wherever it does not encroach on those values.

With that ground cleared, a further step takes us back to the question of citizen virtue. Some theorists have looked to procedural accounts of democracy as a basis for eradicating any gap between people's involvement in the procedure and their acceptance of the outcome as legitimate and binding, even when that outcome adversely affects his or her interests. The fairness of the procedure (which may be variously elaborated) is such that those who subscribe to the procedure acknowledge that they are bound to accept its outcome, whatever that may be. This position is usually accompanied by the recognition that democratic procedures also require a range of background conditions to deliver this compliance. These might include approximately equal rationality; the absence of major social, ethnic, or religious divisions within the community; or (with Rousseau) approximate material equality. An ambitious procedural theory aims to generate binding decisions without specifying independent constraints and by using the least restrictive set of assumptions about the necessary background conditions for the procedure. More plausible pure proceduralist theories, by contrast, may need to specify both independent constraints and quite extensive background conditions—and many critics of procedural democracy are so because modern states fail to secure those background conditions.[43] There is also an issue about whether these background conditions should be taken as brute facts that constrain and shape the participants' attitudes and expectations, or whether they can themselves be willed by those involved in the procedure. Rousseau's solution to this problem, which invokes the legislator, assumes that the people cannot themselves will the background conditions. In contrast, theorists of deliberative democracy suggest that deliberation not only "launders" people's preferences, but also educates them so that brute background conditions become reflectively endorsed background conditions.[44] The value of that claim for our purposes is that it suggests that the virtues we have identified as necessary to the democratic process may emerge, in part, through the process itself. However, while the claim is certainly plausible, it does rely on active and reasonably extensive participation in the practices of politics; that is, deliberative democrats must provide an account of their deliberative practices that demonstrates that they have the complexity and intrinsic qualities (and satisfactions) that mark other practices of which virtue can be predicated.[45] If deliberative democracy has (or could be developed in ways that have) this quality then it does seem possible to speak of citizen virtue in democratic states. Where it lacks this quality, however, the terminology lacks warrant. What, in practice, is required for deliberation to have this quality in practice is debatable. Someone who watches the news, is aware of legislative debates, and is moderately well-informed about the issues in elections does not, on the face of it, seem to have the kind of depth of involvement in the practices of politics that would translate his or her conduct into a set of commitments and activities that exhibit the virtues. Yet someone who acts as a juror on a long-running case and who becomes absorbed in the details of the case and the niceties of legal argument, without losing their own independence of judgment, comes closer to developing certain ethical qualities within the context of the role. Deliberation must be similarly deep, and similarly absorbing, to reach down and engage our sense of self and our ethical judgment, rather than simply involving the expression of more superficial attitudes. Moreover, it needs to connect up to the institutions of the polity in the right sort of way—getting deeply involved in a particular set of debates and disputes, but experiencing these in isolation from the broader political system, may develop aspects of one's character, but not in ways that necessarily lead to the integration of the individual in the political process as a whole. Indeed, narrow involvement may produce a narrow grasp on the intricacies of political life that may in turn issue in cynicism about politics more widely. Mass democracies may allow depth in localities, but they are likely to be systematically weaker at connecting those local issues to a similarly deep understanding of and sense of involvement in the national political process. To accept that deliberation can develop such civic virtues, we need to be able to show that something like this kind of connection is likely to develop (albeit given certain background conditions). That, at least, is the challenge.

I have suggested that the procedural account of democracy as sketched here gives substance to the idea that democracy is, by its nature, open ended; that it is best understood not as an attempt to secure certain given ends or to instantiate certain values, but as a decision-making process that under certain constraints, such as political equality, the burden of proof, free and reasoned assessment of alternatives, together with a range of social and cultural background preconditions, can produce decisions that participants can accept as binding. They accept those decisions not because they get the outcome they want, nor simply because the outcomes respect certain input rights, but because the procedure is recognized as imposing fair and reasonable constraints upon them. Of course, in the absence of those background conditions there is no guarantee that participants in the democratic process will accept the decisions as binding. The argument of much of this chapter has been that given a degree of heterogeneity or atomism in the population, that outcome is more probable. The result will be a compliance problem with people acting opportunistically in relation to the outcomes of procedures and free-riding on participation. Moreover, the language of the virtues will remain something to be deployed only when people's involvement has a certain depth and complexity—and that, I suggest, will inevitably mean with legislatures, executives, central and local government administrations, and in certain areas of interest group bargaining and arbitration, rather than easily among the citizenry at large.

For most people the most attractive justifications for democratic procedures in modern liberal societies are those providing a negative or satisficing account, in which the procedures ensure the basic protection of certain rights or claims, or achieve a certain threshold of such protection. This position has much intuitive appeal, but there can be considerable contention over what minimum should be afforded protection and over whether a minimum protection of rights is in fact being preserved by democratic procedures and constitutional provisions. Consider, for example, the sudden fragility of civil liberties in Western states consequent to the war on terror. Moreover, although a consensus on radical harm might be attainable, this is also a disputable area, and there is no indisputable way of drawing a hard and fast line between matters on which it is legitimate for the people collectively to decide, and matters that have to be ruled off from such collective decision making. As such, the issue of whether a minimum standard of protection can be identified becomes a practical one about what in fact a society can agree on, rather than an a priori matter that can be uncontentiously enshrined legally or constitutionally. And, as a practical matter, it is always potentially open to dispute.

The alternative is to acknowledge that democratic outcomes must be justified by the procedures, but that those procedures need a certain amount of embedding in a common political culture. This seems to me the most promising line of inquiry, the most promising form of justification, and the most promising account of under what conditions participation in the procedures will tend to result in a willing acceptance of the outcomes. It can help us understand how democratic procedures might generate appropriate levels of participation; it can provide us with a justification for democratic outcomes that is pure in character, rather than appealing to some set of potentially contestable ideals or benchmarks; and it offers a way of understanding how reasonableness and reciprocity can develop and become embedded in political institutions in a way that engenders both participation and compliance (two central components of citizen virtue). But for all the promise, this account remains at the level of the ideal theory—and retains that very classical sense that if only we can set the system up right in the first place, not just the institutions but also the culture, mores, customs, and habits of a people (the very components of their interests and their rationality), then we can produce a stable and self-governing state. We can see what we think we want, but our getting there is beset by the very problems we want to use the state to which we aspire to solve. In that sense, the ideal risks becoming a snare and a delusion, since it stops us appreciating that solutions lying far short of this ideal may nonetheless be good enough and may be extremely difficult to improve on!

If the argument in this chapter is right, we can see that liberal democratic cultures are fragile achievements, the more so the more pluralist and atomistic they are. The development of a society in which people participate in the political process in ways that serve to protect their rights and pursue their interests compatibly with a respect for the outcome of democratic procedures is something to be welcomed but not expected. Indeed, the very diversity and difference that politics is in part called upon to negotiate and order testifies to the fragility of liberal democratic solutions. This is not to say that they are under threat of collapse, but they remain open to destabilizing contestation and, even when not so threatened, they face issues of how effectively they are able to control and hold to account those who govern them, and how far they are able to maintain themselves without recourse to coercion that may lay the ground for future controversy and protest. The thought that the answer to such concerns might not lie with the citizenry but with aspects of institutional design is one I address in the next chapter.

CHAPTER 10

Institutions and Integrity

Politics is a rule and norm governed activity; sometimes the rules are clear and explicit (although they are never exhaustive), sometimes they are few and far between, almost wholly implicit, and very much forged in the process. The attempt to exercise political authority comes with prudential and categorical constraints built in—prudential, because not every means is equally effective to that purpose; and categorical, because not every act is compatible with making one's commitments authoritative for others, and rules and norms are part of the background against which authority is claimed. Even in Machiavelli's disordered world there are guidelines as to how princes should act and clear injunctions, both prudential and ethical, against acting in certain ways. There are also, however, stochastic elements in political life that make it not wholly reducible to existing rules, procedures, and norms: the existence of persistent dimensions of conflict that must be ordered authoritatively and the tendency of that very ordering process to engender new conflicts; the reliance of politics on innovation, agency, and will in shaping the attitudes and dispositions of those who are critical to rendering particular political solutions viable; the importance of loyalties and particular relationships in the development of political careers and the creation of coalitions of support; and the irreducibility of value conflicts in political life. Political life is, in this account, open-ended; it is susceptible to agency but also to hubris; it reaches for authoritative solutions but can destroy them by the exercise of power; and while it may aim for impartiality it often does so building on particular, local, and fundamentally partial relationships. This is not simply a story of human weakness in the face of temptation, it is, more seriously, a function of the conflicts and irrationalities inherent in acting to set the pattern of action for others against a history of previous attempts and their intended and unintended consequences.

As the last two chapters have emphasized, even modern democratic systems have difficulty in generating the right level and type of participation both to support the institutions and procedures of government and administration and to act as an appropriate accountability mechanism for those in power. Accountability can become politicized and destabilizing, and the motives that are likely to prove most resilient for citizens of modern democratic states are those that further their interests relatively directly, rather than those that support just institutions. This has a corresponding impact on those in public office. Even where states act to rectify abuses and correct injustices, they may do so (unwittingly) in ways that generate further conflicts or sensed injustices elsewhere in the polity. There remains a concern that successful democratic procedures must rely on more or less demanding background conditions. The assumption that there is a set of values upon which we can agree that can provide a basis for a wholly legitimate and thus stable system of government, or that there is a set of institutions that can provide a solution on an enduring basis to order within any polity, seriously understates the complexities of social and political conflict, the difficulties of designing institutional orders for mass democracies that systematically unite the interests of rulers and ruled, and the importance of the social, cultural, and structural preconditions under which those values and institutions could serve as a basis for consensus and the management of conflict. Yet the hope that there can be an institutional solution to the potential for political misrule or majority tyranny has a long history and, even if its prospects as a panacea are less rosy than many of its advocates have suggested, it remains the case that institutions matter.

Although political conduct is concerned with agency, laws and institutions are an essential part of the context in which men and women act. Institutional design is partly what political innovation produces, and partly what creates and frames the context within which most modern political agents act. In contrast to *fortuna*, who malevolently stalks Machiavelli's prince, institutions stabilize and routinize public office and political conduct takes a more regulated and constrained character. The prince defines the parameters of his office by his will and agency. He sets the pattern of action for others by his personal qualities, not by his formal standing (since, by hypothesis, no formal structures or norms are authoritative in the context within which he acts), and he attempts by his will to create precisely the institutions and patterns of action that will structure his city and moderate the play of *fortuna*. While Machiavelli was pessimistic about how easily such institutionalization could be achieved and how far it would eliminate the need for innovative political agency, the spread of legal-rational forms of administration and the rise of a liberal democratic culture have enabled politicians increasingly to draw their authority, not from their innovative political will (and brute power), but from their institutional location and the powers formally conferred on them by virtue of their office. The sense that authority comes largely from their position within an institutional order, rather than simply from their personal capacities to make effective their commands, plays a central role in modern democratic states and is an essential element in stabilizing, sustaining, and legitimating political authority.

Public office entails a formal position whose holder is accorded certain rights and powers so as to fulfil associated responsibilities vis-à-vis members of the general public.[1] It creates the basis for a distinction between the rights and duties of the agent as a private person and those that arise in virtue of his or her appointment to a position with accompanying formal and informal responsibilities and powers. Private, personal, or contractual relations may involve relations of trust associated with responsibilities but they are not thereby public offices. Nor is the formal designation of rights and duties, powers, and immunities a necessary feature of public office since, although they are common to modern conceptions of office, historically such duties have sometimes rested wholly on informal or implicit norms. The crucial element in defining public office is that it is devoted to public rather than private ends; that is, to the public interest, rather than to the occupant's private interests, and to recipients as members of the public, not as private individuals. Of course, the public official may be answerable for the conduct of the office to particular individuals or institutions, but the office itself is ultimately referenced to the public rather than to those to whom it is directly accountable.

Holders of public office may exploit their office for their personal advantage, they may be lazy or incompetent, or they may exercise it capriciously or malevolently. That there is public office does not entail that the trust involved is always well placed. Nonetheless, the criteria for whether a public office is exercised well or badly are rooted in the trust that is reposed in the office; not in whether or not people actually trust it, but in on what its claim to authority and public support is based. When the Committee on Standards in Public Life in Britain sought to articulate the basic principles of public life, it arrived at seven principles: selflessness, integrity, objectivity, accountability, openness, honesty, and leadership.[2] For the committee, it was central to their idea of public office that officials are there to pursue the public's interest, not their own, and it took a very strict and modern view of the incompatibility between public office and private gain, and of the nature of "merit" in making public appointments, in policy formulation, and in the awarding of contracts.[3] These latter concerns are, in fact, conceptually contingent for the definition of public office: public office requires that the public's interest be served in some way but whether this aim is seen as compromised by personal gain or deviations from meritocratic or other principles varies widely. This is not just because some systems see a conflict and others do not, but because historical context has an impact on what is, in fact, compatible or incompatible. Depending on how one understands the character of politics, all kinds of personal gain may be regarded as legitimately combined with public office, and all kinds of features could be rolled into the idea of merit. But the case for such elements will revolve around a prior conception of an office whose ends refer beyond the satisfaction of the . post-holder's interests and preferences. That much is core to public office, even if the articulation of that core, the recognition of its intimate dependence on its context, and the sense of the range of factors that can obstruct or derail its proper exercise, fluctuate dramatically over time.[4]

A major precondition for the autonomy of the political sphere concerns its institutional consolidation.[5] This refers to the extent to which organization of offices and responsibilities in the state enable effective policy formation, implementation, and administration. The considerations relevant to this include: that a clearly understood structure of authority exists that specifies individuals' institutional responsibilities; that this authority structure is normative over its members' behavior; that the tasks and goals of the institution are clear and derive from a clear process either internal or external to the institution; that the institution has formal access to the resources it needs to meet those tasks and goals and is not dependent on informal deals and arrangements; that officials are managed so as to ensure that they meet their institutional responsibilities (and have some protection from pressures from outside the institution that work against that end) and that they subordinate their private concerns and interests to the performance of this role; and that there is an accountability structure for the institutions within the state that protects the independence of their activities. Consolidated institutions provide regulated and ordered patterns of policy making, implementation, and administration, and they delimit the extent of legitimate interest representation within the area of their activity.

To achieve consolidation a range of elements comes into play. It is not simply a case of getting the institutional structure right. It needs a culture that sustains a high degree of proceduralism or "vertical integration" (i.e., that people's activities are constrained by higher order procedures and decision rules);[6] it requires a political culture that can generate personal, professional, and institutional loyalties that are conditional rather than highly exclusionary; it depends on people being able to deal with their history in ways that work toward tolerance and integration rather than exacerbating difference and a nonnegotiable politics of identity; and it needs a process of accountability that supports rather than erodes trust, and yet does so in ways that retain a critical dimension to the relationship between rulers and ruled.

This sketch of the autonomy and authority of the liberal democratic state has powerful normative appeal. Such political systems exercise authority (that is, they are capable of eliciting willed compliance, rather than having to rely on force or coercion), they facilitate access to the political system for their citizens, and they are regulated to ensure that those in authority are accountable to those they rule. The accountability of those in public office to the electorate can enhance their authority, and the existence of widely legitimated formal procedures for election or appointment to office, and a degree of transparency in the execution of these procedures, provide grounds for compliance even among those who dissent. Legitimacy streamlines access and representation, ensuring that it is channeled appropriately and normatively regulated, and it reduces friction and noise in the political system, making it more efficient, which in turn consolidates its legitimacy and enhances its authority. Liberal democratic states with clear rules that are acknowledged as legitimate and whose officials and politicians are seen as compliant with these rules will be better able to order conflict within the state. Moreover, where such states justify policies and practices on grounds that meet the criterion of neutrality, they moderate the impetus for sectional conflict and establish the principle that claims against the state be justified in similarly nonsectarian terms.[7]

This portrait of the self-reinforcing character of liberal democratic institutions is extremely attractive, but it places a good deal of weight on the power of institutions to direct their members' expectations and conduct, it underplays the indeterminacy in the interpretation of responsibilities and the place of innovation in political action, and it tends to make strong assumptions about the degree to which institutional design can resolve in advance the most pressing strains in a polity.[8] It also tends to play down the fallibility of those who occupy office, or it compensates for fallibility in one domain, for example, among politicians, by exaggerating the positive contribution of others, such as a mobilized and virtuous citizenry, or an upright public service, or a set of prescient institutional designers! In reality, things can go the other way: leaders may exceed the bounds of their office, especially when they risk losing it; public officials may lack the commitment and the courage to insist on their peers' or superiors' compliance with the norms and rules of public office; and rules and institutions may be twisted in ways that ensure that members of the public support movements against the system rather than playing their part in constraining those in power. There are different objects of loyalty within the state and people may reject or accept some or all—policies, the government of the day, the administrative order, the system of government, or the nation itself. Indeed, lining up and sustaining commitment to all levels simultaneously is a fragile achievement. It is also the case that in all political systems, but perhaps especially in democratic states with frequent electoral cycles, the ends of public office can become a secondary consideration to the practical struggle to attain and secure power; the means can become the end. As we have seen, the civic participation required to sustain political accountability is not easily generated, and, where it is generated, it is not necessarily civil in character. Even if there is a dimension of civic mindedness, it may nonetheless contribute to the weakening of trust and the diminishing of professional standing if accountability mechanisms become increasingly intrusive and politicized.

Institutional design is not a panacea for politics: it relies on political leadership and innovation to bring it about; it can become a bone of contention between rival political groupings, resulting in partisan legislation and implementation; and it depends for its success on a range of background conditions. That success must be measured with care. The Roman and Spartan republics were in many respects extraordinarily successful, on both the grounds of longevity and in terms of their ability to resist outside subjugation while imposing domination on others. Nonetheless, they collapsed. The U.S. Constitution is often held up as a model of institutional design, but because it has been in existence for barely 200 years, has had one major civil war, and is increasingly experiencing the pressures of something like imperial rule in the international arena, we ought not to rush to premature judgments on its stability or on the resilience of its institutional design. In many respects, the work of the Founding Fathers and their subsequent commentators and interpreters should encourage us to recognize that institutional design is not a one-off moment, but an ongoing process that is an integral part of the political process and, as such, is subject to its dynamics and irrationalities, and to its successes and failures.

The ability to hold those who rule to account is a touchstone for liberal democratic thought. The rights of citizens to reject politicians at the end of their term of office—to throw them out, to seek redress for official wrongdoing, and to resist the extension of political power into areas deemed properly private—provide the core to many modern conceptions of an appropriately liberal democratic process.[9] We want government and the administrative order to be answerable for what they do and we tend to think that in democratic governments leaders rule in the public interest *because* they are in some way accountable to those whom they rule. Yet it is not clear how who most appropriately holds whom accountable for what. Even recognizing these four dimensions—how, who, whom, and what—leaves untouched the question of what precisely is involved in being accountable. When the impetus for institutional design derives from mistrust of those who rule, these subtleties and distinctions are easily overridden. Moreover, discussions of accountability tend to inflate the content of the concept by equating what something is with what makes it valuable. Accountability is not unique to democratic governments and whether or not a given accountability mechanism adds value in an institutional setting is a contingent and empirical issue, not something that follows automatically from its being an accountability mechanism. Indeed, principal-agent theory, the dominant model used today to analyze political accountability, only exacerbates these mistakes. Consider, for example, the definitions of accountability offered in a recent collection of essays on the subject:

> Governments are "accountable" if citizens can discern representative from unrepresentative governments and can sanction them appropriately, retaining in office those incumbents who perform well and ousting from office those who do not. An "accountability mechanism" is thus a map from the outcomes of actions (including messages that explain those actions) of public officials to sanctions by citizens. Elections are a "contingent renewal" accountability mechanism, where the sanctions are to extend or not to extend the government's tenure.[10]

Later in that volume, James Fearon offers a formal definition (similarly based on principal-agent thinking): "We say that one person, A, is accountable to another, B, if two conditions are met. First, there is an understanding that A is obliged to act in some way on behalf of B. Second, B is empowered by some formal institutional or perhaps informal rules to sanction or reward A for her activities or performance in this capacity."[11] The first definition, which gives a wholly electoral account of accountability, implies a strikingly majoritarian view of what it is for a government to be accountable (and assumes that accountability should be understood wholly in terms of political accountability).[12] In effect, the government is seen as an agent of (and accountable to) its majority "principal." Fearon's definition more formally states that model.[13] The model is not especially subtle, which is not always a fault, and it might be thought that the clarity of its vision concerning the accountability of rulers to the ruled through the democratic process is commendable. Nonetheless, the definitions cited above are over-encompassing, treating relationships of accountability as necessarily principal-agent relationships. In fact, there are at least four grounds for resisting the equation of democratic accountability with a principal-agent relationship between ruler and ruled.

The principal-agent model treats government as the agent of its principal—the people—and accountability does not have to be construed in this vertical fashion. Unless we define the principal as the person to whom A is accountable (which is a straight tautology), we have to recognize that the beneficiaries of the agent's actions may not be those who direct them or hold them accountable. To use Plato's habitual example, the beneficiaries of doctors are their patients, but there are serious problems involved in making doctors directly accountable to patients (and systems that try to do so in fact end up by making both accountable to the law).

Second, principal-agent analysis uses a very broad definition of accountability, treating elements as essential that are in fact contingent: A may be accountable to X without X having the power to sanction A. It may make accountability serve democratic principles better if X has the power to sanction, but it is not a necessary condition for A to be accountable that this be so.

The third problem is that principal-agent models of democracy import considerable freight by drawing on several different sources. The democratic principle is something like "rulers should rule in the interests of the people;" but the economic model of principal-agent theory is a way of designing incentives for agents in conditions of imperfect information where the principal entrusts the agent with resources and where each seeks to maximize their return. It is an empirical question whether relations between politicians and citizens are usefully modeled in this way; but the normative principle that rulers should rule in the interest of the ruled certainly does not require that the relationship be modeled in principal-agent terms. The legal literature in contrast focuses on when and how far an agent's acts can be taken to be the acts of his principal. Attempting to build models with explanatory power, trying to determine the exact parameters of relationships of agency that the law should enforce, and trying to establish normative relationships are significantly different activities. While one dimension may inform the others, they are importantly disjoint and when people argue that democratic institutions involve a principal-agent relationship this is usually a normative claim, rather than one that follows the contours of economic or legal analysis.

Finally, by treating accountability as an economically defined principal-agent problem, we tend to run together the issue of what accountability is with what is necessary for an accountability relationship to have certain outcomes under certain conditions. A good deal of recent writing is based on the essentialist concept of whether someone or some thing is *really* accountable, when the question is better put in terms of what types of accountability exist and whether these deliver the results that meet our concerns about sustaining democracy, or political stability, or legitimacy, or whatever. Accountability is not the value—forms and methods of accountability are instruments to secure other values. Institutional design that aims to maximize accountability itself essentially mistakes the means to particular ends for the end itself.

A more parsimonious understanding of accountability runs as follows: A is accountable with respect to M when some individual, body, or institution, Y, can require A to inform, explain, or justify his/her conduct with respects to M. The definition has three dimensions: (1) "A," the agent or institution who is to give account; (2) "Y," the agent or institution to whom they give an account; and (3). "M," the responsibilities that are the subject matter of the account they give. The relationship among them is that A can be required to inform, explain, or justify his/her actions regarding M to Y. The following conditions may be present but are not strictly necessary for A to be accountable to Y.

The beneficiary of M may (or may not) be identical with Y. We may submit our "accounts" to Y who is acting for another party, or who may be (or may act for) a third party who has a responsibility to protect both A and the beneficiary of M.

Y may or may not be able to monitor A's conduct with respect to M, since Y may simply lack the capacity or may rely on other bodies to monitor A. Lacking the capacity to monitor weakens the *effectiveness* (or outcome) of Y's holding A to account, but retains sufficient elements of the requirement that A give an account for us to acknowledge an accountability relationship.

Y may or may not be able to sanction or reward A for her conduct with respect to M. That is, we must distinguish between cases in which Y can require—and sanction A for failing to provide—an account, even if he cannot sanction her for the content of the account she gives.

A *may* also have an *obligation* to explain or justify (give an account of) her conduct to Y with respect to M (or Y may simply have the power to elicit A's account). When we say that A is accountable to Y we usually imply that A has an obligation to Y, but we also talk about Y having the power to hold A to account, which means that A may be obliged to give an account, despite not formally having an obligation.

In each case, these additional features may enhance the outcomes for Y of being able to hold A to account, but they are not necessary conditions for A to be formally accountable to Y. Institutional design needs to be acutely sensitive to these distinctions, especially that between whether accountability exists and under what conditions it will produce a certain set of outcomes. In thinking about what outcomes it wants, design must also focus on the different elements of accountability, paying careful attention to what it means for A to be accountable and *how*, considering the various possibilities raised above, *who* might hold *whom* accountable for *what*. Each variable has its part in designing democratic accountability. Understanding accountability in terms of an obligation on the part of A to explain or justify to Y his or her conduct with respect to M, should lead us to explore, given the potentially disjoint relationship between Y and M, the grounds for choosing Y. Should Y be chosen because she is a beneficiary of M or because she has the technical expertise to audit the account A gives? And is the relationship between A and Y to be understood as horizontal—peer review—or vertical, either answerable up to a superior body or down to the client group? In addition, we need to consider with *whom* it is appropriate to lodge what degree of independent authority in respect to holding A accountable. Which institutions do we trust? Which sustain an ethic of responsibility? Which fail to do so? We must also consider how far the accountability relationship between A and Y should be understood as formal (in terms of A complying with the rules of office), political (meeting Y's expectations concerning the outcome of the office), or technical (where Y sets regulatory standards for a group of As on the basis of technical judgments).

In asking *how*, we need to consider the motives that A brings to his responsibilities.[14] Principal-agent models in economics assume that the gains of principal and agent are in the same coin—literally. Yet there are potential incommensurables in politics: honor and glory are goods for the politician but they are not in direct conflict with the interests of those they serve, indeed, the individuals involved may all gain in ways that are not fungible between them. We must ensure that the way we secure an account from A dovetails with the motives that drive him with respect to M. Someone who regards his conduct as a matter of honor should not be held to account in ways that are in themselves perceived as dishonoring or shaming—even if his failure to account appropriately for his conduct might subsequently issue in disgrace. How is, then, linked to who—those who benefit from A's conduct are not necessarily those who should hold A to account for it. Prison guards should not be held to account by prisoners; teachers by pupils; judges by defendants, prosecutors, and the beneficiaries or victims of crimes; and so on for a wide range of other public officials!

Whom should be held accountable raises substantial questions about the proliferation of accountability and audit in modern democratic states. This is related to the how question—for whom should we have alarm bells (minimizing proliferation) and for whom intensive surveillance?[15] But it is also an issue about who owes account for what. The question tends to be given powerful moral overtones by people who insist that those in receipt of public funding should be held to account for the way it is used, which is certainly one principle, but outcomes and efficiency are also relevant. We should also ask how far the good sought is affected by the type of accountability applied to those responsible for its production. Those who believe in public funding for art might demand detailed accountability for every element of expenditure; or might take the view that you give people money and see what comes out of it. The audit society—the validity and efficiency of which the collapse of Enron and World Com might be thought to throw into question—is often frankly stupid in its proliferation of systems of regulation and accountability that have little pay-off or purpose and whose costs can be huge, as is powerfully illustrated in Anechiarico and Jacobs's *The Pursuit of Absolute Integrity.*

The existence of an accountability mechanism does not ensure that people will always tell the truth but the form their accountability takes should not itself militate against their doing so. However much we may dislike "spin" in modern politics, we have to ask whether it is really a function of politicians' declining veracity, rather than a result of the demands made by an increasingly public accountability, not least to a voracious and often irresponsible popular press and media. In the House of Commons in the nineteenth century, parliamentary questions followed a particular protocol and were a matter of public record; the questioning was framed by procedures and traditions and could not stray off the path of the particular responsibilities of the minister. It was a subtle and complex engagement that was heavily rule-governed, and yet it could ruin ministers and bring down governments through exposing their failures in office. In contrast, modern media interviewing cuts across political and personal life; refuses to take no for an answer; and is hugely more intrusive, combative, and personally directed and vindictive than was the case for parliamentary routines. This power is legitimated by its claim to be acting in the public interest by holding politicians to account, yet the result does not seem to be higher probity so much as the subversion of political integrity into practices that involve "economy with the truth" and spin on the one side, and salacious gossip and a lack of real knowledge or interest in the intricacies of political life and its responsibilities or in the substance of public policy on the other.

Institutional design has to recognize that those in power often have reasons to resist their accountability, but accountability is a game with two sides and those who hold others to account must do so for the right reasons, to the appropriate standards, and in ways that safeguard their standing. When Przeworski answers Juvenal's question "Who guards the guardians?" by referring to "those forces in civil society that find it in their self-interest," he dramatically overstates the extent to which such interests among the people at large are ever organized and channeled in an appropriately civic-minded form and underestimates the extent to which populist accountability and regulatory mechanisms can destroy the very institutions and virtues they are intended to monitor.[16]

These difficulties with accountability underline that regulatory and accountability procedures and instruments cannot substitute for integrity on the part of those who rule, and on the part of those who hold them accountable. Moreover, the design of regulatory and accountability systems presumes integrity on the part of the designers—Juvenal's "who guards the guardians?" cannot be answered wholly by institutional design. Although there is longstanding support for the idea that a mixed government and the separation of powers can be used to ensure a balance between institutional components that renders those in government accountable, this line of argument curiously underestimates the problem of design. Mixed systems of government work on the basis of competing societal interests. A balance of power is maintained by the interest that each component of government (traditionally rooted in a different social class—hence the mixing of rule by the one, the few, and the many) has in resisting the encroachments of other branches. In Polybius's account, which begins the tradition, the assumption is that this device can balance any deviation from the pursuit of collective interests on the part of one element of the government. For example, motives in support of the common good are used to explain the ability on the part of two sections of the political order to resist a third component of rule temporarily swayed by tyrannical ambitions. But, if the tradition begins in this way, mixed government comes increasingly to be seen as a way of balancing competing interests within the state. This perspective inherits the assumption that self-interest cannot break down institutional framing, but it lacks the background assumption of the commitment to the public good among the different elements that is central to resisting that breakdown. If we start with the assumption of self-interest, even if we can see that a system of balanced and mixed government would produce benefits for all, there is no reason why those participating in the system should give priority to the benefits that accrue to the broader system rather than seeking to maximize their own particular advantage. The Polybian self-equilibriating model of balancing interests assumes that some broader vertical integration exists, where people treat the procedures, practices, and outcomes of the system as having a legitimacy that is independent of whether the system maximally serves their interests. In the absence of that assumption, the model of mixed government driven by a conflict of interests view must assume a depth of prescience and wisdom on the part of the designers that is wholly implausible and is in deep tension with the contrastingly negative assumptions made about the characters and motivations of those who will inhabit the institutions. This suggests that any adequate theory of design has an ineliminable need for integrity in those who design, those who exercise public office, and those who hold politicians and public officials accountable. But the thrust of this and the previous two chapters is that it is difficult to believe that the *populace* of modern democracies can function adequately as the key component for holding those who rule and exercise public office accountable and responsible.[17]

This returns us forcefully to the anxieties voiced by Constant and Tocqueville (discussed in the previous chapter), but it does so without much prospect that citizenship will provide an answer: Liberal democracies are at risk unless there is integrity in politics, but no convincing case can be made for believing that citizens alone can generate and sustain that integrity among those who rule. Similarly, institutional design faces a basic conundrum in presupposing that its designers have virtues that its institutions are either meant to generate (the conundrum), or presupposing virtues among its designers the need for which is eliminated by the design (suggesting a fundamental implausibility in motivational assumptions). How then can we explain the existence of integrity in the political orders of at least some liberal democratic states, and what resources exist for its promotion?

One assumption that Constant makes that needs challenging is the view that we are dealing with two groups—citizens and elite.[18] It needs challenging because a wide range of mediating players and institutions exists between citizens and the political elite that both set constraints on the élite and help overcome collective action and threshold problems for ordinary citizens. Just as an effective judiciary and system of law enforcement work to ensure procedural compliance as much on the part of the élite as among the citizenry, so too can professional and semiprofessional groups and institutions, such as lawyers, professional watchdogs, journalists, commentators, academics, and the intelligentsia, serve both as a constraint on the political elite and as a source of information, signaling, and guidance to the citizenry more broadly. Organizations, professions, civic institutions, social networks, and broad cultural and political norms all work both to render the conduct of the political elite more accountable, and to lower the threshold costs of participation for members of the public. Information networks, a free press, and a relatively free flow of information through a variety of media can help generate and sustain a public sense of political propriety, which constrains leaders seeking to redefine those standards to their advantage while informing members of the public of the appropriate level of expectation they should have. But does emphasizing such groups simply cascade down the integrity problem—why should these groups have any greater integrity than those who lead? I am certainly not suggesting that these groups uniquely hold the key to the integrity problem in the political life of modern democratic states but they are significant players in the broader political system and can help both to sustain an understanding of the rules of the game in contemporary politics, and to serve certain functions, traditionally assigned to citizens, more efficiently and with fewer and less demanding motivational assumptions.

In asking for integrity, we are not necessarily asking for wholly disinterested or altruistic action. We want responsible and professional conduct, not self-sacrifice. Conduct needs to be driven by a respect for and commitment to the standards of the activity. The existence of professional communities in which these standards are sustained create powerful incentives for compliance, since the face-to-face character of many of these intermediary groups and subcommunities makes enforcement of collective norms relatively costless.[19] What matters most, then, is that a civil society exists in which a variety of institutions and bodies have an interest in scrutinizing and monitoring the activities of the state. Whether such groups exist depends on the history and political and cultural traditions of the society; the strength of its civil institutions; the standing of its press and universities; the degree of professionalization of lawyers, accountants, and policy analysts; and the extent to which these groups operate in a context in which the expectations of those in public office are clear and well-formulated.

On this account, the press, the judiciary, the police and legal profession, professional systems of audit and control, and a wide range of both public and private interest groups and watchdogs involved in the ongoing reaction to and scrutiny of government policy and administration can substitute for the role that classical republicans ascribed to an active citizenry and can do so without demanding exceptional virtue or heroism.[20] These institutions provide their members with employment and with personal incentives to work effectively in the public interest. They create a professional ethos with a set of standards and loyalties such that those involved make the interests of scrutiny their own. There is no difficulty in motivating participation and, although they may require guidance and reminders of their responsibilities within the political domain, there are formal and informal mechanisms to exert such pressure, coupled with their need, in a democratic and open society, to sustain their own standing with the public. Indeed, the arguments that we have used for the way that motives may be transformed through procedural involvement and the need to defend proposals in public apply powerfully in the case of such agencies in their interaction with the political system. In both cases, various interests may bring people into the political system, or involve them in the work of the social and civic institutions associated with politics, but these institutions shape their members' behavior and preferences and play a formative role in the values they pursue. The ethos of an institution takes shape within a broader context of institutional pluralism in which the ethical integrity of the institution and its practitioners is both at a premium and remains open to challenge by competitors, by the political institutions with which they interact, and by the members of the public whose interests they affect. The professionalization of these activities gives people the opportunity to make a career out of participation, but it also gives them a range of responsibilities. Of course, there are risks. The legal profession may become out of touch with public attitudes, or we may develop an unimaginative, obstructive, and inefficient administrative service, a sensationalist and irresponsible mass media, or an entirely self-serving lobby.[21] We should not underestimate these dangers, but nor should we think that we can guard against them only by developing a mobilized citizenry.

The four elements that militate against the subversion of these intermediary institutions by those in power, or by those within who come exclusively to pursue their own ends, are transparency in the political process, professional loyalties, a context of institutional pluralism, and a culture of tolerance for value pluralism. The first makes accountability more easily enforced; the second underpins people's identification with the responsibilities of their office and provides a powerful reference group for their conduct; the third sets institutions partly in competition with each other (both within and between professional groups) so that each has incentives to ensure that their own standards are unimpeachable and that others are similarly constrained; and the last ensures that, in principle at least, the political system (in the broadest sense; i.e., including these groups) remains open to challenge by those whose concerns are excluded or given short weight. In a stable liberal democratic polity the competition between mechanisms for public scrutiny and accountability creates a context in which standards are clarified and questioned on a regular basis.

Moreover, there is no puzzle about what is to motivate political participation on the part of members of the public whose interests are affected by such institutions, since we need not look beyond self-interest. Citizens can act self-interestedly with respect to challenging the activities of the government, or these other institutions. These institutions must defend their conduct (insofar as they can) by reference to their responsibilities, procedures, and their ethos more broadly. Their defense can appeal to the responsibilities of their office and the manner in which it must be exercised, but it must do so publicly and appeal to standards of public reason, loosely understood. Liberal democratic political systems can, then, accept that there is no need for a general *duty* of political participation on the part of citizens, so long as those with grievances can find institutions that can represent and resolve their grievances in public (that is, so long as there is a *right* to participation, and some civil commitment to facilitate such participation when desired).

One concern with this account is with how genuinely pluralistic liberal democratic societies are. Critics of pluralist accounts of democracy argue that the unequal access to resources for collective mobilization prove that liberal democratic societies are not truly pluralistic—hence Dahl's acknowledgement of "polyarchy."[22] However, the account I offer here is of *institutional* pluralism, it is not a claim about the socially pluralist character of modern democracies. Against the view that there is a widespread need for virtuous political participation on the part of citizens to act as a bulwark against forms of corruption and tyranny, I am suggesting that a plurality of institutions, together with a climate of transparency, can draw support from citizens who use these diverse institutions to represent their interests or express grievances against their treatment by the political system. We do not need equal capacities for mobilization among diverse citizen groups, but facilitated individual access to these institutions. Institutional design can ensure certain types of protection for individuals, and can provide access to the political process through institutionalizing intermediary bodies, the creation of ad hoc scrutiny bodies and complaints procedures, and free legal advice. In each case we promote the capacity of citizens to defend their rights by creating access to institutions that have an interest in protecting those rights and a responsibility to account for their activities publicly.

A second concern voiced with respect to pluralism concerns the unequal standing of minorities. Again, however, the concern is to ensure the protection of civil rights, and the kinds of mechanism I have outlined, when rooted in a culture that demands public accountability and the public defense of its procedures, should meet this purpose. How adequate that defense is as a compensation for past injustice (as discussed in Chapter 8) is another matter, but if that injustice is to be addressed within the political procedures of the modern state, rather than through attempts fundamentally to change its character, the mechanisms I have indicated are likely to ensure that these broader issues will be broached, even if the struggle is often a long one.

The picture I have sketched here offers, as an alternative to civic virtue, a view of *surrogate participation*. In most Western polities, most people, most of the time, rely on others to participate on their behalf on issues of access (where parties, interest groups, and other organizations play a formative role in defining and realizing one's interests); to provide feedback on political performance and proposals; and systematically on matters of formal accountability. These surrogate participants are people and institutions with incentives to scrutinize the activity of government and administration. They can serve both as a constraint on government and as a signaling device for the broader public as to the reliability and impartiality of public procedures and judgments. These signals may prompt acts of broader popular participation—at elections or in demonstrations or other political activity—but they also provide feedback to those in public office, who have powerful incentives to correct abuses in order to preempt popular censure. Such surrogate participants are the mainstay of the accountability mechanisms of modern democracies and include elements of the elite political culture, such as judges, investigatory tribunals and commissions, ombudsmen, and select committees; various semi-governmental organizations, such as regulatory bodies for public industries; the press and the media more generally; and political commentators and critics. I make no claim about their automatic efficacy, but they certainly play a key part in contemporary liberal democracies and where they fail to do so, we become more dependent on still less secure and more volatile elements, such as innovative political leadership or direct popular participation. While there are occasions when these elements may work, neither singly nor together do they constitute a sufficient and secure source of both political integrity and the protection of civil and political rights in the absence of a culture of competitive institutional pluralism.

Mobilized popular sovereignty may have been a requirement of stable government in classical republics that relied on their citizenry for their defense and for whom war was an omnipresent threat, but the more pressing concern in modern states is to produce governments that are responsive to the rights, needs, and interests of its citizens. To achieve this, as discussed in Chapter 7 in relation to public officials, there are two distinct (although not wholly mutually exclusive) approaches: we can look to regulatory, accountability, and corruption-control mechanisms, or we can look to ways of ensuring the professional integrity of those in public office. The first approach focuses on the scrutiny and supervision of governmental functions, the second on the political and professional culture of those in authority. The same models can be generalized to the political system more widely: either we look for mechanisms to limit and regulate political power, or for ways of developing and supporting the integrity of those in office (although the "moment" of sovereignty in high political office ensures that the first route can never be exclusively adopted). The tendency in accountability mechanisms is to provide indirect rather than direct incentives for integrity. Technically speaking, a successful indirect set of incentives would result in civil servants and politicians acting appropriately but without any commitment on their part to such behavior, they would simply respond to the pattern of incentives. Clearly, indirect means can be hugely sophisticated but they may always be inadequate for determined fraudsters and opportunists.

In contrast, direct mechanisms are designed to ensure that those in public office value their professional integrity and their integrity as politicians and public officials above other interests or rewards. Direct means must be supported by background material conditions—such as pay and status[23]—as well as by the creation of a political culture that takes professional values, public integrity, and loyalty to the public service seriously. This applies both to those formally in public service, and to those whose professional lives are concerned with regulating and scrutinizing the activities of government. Moreover, the broader population has to respect and trust this culture if political authority and legitimacy are to be sustained.

The direct route to public integrity is not easy to establish when it has no foundations. It aims to ensure that people's activities are guided by the desire to act in ways that are in keeping with their sense of personal, political, and professional integrity. For most of us, our sense of what integrity demands comes from our involvement in practices and rule and norm governed activities that are generative of standards for public and professional standing, status, and respect. Those involved have to value these marks of recognition and their standing in public office more highly than profit or other incentives and rewards, and their status must be seen to be positively related to their integrity and dedication.[24]

The basis for components like "consciousness of integrity" and a "satisfactory review of our own conduct," as far as political and professional conduct is concerned, derive from upbringing and family values, the professional and political culture one inhabits, the responses of colleagues and occupational acquaintances, and the attitudes of those within the political or professional world whom the individual respects. A stable political culture requires a system of values and standards of conduct that are expressed in the actions of those in the system, and that prescribe behavior that is adequate to ensure the authority and legitimacy of the political system. In the absence of these conditions, the system faces disorder, and only innovative political agency that is able to set the pattern for action at an appreciably higher level will be able to stem this disorder.

This is not an argument for an elite technocracy. Rather, it is to appreciate the need for a public service that is highly professional and in which the institutions that scrutinize the political activities and policies of a government are involved in a competitive market for integrity. That market must reward people in ways that are consistent with sustaining their integrity and that public life. Rewards should not lead people to prefer the reputation for integrity rather than integrity itself; nor should they result in a style of life and set of connections that vitiate the qualities that brought them those rewards; nor should the way that they are treated undermine the value they attach to their integrity and conduct (as mudslinging reporting may do, but investigative journalism may not). Only with these caveats can we expect this competitive political culture to avoid undermining its own basis and the accompanying trust in those in public office.

These are not simple requirements. The professionalization of government, administration, and accountability over the last three centuries in the West has involved a movement from informal networks, practices, and norms based on rank and class solidarities, friendships, and kinship, to a wide range of political and administrative systems in which professional credentialism plays a much more significant role in securing people's entry into the administration and the political culture. Nonetheless, relationships and contacts based on loyalty, friendships, and reciprocity remain extremely important in the building of political capital and retain a role in the professional world; in fact, these elements remain central to the way that politics works. The difficulty is to ensure that codes of conduct, regulation, and professional ethics recognize that a reliance on intensive formal accountability mechanisms may clean up politics at the cost of destroying many of the mechanisms of political coordination.

The less rational elements of politics, such as friendships and loyalties, place constraints on the extent to which we can look for a perfect regulatory framework. Moreover, the picture I have sketched in this chapter leaves out or plays down a great deal of the substance of politics, emphasizing procedures and institutions rather than the substantive values that engage these procedures, motivate those in politics, and around which opinion and commitment more widely are mobilized. As we have seen, fundamental conflicts between values is a basic fact of political life. Such conflicts are inextricably entwined with the history of particular states. Each political generation reinforces, redivides, or reconstitutes some of the basic lines of conflict and potential bases for consensus within the state, and between the state and its partners or enemies in the international arena. On the one hand, the ability of liberal democratic states to contain these conflicts cannot be guaranteed. On the other, the histories of these conflicts mean that each political order will develop its own particular institutional character that will have a profound impact on the detailed organization of politics and public office, so that prescriptions for institutional design must be acutely sensitive to the path dependency of the institutions and practices that they address least they exacerbate these conflicts.

Prescriptions that make eminent sense in one set of institutions and traditions will not necessarily do so in another. Accountability mechanisms that play a positive role in one context may play a negative role in another. This principle applies more widely and points to the dangers of some dimensions of globalization, particularly those where international agencies attempt to identify in detail standards of good governance that they expect to be adopted by all states. For example, applying a perspective from the U.S. context that expects high levels of access to the political system and high levels of formal accountability for officials, but that couples this with intensive, individualized political accountability in elections, can be very damaging in democratizing states, such as in Eastern Europe. Such expectations would entangle already highly bureaucratic systems with still further regulation, little of which has purchase since the judicial capacity is often inadequate. Further, it would overstate levels of corruption by applying norms and standards that derive from a distinctive, indeed unique, if economically successful, political system. It would assume the existence of an independent civil society and economy to act as a source of autonomous demands on the political system, when, in fact, state and society are so linked by clientelism that representation and accountability are enmeshed in relationships of dependency. Finally, the U.S. perspective of confidence that freestanding political agents are only created within free-market systems is such that it promoted rapid privatization in former communist states without ensuring that adequate political controls were in place. The result of democratization, coupled with marketization, under the tutelage of largely North American advisers resulted, for the most part, in widespread corruption in the acquisition and subsequent management of former state assets, dramatic slumps in GDP with negative growth, an evaporation of confidence in the new political institutions, and a need for increasing reliance on clientelism and unofficial forms of exchange that had served as an alternative to open markets in the last decades of the communist system. Moreover, since about 1996, Eastern Europe has been taught a lexicon of corruption that has became an essential resource for aspiring politicians—politicizing formal accountability and exacerbating the confusion over the rules by which politicians and their patrons should be judged. The institutions in civil society have been equipped to attack the semblance of legitimacy that attaches to those in government, but they lack the strength and support needed to play a more constructive role in the reconstitution of the political system with more tightly regulated access and clearer systems of formal and political accountability that can command wider legitimacy. There may not be much integrity among those who work in the political systems of Eastern and Central Europe but it is more significant that there is huge confusion over what it would be to have such integrity, and that confusion is substantially increased by the importation and politicised use of Western models of corruption.[25]

The problem of institutional design is not essentially different from the problems I have discussed in relation to political leadership and the character of politics. It is a problem of how to frame and establish institutions that will enable those in politics to negotiate and authoritatively to resolve the range of conflicts that beset their society. The phrase *institutional design* implies that the task of design is somehow extra-political, rather than being mired in the same conflicts and the same need to generate commitments that accompanies the activities of politicians, but that involves a sleight of hand. Clearly, design matters and institutions play a powerful role in shaping the behavior of their members. However, the process of design, argument, and implementation is itself a political process and faces similar issues respecting the political purposes of those involved, their commitment to their objectives, and the integrity with which they see through the implementation of their proposals. Institutional design has no more neutral, impartial, or objective position from which to work than does politics itself, although that is not to deny that appeals to such values play a central role in the strategies adopted by many designers to secure certain goals. Institutional design cannot be an answer to the problem of political integrity, whether among leaders, public servants, or citizens, since it is not itself independent from that problem.

I argued in the first part of this book that political integrity is a demanding requirement for those in public office because neither egoism nor moralism is adequate in responding to the demands that politics makes of the judgment and conduct of those who take its practices seriously. Political integrity demands very much what Weber thought it demanded—responsibility and proportion, passion and commitment. In a fractured and conflict-ridden world, personal morality is not adequate to the challenges faced by those who attempt to set the pattern of action for others, to exercise authority, and to negotiate and settle the antagonistic forces around them. In a pluralist society what morality requires may be subject to wide contestation; while in a homogeneous culture the injunctions of morality may threaten to deprive public officials and politicians of the capacity to act responsibly and with proportion.

Those who insist on the strict reducibility of politics to morality understate the potential for divergence on exactly what morality demands, they ignore the fact that political office and the exercise of authority both come with certain demands and standards built in that are neither egoistic nor strictly moral, and they leave no space for recognizing that those in politics must sometimes act where moral injunctions are conflicting. To insist on moralism as authoritative over political conduct is to ignore the fact that it is through the political institutions of a society, their capacity to establish and maintain order, and their ability to forge a basic consensus on procedures and principles that the contexts within which individual moral beliefs take root and are nurtured and protected. As Hobbes postulated, without sovereign political orders, life for many people would be nasty, brutish, and short. When Weber wrote of the state beginning as a body of armed men who subsequently attempt to legitimate their power, he was also thinking of the establishment of sets of practices linked to the public realm that take their participants beyond their primordial attachments and familial and group loyalties, and generate norms and rules that can cross the grain of our passions and instinctive commitments and successfully constrain their expression and pursuit. In the process of legitimating power, principles and norms develop that offer us a degree of critical purchase on the political system, allowing us to make demands of it and of those who take office within it; but, properly understood, these norms do not provide a set of universal principles with which to assess political integrity so much as a series of contextually generated claims whose weight depends on their being sustained by, acknowledged within, and integrated into the political order. They provide the starting point for evaluation that must be filled out in considerable detail and in the light of a more general grasp of the character and purposes of political rule, but they do not provide an Archimedean point outside politics itself.

The integrity we want from those in public office is properly understood as an integrity within politics—within the particular set of historically conditioned constraints and conflicts facing distinct challenges, to which we expect them to respond appropriately and imaginatively, and by attempting authoritatively to order the world in ways that provide the basis for a broadening consensus. Those who have the virtues to play this game well are those who grasp the point of their activity in this way (while knowing that it is not a game), who recognize the seriousness of the challenges their communities face, and who have the humanity, imagination, and intuitive abilities to find ways of negotiating conflict, broadening constituencies of support for the order, and responding to the demands of rule in ways that provide citizens and subjects with security and well-being, rather than those who react with great acts of state that redivide society and exacerbate the conflicts within the social and political order. Those in subordinate positions similarly have responsibilities associated with their position and their loyalties and we judge their conduct by the extent to which it responds proportionately and continently to the demands they face. There is, however, no place outside such positions to stand and legislate, reconstituting the institutions to enhance the position of citizens or to integrate them more fully into the political process and its practices. There is no such place simply because the attempt to act in this way, to set the pattern for others, is necessarily a political act and, as such, is inherently part of the game.

The demands of politics are considerable. There is a good deal of luck at play and the attempt to rule others makes demands on one's character and intellectual and emotional resources that are not always met. Men and women overreach—indeed, I have suggested, there are features of some modern states that encourage them to overreach and treat them with such suspicion that overreaching is almost inevitable, introducing strains into modern democratic systems whose final outcomes remain unclear. The rules to which political office is subject may also defeat the ends of that office; for example, by rendering the official so rule-bound that he or she cannot serve the purposes the office implies. Moreover, ordinary people's inchoate grasp of many of the central ingredients of political life can produce misconceived attempts to institutionalize and regulate its conduct: we can appreciate the importance and value of personal and political loyalty, but we don't see how to square it with the impartialist demands of modern political systems; we can see the need for loyal and dedicated public service, but we cannot achieve it wholly through regulation or modeling the public service on commercial enterprises; we need citizen participation in modern democracies, but it has to be suitably civic in character and this is not easily generated or sustained; we want to attract people to take high public office, but we are systematically suspicious of their motives and their activities thereby both deterring their entry and restricting them in office. Liberal democratic orders may moderate the impact of some of these problems, but it is not obvious that they will contain them indefinitely.

In politics, I have argued, there is much that remains undefined. At the same time, while recognizing this complexity and indeterminacy, we must also acknowledge the importance of individual agency and its decisionist and performative character, which makes things right by the way they are conceived, initiated, and seen through. Rather little in contemporary political philosophy acknowledges and responds to this, and I do not claim to have done more than scratch the surface of this "gray" practice. I am also aware that I have complicated my task by eschewing the approach, common to those who have addressed the problem of political conduct in recent years, which starts from the principles, practices, and values of a liberal democratic constitutional order.[26] I have done so because liberal democratic politics is a type of a more general activity that we should try to understand, and in restricting the scope of the enquiry to a particular system we are in danger of missing or playing down features of politics that should inform our analysis of all systems—such as the importance of leadership, innovation, and decisionism; the force of personal and professional loyalties and commitments; the fragility of institutional design; the consistent tendency of political decisions themselves to generate contentious political action; and the extent to which the taking and seeing through of political decisions with huge consequences for societies, indeed for the future of the planet, rest on the character, political integrity, and abilities of relatively small numbers of men and women. Liberal democratic regimes are plural, not singular; they vary greatly, and their political processes are organized differently, weighing aspects of office differently. The tendency to treat the liberal democratic model as a unified one is partly testimony to the hegemony of the United States in contemporary political philosophy, and partly a function of its writers to see their own case as the standard. Europeans, Asians, indeed, each nation, might reasonably see things differently.

Yet it is also a function of the tendency of political philosophy to treat abstract normative ideals as regulative models—so that the ideal of liberal democracy and its associated principles come both to represent the complex and plural reality of liberal democracies and to set standards for how they should operate. One reason for resisting such an ideal and for resisting the view that the principles of that ideal provide an appropriate standard of evaluation is that, in keeping with the arguments of this work, we have to ask what those principles demand (and with what realism) in terms of the motives and ambitions of their members, and we have to recognize that the process through which institutions are created, interpreted, and progressively reworked is itself a political process, rather than a merely deductive one. The instruments we use in politics instantiate particular interpretations of the principles they take to underlie their task, they shape the design and they shape the product. Liberal democracies certainly have features and tensions in common because they are trying to combine political rule with democratic participation, popular legitimation, and some form of legal and constitutional protection, but the ways in which they resolve these tensions are various, and are framed by the particular historical experiences and the ambitions and concerns of those attracted into the political process. There is no "one size fits all" system of accountability or regulation, no single right way of balancing the relationship between money and politics or of securing the political, civil, and personal rights of citizens against political authority. As political problems they call for political solutions, and political solutions, even when they are inspired by grand ideals, have a local and contextually shaped character.

Politics makes many demands on those who practice it, although, as in some other complex practices, it may be a disadvantage to the practitioner to have too intellectual a grasp of the character of this activity. Those of us who merely try to comprehend it are not necessarily so constrained. The approach I have adopted is to ask what makes the activity intelligible to those who act and to those affected by those actions. I have attempted to describe at least some of the range of actions and associated meanings, institutions, and practices that taken together make up the practices of politics. These elements encompass innovation and loyalty, *dignitas,* glory and standing, decisionism and the identification with procedures, and much else besides. In each case, it is necessary to identify as far as one can the intelligibility and meaning of political options to those who act and respond in their particular political context and, in doing so, to explore the extent to which their actions also imply commitments and judgments on their part and/or on the part of those whom they associate with, or lead, or rule. That does not wholly settle the evaluative issue—as I have shown, action that is recognizably political in form is sometimes simply abhorrent, its outcomes so obscene that a basic sense of human values and well-being demands its condemnation. Sometimes we can argue that those involved are driven by passions, resentments, and interests that ride roughshod over facts that they should consider and weigh, and that they could have recognized as relevant had they been less disturbed, arrogant, or insouciant. More troublingly, on occasion, we may simply have to accept that, while things could not feasibly be otherwise, they are nonetheless repugnant—much in the way, I think, in which Colin Turnbull came to see the lives of the Ik.[27] Of course, in making such a judgment we are somewhere on a continuum from horror to tragedy—horror insofar as we find people incapable of behaving humanly to each other (whether by force of circumstance, or by the depth of ideological, ethnic, or racial hatreds), tragedy when they themselves can see the awfulness of what they are bringing about but are impotent to prevent it.

Often, however, there is no incompatibility between these very broad values on the one hand and politics on the other. Indeed, when people show loyalty to causes and concerns that have a more universal character, when their tenacity of purpose wins through to secure their objectives, or when they commit themselves to ends in ways that galvanize and mobilize others sufficiently to achieve their goals, then the meanings and understandings of those involved are acting as the medium within which such values are interpreted and spelled out in detail. As such, no external standpoint is required: the meanings and values generated within the institutions and context of political action are playing a defining role in people's understanding of the nature of the good life or of the types of values or order they wish to see realized. Just as particular relationships in families are such that we regard them as trumping many more universal claims, so too the particular skills, virtues, and strengths of character associated with political action and the negotiation and resolution of conflict should be acknowledged as part of a distinctive domain of action, meaning, and value. That domain often stands apart from more general moral principles, may sometimes come into shocking conflict with them, but may also, and more often, play a fundamental role in both shaping and realizing our conception of the kind of life we want to live and the kind of institutions and values we want to see regulate it.

Notes

Introduction

1. Harold Dwight Lasswell, *Politics: Who Gets What, When and How* (New York: Meridian Books, 1958). See also John Dunn's characteristically eloquent *The Cunning of Unreason: Making Sense of Politics* (New York: Basic Books, 2000), especially part 1.
2. By "to make normative" I mean to inform and help determine people's understanding of their most basic commitments and thereby to condition their understanding of their interests and their motives for acting. "Making normative" can range from cases in which people develop a more acute sense of where their interests lie to cases in which they embrace and pursue new values and goals (which may dramatically redefine their sense of their interests).
3. Giovanni Sartori, *Democratic Theory*, 2nd ed. (Westport, Conn.: Greenwood Press, 1976), p. 182—to which I was prompted by Yves Meny's "Politics, Corruption and Democracy; The 1995 Stein Rokkan Lecture," *European Journal of Political Research* 30, no. 2 (1996): 111–123.
4. Although Sartori does not fill out the claim, others have sought in various ways to do so, most recently Andrew Sabl, *Ruling Passions: Political Offices and Democratic Ethics* (Princeton, N.J.: Princeton University Press, 2002) and J. Patrick Dobel, *Public Integrity* (Baltimore: Johns Hopkins University Press, 1999).
5. I develop this account in Chapter 2, drawing on Machiavelli and on Alasdair MacIntyre's *After Virtue* (London: Duckworth, 1981), even while departing from them in a number of significant respects, not least with respect to the grounding of political virtue. See also chapters 2, 3, and 4.
6. Karl Marx, "Eighteenth Brumaire of Louis Bonaparte," in *Surveys from Exile: Political Writings*, vol. 2, ed. David Fernbach (Harmondsworth: Penguin, 1973), p. 146.
7. Max Weber, "Politics as a Vocation," in *From Max Weber*, ed. H. H. Gerth and C. Wright Mills (London: Routledge and Kegan Paul, 1948), p. 128.
8. The most influential scholar in the field is Dennis Thompson, in his *Political Ethics and Public Office* (Cambridge, Mass.: Harvard University Press, 1987), *Ethics in Congress* (Washington, D.C.: Brookings Institution, 2000), and *Restoring Re-*

sponsibility (Cambridge: Cambridge University Press, 2005). See also Sabl, *Ruling Passions,* and Dobel, *Public Integrity.* Michael Walzer's work *Obligations: Essays on Disobedience, War and Citizenship* (Cambridge, Mass.: Harvard University Press, 1970), *Just and Unjust Wars* (New York: Basic Books, 1977), and *Spheres of Justice* (Oxford: Blackwell, 1983), especially chapter 5, has also explored a range of themes focused on more practical political concerns. See also Joel L. Fleishman, Lance Liebman, and Mark H. Moore, eds., *Public Duties: The Moral Obligations of Government Officials* (Cambridge, Mass.: Harvard University Press, 1981) and Arthur I. Applbaum, *Ethics for Adversaries* (Princeton, N.J.: Princeton University Press, 1999). Political theorists (in the broadest sense) who have addressed in detail particular practical problems as they relate to political office include Andrew Stark, *Conflict of Interest in American Public Life* (Cambridge, Mass.: Harvard University Press, 2000) and John T. Noonan, *Bribes: The Intellectual History of a Moral Idea* (Berkeley: University of California Press, 1984).

9. *Oxford Dictionary of Political Quotation,* ed. Anthony Jay (Oxford: Oxford University Press, 1996), p. 239. There is a tradition of using games to illuminate features of social practices—as in Wittgenstein—but, as the following discussion emphasizes, this is an analogy, one that breaks down in a number of major respects.

10. The 2000 U.S. presidential election suggests that even institutions that are highly rule bound are not necessarily immune from highly contentious results.

11. "Hardwired" in the sense that they are part of what it is to be that agent, rather than something that the agent chooses to have or to be.

1. Rendering unto Caesar

1. Niccolò Machiavelli, *Discourses on Livy,* ed. J. C. Bondanella and P. Bondanella (Oxford: Oxford University Press, 1997), I (10), pp. 50, 48. The point of the last sentence is not to deny that intention matters, but to say that evil intent and success in action are more blameworthy than simply evil intent.

2. Erich S. Gruen, *The Last Generation of the Roman Republic,* 2nd ed. (Berkeley: University of California Press, 1995).

3. "[A] criminal enterprise which I consider specially memorable as being unprecedented in itself and fraught with unprecedented dangers to Rome." In Sallust (Gaius Sallustius Crispus), *Sallust: The Jugurthine War and the Conspiracy of Catiline,* ed. S. A. Handford (Harmondsworth: Penguin, 1963), p. 177.

4. See R. Seager, *Pompey: A Political Biography* (Oxford: Blackwell, 1979), p. 82, who credits Cato with driving Pompey into Caesar's arms.

5. "Lesser" partly in Roman terms because he does not come from a noble family. His election as consul in 63 BC was the first election of a *novus homo* for thirty years and could be seen as symptomatic of the changing order. "Lesser" also because he was both more conciliatory to suspect political movements than Cato and less continent in respect of his hopes and fears. See *Ep. Att.* (Letters to Atticus) I.18 and II.1, for his judgment of Cato. For his own willingness to adapt, see *Ep. Fam.* I.9: "I believe in moving with the times."

6. Plutarch, "Caesar," in *Fall of the Roman Republic,* trans. R. Warner, ed. R. Seager (London: Penguin, 1972), section 15, p. 258. Plutarch relates many anecdotes of Caesar's early ambition, but he also suggests that Caesar "seems to have made a new start, and started upon a different way of life and of achievement" after assuming command in Gaul.

7. Plutarch, "Caesar," sections 3–5, pp. 245–248. See Robert A. Kaster, *Emotion, Restraint and Community in Ancient Rome* (New York: Oxford University Press, 2005), chapter 2.

8. Dio Cassius is more negative, seeing him as an artful strategist undermining the power of others. Dio Cassius, *Dio's Roman History,* trans. E. Cary (Cambridge, Mass.: Harvard University Press, 1914), vol. 3, book 36, section 43, lines 3–4, p. 70; book 37, section 22, line 1, pp. 134–136 and section 44, line 3, pp. 168–169. Suetonius suggests that Caesar was involved in a conspiracy with Crassus to overthrow the elected consuls in 65 BC, but the evidence does not support this. Suetonius, "Caesar," in *The Twelve Caesars,* trans. R. Graves, ed. M. Grant (Harmondsworth: Penguin, 1979), section 9, p. 16. See M. Gelzer, *Caesar: Politician and Statesman,* 6th ed. (Cambridge, Mass.: Harvard University Press, 1968), pp. 39–41.

9. The laws were believed to have been passed illegally because they were enacted *per vim,* against the auspices and contrary to *lex Caecilia Didia* (*Ep. Att.* II.9.1; *Ep. Att.* VIII.3.3; *In Vatinium* VII.15). See A. Lintott, *Violence in Republican Rome* (Oxford: Oxford University Press, 1999), pp. 135, 189–190. See T. P. Wiseman, "Caesar, Pompey and Rome, 59–50 BC," in *Cambridge Ancient History,* vol. 9, 2nd ed., ed. J. A. Crook, A. Lintott, and E. Rawson (Cambridge: Cambridge University Press, 1994), p. 369.

10. That is of being prosecuted for *vis* or *ambitus*—force or bribery.

11. Gelzer, *Caesar,* p. 84.

12. Other achievements included the agrarian law and a later distribution of land to veterans, the resolution of tax farming issues, the creation of a settlement in Asia, and the establishment of an alliance with Ptolemy XII of Egypt. See Gelzer, *Caesar,* chapter 3.

13. He may also have distrusted those involved, aware that as he set out Cicero was being driven into exile by Clodius for his actions as consul in the Catiline conspiracy.

14. His military successes have also been described as involving the death of over a million Gauls, the enslavement of another million, and punitive devastations which produced a human, economic, and ecological disaster probably unequalled until the conquest of America. See *The Oxford Classical Dictionary,* 3rd ed., ed. Simon Hornblower and Anthony Spawforth (Oxford: Oxford University Press, 2003), entry on Iulius Caesar. See similarly C. Hignall, "The Conquest of Gaul," in *Cambridge Ancient History,* vol. 9, 1st ed., ed. S. A. Cook, F. E. Adcock, and M. P. Charlesworth (Cambridge: Cambridge University Press, 1932), pp. 572–573. Such a judgment is relevant to our assessment of Caesar's political conduct, but it also has to be contextualized. Rome was a military culture: it

saw itself as either commanding these domains or remaining at risk from them, and it had little sense that its civilizing mission was in any way flawed. We can regret the outcome in human and moral terms without thinking that the political order of the day could have recognized the reasonableness and probity of that judgment. For Caesar, the question would have to be how uniquely bellicose he was—and that is a hard case to prove, although Hignett presents him as distinctively so and late to attempt conciliation.

15. Julius Caesar, *The Civil War*, trans. John Carter (Oxford: Oxford University Press, 1997), book 1, section 32, pp. 20–21. Albeit the ruling's legitimacy was open to question. See the detailed discussion in Gruen, *Last Generation*, chapter 11, especially pp. 455–460, on the impact of Pompey's reforms of 52 BC on Caesar's position. Against the traditional view, Gruen argues that Pompey's legislative innovations were largely sound policy decisions that protected Caesar's special position and interests.

16. See Gruen's careful analysis in *Last Generation*, pp. 451–497.

17. Niccolò Machiavelli, "Tercets on Ingratitude," lines 151–156, in *Machiavelli, The Chief Works and Others*, vol. 2, trans. A. Gilbert (Durham, N.C.: Duke University Press, 1958), p. 743.

18. Caesar, *The Civil War*, book 9, pp. 8–9.

19. Ibid., book 1, sections 7, 9, and 32, pp. 7–9, 20–21.

20. More strictly, it would have had to seem to him to be plausible to his intended audience—but as an acknowledged expert in rhetoric, Caesar was a good judge of the effect of what he said and wrote. See Gelzer, *Caesar*, p. 191n1 on the issue of the veracity and intent of Caesar's *The Civil War* and Elizabeth Rawson's comments in her "Caesar: Civil War and Dictatorship," in *Cambridge Ancient History*, vol. 9, 2nd ed., ed. J. A. Crook, A. Lintott, and E. Rawson (Cambridge: Cambridge University Press, 1994), pp. 425–427.

21. His troops might have had other motives, as suggested by Lucan: "Their swelling minds and spirits made fierce in slaughter are crushed by love of country and ancestral gods, but they are recalled by their hideous love of the sword and by their terror of their leader." Lucan, *Civil War*, trans. Susan H. Braund (Oxford: Oxford University Press, 1992), book 1, lines 353–356, p. 12. But see also Gruen, *Last Generation*, p. 502.

22. *Partitiones Oratoriae* 90, quotation from John Carter's notes to his edition of Caesar's *The Civil War*, p. 274.

23. On *verecundia*—this sense of the self's claim in relation to others—see Kaster, *Emotion, Restraint and Community*, chapter 1.

24. See Charles Wirszubski, "Cicero's *Cvm Dignitate Otivm*: A Reconsideration," *Journal of Roman Studies* 44 (1954): 1–13.

25. *Pro Sestio in Vatinium*, trans. R. Gardner (Cambridge, Mass.: Harvard University Press, 1958), book 46, section 98, pp. 168–170; "cum dignitate otium." Loeb edition, but slightly adapted in the light of Wirszubski's version, p. 10.

26. *Pro Sestio*, book 49, sections 99–100.

27. *Ep. Att.* VII.11—translating *dignitas* as dignity (not honor).

28. See Z. Yavetz, *Julius Caesar and His Public Image* (London: Thames and Hudson, 1983), p. 175. Curio claimed that his *clementia* was entirely opportunist, but Curio is not entirely reliable—see Rawson, "Caesar," p. 428.

29. Plutarch, "Caesar," section 54.

30. Ibid., section 46; Suetonius, "Caesar," section 30, p. 4.

31. Seager, *Pompey*, pp. 152–155, 156, 161. See also Lucan, *Civil War*, book 1, lines 124–125.

32. Caesar, *The Civil War*, book 3, section 82.

33. See Gelzer, *Caesar*, pp. 290–291, 314–315.

34. He did not, however, take every office offered: He refused honors such as full *tribunicia potestas*.

35. Dio Cassius, *Dio's Roman History*, book 43, section 26, is cited by Yavetz to support the view that "Caesar did not act unilaterally. In all matters, he made a habit of taking advice from leading members of the Senate, and frequently brought questions before the full body" (*Julius Caesar*, p. 59, but see also comments at p. 196). Dio's comments are not unambiguous. Gelzer's view is that "he shortened the transactions of the Senate by merely informing senior members of his plans and, if he called a meeting of the whole body, he simply announced his decisions to it and without any discussion these were then entered into the archives as senatorial decrees" (*Caesar*, p. 290).

36. Yavetz, *Julius Caesar*, pp. 196–197, 207, 213. However, Caesar himself sensed that he was becoming hated for his inability to treat people as he ought: "Can I be foolish enough to think that this man, good natured though he is, is friendly to me, when he has to sit and wait for my convenience for so long." *Ep. Att.* XIV.1.

37. See C. Meier, *Caesar*, trans. David McLintock (London: HarperCollins, 1995), p. 476 and chapter 14 more generally for a shrewd analysis of the tensions in Caesar's final position.

38. It should be noted that Machiavelli's misleading contrast is with Romulus who founded the city. Romulus could hardly have reorganized Rome since it did not exist.

39. His actions in 59 BC can be interpreted as intended to reform the city, although they were systematically misunderstood by others.

40. Cf. Gelzer, *Caesar*, pp. 299–300.

41. Some commentators suggest that the risk of collapse might have been averted for some time had Antony been eliminated at the same time as Caesar. Cf. P. A. Brunt, *The Fall of the Roman Republic* (Oxford: Clarendon Press, 1988), p. 86.

42. R. Syme, *The Roman Revolution* (Oxford: Clarendon Press, 1939), pp. 51–52; Yavetz, *Julius Caesar*, p. 182.

43. Not that there was no temptation to exact revenge, but such temptation was resisted. See, *Ep Att.* X.4, but see also *Ep. Att.* IX.7c (Caesar to Oppius and Cornelius).

44. Plutarch, "Caesar," section 22. See note 13 above.

45. Of course, any order that gives that much weight to dignity may systematically

be more prone to certain types of conflict and disorder. Which is not to say they are easy to change; and, as we shall see, it may be that all political orders share some elements of this problem.

46. G. W. F. Hegel, *Lectures on the Philosophy of World History,* ed. D. Forbes and H. B. Nisbet (Cambridge: Cambridge University Press, 1975), p. 89.

2. Machiavelli and Political Virtue

1. See Machiavelli's claim about the emergence of the professional soldier and general who puts the republic at risk, as under Caesar and Pompey, and his distinction between the brave and the good in the "Art of War," *Machiavelli: The Chief Works and Others,* vol. 2, trans. A. Gilbert (Durham, N.C.: Duke University Press, 1958), pp. 575–576. See David Hume's *Treatise,* III.2.1: "tis evident, that when we praise any actions, we regard only the motives that produced them, and consider the actions as signs or indications of certain principles in the mind and temper."

2. A *vivere civile e politico* involves the rule of law directed to the common good. See Maurizio Viroli, *From Politics to Reasons of State: The Acquisition and Transformation of the Language of Politics 1250–1600* (Cambridge: Cambridge University Press, 1992), chapter 3, and *Machiavelli* (Oxford: Oxford University Press, 1998), chapters 2 and 4.

3. Machiavelli, *The Prince,* ed. Q. Skinner and R. Price (Cambridge: Cambridge University Press, 1988), p. 31. See also Price's comments in his "The Theme of Gloria in Machiavelli," *Renaissance Quarterly* 30, no. 4 (1977): 611. A coda to this judgment comes at the end of the chapter when Machiavelli says that there is a difference between cruelty used well and badly. What accounts for Agathocles's success was that he did everything at once and at the beginning—those who do this can "in some measure remedy their standing both with God and with men as Agathocles did" (*The Prince,* p. 33). The tension between this claim and Machiavelli's earlier condemnation is not resolved but would seem to turn on the desirability of the ends pursued, on the much more difficult counterfactual judgment about what else could have been brought about or achieved, and on the extent to which Agathocles's ambition was an ambition related to the security of Syracuse, or was entirely self-seeking.

4. Max Weber, "Politics as a Vocation," in *From Max Weber,* ed. H. H. Gerth and C. Wright Mills (London: Routledge and Kegan Paul, 1948), pp. 115–117.

5. The most sustained discussion is Price's "The Theme of Gloria in Machiavelli."

6. "Impress" in the double sense of winning their respect and imposing a form upon them. Cf. J. G. A. Pocock, *The Machiavellian Moment* (Princeton, N.J.: Princeton University Press, 1975), chapters 6 and 7.

7. See Bernard Williams. *Ethics and the Limits of Philosophy* (London: Fontana, 1985), p. 10. One formulation, common in essence to both Williams and Hursthouse, is: "the virtuous agent chooses virtuous actions . . . for at least one of a certain type or range of reasons, X, where 'the type or range X' is typical of, and

differs according to, whichever virtue is in question." R. Hursthouse, *On Virtue Ethics* (Oxford: Oxford University Press, 1999), pp. 127–128. See B. Williams, "Acting as the Virtuous Person Acts," in *Aristotle and Moral Realism*, ed. R. Heinamen (London: UCL Press, 1995), pp. 13–23. Hursthouse does not want to rule out reference to the virtue in the reason given—as in "it was the honest thing to do," but it is crucial that the deliberation is not about whether I, as the agent, should be V (where V is the virtue), even if some judgment about whether a given act does meet what V demands might be made, as when a modest person might demur from an action on the grounds that it would be improper. For some virtues, such as modesty, claiming to act from the virtue does seem self-defeating.

8. Machiavelli, *Tercets on Fortune*, in *Machiavelli: Chief Works, and Others*, vol. 2, trans. A. Gilbert (Durham, N.C.: Duke University Press, 1958), pp. 100–119. See also Letter 121, Niccolò Machiavelli to Giovan Battista Soderini, Perugia, 13–21 September 1506, in *Machiavelli and His Friends: Their Personal Correspondence*, trans. and ed. James B. Atkinson and David Sices (DeKalb: Northern Illinois University Press, 1996), pp. 134–136.

9. As does the comment in *Discourses on Livy:* "those men are infamous and detestable who have been destroyers of religion, wasters of kingdoms and republics, enemies of the virtues, of letters, and of every other profession that brings honor and advantage to the human race, such as the impious, the violent, the ignorant, the worthless, the lazy, and the cowardly." *Discourses on Livy*, ed. J. C. Bondanella and P. Bondanella (Oxford: Oxford University Press, 1997), I (10), p. 47.

10. Weber, "Politics as a Vocation," p. 127.

11. See R. Price's glossary to the Skinner and Price edition of *The Prince*, p. 103, and Price's "The Senses of *Virtú* in Machiavelli," *European Studies Review* 3 (1973): 315–345.

12. See the discussion of these components in Chapter 4.

13. See Hursthouse, *On Virtue Ethics*, chapters 6 and 7.

14. As Price remarks in his essay on "Gloria in Machiavelli," Machiavelli does not spell out the details of his account, leaving much to the reader's inference. Nonetheless, the account given here does seem to do justice to a number of the central themes in *The Prince* and *The Discourses*, even if it draws on some distinctions and tools from virtue ethics that initially seem foreign to Machiavelli. I return to this in Chapter 4.

15. See Sebastian de Grazia, *Machiavelli in Hell* (Basingstoke: Pan Macmillan, 1992), p. 135, on Madonna Caterina of Forlí.

16. On "roving" as against "stationary" bandits see Mancur Olson's *Power and Prosperity: Outgrowing Capitalist and Communist Dictatorships* (New York: Basic Books, 2000).

17. See Aristotle's *Nicomachean Ethics*, ed. T. Irwin (Indianapolis: Hackett, 1985), 1095b18–1096a10, where Aristotle indicates that his inquiry is to go beyond the excellence of the political life and will focus instead upon the life of reflec-

tion as the highest and best life. Machiavelli's account is clearly not such an account, but the more one either doubts the existence of such a higher form of life, or thinks that an absolute precondition for starting on that inquiry is the creation of the state that calls on a range of other types of virtue or excellence, the less easy it is to see Machiavelli's account of virtue as falling short as an ethical doctrine. I return to this issue below.

18. As in the implicit debate with Cicero emphasized by Quentin Skinner in *Machiavelli* (Oxford: Oxford University Press, 1981), especially pp. 35–47.

19. Alasdair MacIntyre, *A Short History of Ethics* (London: Routledge and Kegan Paul, 1967), p. 125.

20. Ibid, p. 123.

21. Although determining what can be ascribed to human agency in politics is by no means easy—this is a recurrent theme throughout John Dunn's *The Cunning of Unreason* (Cambridge, Mass.: Harvard University Press, 2000).

22. Aristotle, *Nicomachean Ethics*, 1105a28–1105a30.

23. Adapted from *Nicomachean Ethics*, 1105a30–1105a35. The commentary that follows has been aided considerably by the sophisticated discussion of the problem by Sarah Broadie, *Ethics with Aristotle* (Oxford: Oxford University Press, 1991), pp. 78–90.

24. See *Nicomachean Ethics*, 1115b10–1115b13 and 1120a23–1120a27, in which the suggestion is that we do what is right and stick by our commitments for the sake of what is fine (Irwin edition) or noble (Broadie, *Ethics*, p. 92 and Rogers Crisp's translation of the *Nicomachean Ethics* [Cambridge: Cambridge University Press, 2000]). This helps ground the judgments on which virtue rests, but it needs factoring into the explanatory account of action with care, since Aristotle does not seem to advance the view that a person cannot act from virtue unless she sees herself acting from virtue (see Broadie, *Ethics*, p. 94).

25. See Hursthouse's discussion in chapters 6 and 7 of *On Virtue Ethics*.

26. *Nicomachean Ethics*, IX.8, for example.

27. *Nicomachean Ethics*, 1095b31 and I.5 more generally.

28. In addition to Broadie's discussion see Williams, "Acting as the Virtuous Person," and R. Hursthouse, "The Virtuous Agent's Reasons: A Reply to Bernard Williams," in Heinaman, *Aristotle*, pp. 13–33.

29. Alasdair MacIntyre, *After Virtue* (London: Duckworth, 1981), p. 174 *passim*.

30. Ibid., p. 178 (originally in italics).

31. See Weber, "Politics as a Vocation," p. 115. On the intrinsic goods of politics, see Chapter 4.

32. The fragmentation of the virtues has been resisted in other ways. Hursthouse, for example, argues that virtues are excellences of character, so that they cannot come to the aid of vices: the courage of the thief is not true courage, generosity to a fault is not true generosity. Against the view that these traits can be put to good or bad ends, she endorses the Aristotelian idea that each of the virtues involves practical wisdom, which is the ability to reason correctly about practical matters. This means that the reasoning that individuals engage

in with respect to one situation in which a given virtue is called for must have an impact on their reasoning in other situations in which other virtues are called for. Hursthouse, *On Virtue Ethics*, pp. 12–14, 153–57.

33. I. Berlin, "The Originality of Machiavelli," in *Against the Current: Essays in the History of Ideas*, ed. H. Hardy (Oxford: Clarendon Press, 1979), pp. 25–79.

34. Williams, "Acting as the Virtuous Person," p. 21; see also *Ethics*, pp. 140–145, 200, and *In the Beginning Was the Deed: Realism and Moralism in Political Argument*, ed. Geoffrey Hawthorne (Princeton, N.J.: Princeton University Press, 2005), pp. 45–50.

35. Contrast, for example, Christian Meier's striking account of ancient Greece's experience of politics, *The Greek Discovery of Politics* (Cambridge, Mass.: Harvard University Press, 1990), p. 22.

3. The Character of Political Rule

1. "The authoritarian relation rests neither on common reason nor on the power of the one who commands; what they have in common is the hierarchy itself, whose rightness and legitimacy both recognise and where both have their predetermined place." Hannah Arendt, *Between Past and Future: Six Exercises in Political Thought* (Harmondsworth: Penguin, 1992), p. 93. This means that for authority to be exercised we need two distinct components: a type of command and a type of compliance. A's command claims a right to be taken as authoritative over the agent (B), and B responds to A's authority if and only if he recognizes A's right to command him in this respect and acts accordingly on the basis of that recognition.

2. " 'Public' referred to the state that . . . developed under absolutism, into an entity having an objective existence over against the person of the ruler." Jürgen Habermas, *The Structural Transformation of the Public Sphere: An Inquiry into the Category of Bourgeois Society*, trans. T. Berger (Oxford: Polity Press, 1989), p. 11.

3. With apologies to Thomas Kuhn, *The Structure of Scientific Revolutions*, 2nd ed. (Chicago: University of Chicago Press, 1970).

4. David Easton, *The Political System: An Inquiry into the State of Political Science* (New York: Knopf, 1953), p. 129.

5. *The Rise and Fall of Athens: Nine Greek Lives by Plutarch*, trans. Ian Scott-Kilvert (Harmondsworth: Penguin, 1960), section 25, pp. 67–68.

6. See John Rawls, *Political Liberalism* (New York: Columbia University Press, 1993), pp. 40–41, where the author effectively rules out immigration as a possible source of entry to his society—a rather peculiar starting position for an American political philosopher.

7. Drawing on Pasquale Pasquino, "Political Theory of War and Peace: Foucault and the History of Modern Political Theory," *Economy and Society* 22, no. 1 (1993): 77–88; and Carl Schmitt, *The Concept of the Political*, trans. G. Schwab (New Brunswick, N.J.: Rutgers University Press, 1976). See my "Defining Political Corruption," *Political Studies* 45, no. 3 (1997): 436–462.

8. Thomas Hobbes, *Leviathan* (London: Andrew Crooke, 1651), pp. 60–64.

9. Depending, that is, on whether one takes a prisoners' dilemma or an assurance game reading of the Hobbesian state of nature, see Jean Hampton, *Hobbes and Social Contract Theory* (Cambridge: Cambridge University Press, 1986).

10. Carl Schmitt, *The Concept of the Political,* trans. George Schwab (New Brunswick, N.J.: Rutgers University Press, 1976), p. 67.

11. The classical commitment to *isegorea*—the right of each citizen to a voice in the determination of public affairs—and the Aristotelian concept of taking turns at ruling and being ruled both capture the concern with elevating political rule over other forms of rule (particularly the household). Political rule becomes, ideally, the rule of reason: a rule which can be justified to each and which each can endorse. It substitutes self-rule (which is flawed because we lack true self-sufficiency when acting in isolation) for self-rule-in-community. For the Greeks, to lack this form of rule was to be enslaved. John Dunn, *Western Political Theory in the Face of the Future* (Cambridge: Cambridge University Press, 1979), p. 17.

12. For example, enthusiastic communitarians have argued against the political norms of impartiality and justice in favor of the emotional, communal, and fa-milial attachments of individuals, on the grounds that these abstract values fail to take into consideration the constitutive character of the attachments that people have. To give priority to political norms over constitutive attachments is, on this (for me mistaken) view, to make a fundamental error about the nature the self and moral life.

13. In Slagstad's apt phrase, "the Machstaat overrides the Rechsstaat." "The state of emergency clearly reveals the nature of the state's authority. Here, the decision separates itself from the legal norm and (put paradoxically) authority shows that it creates Recht but does not have to be Recht." Cited by Slagstad, "Liberal Constitutionalism and its Critics," in *Constitutionalism and Democracy,* ed. Jon El-ster and Rune Slagstad (Cambridge: Cambridge University Press, 1988), p. 116. Compare the translation by George Schwab in his edition of Carl Schmitt's *Polit-ical Theology: Four Chapters on the Concept of Sovereignty* (Cambridge, Mass.: M.I.T. Press, 1988), p. 13.

14. This approach is similar to that which the late Judith Shklar described as "The liberalism of fear," in *Liberalism and Morality,* ed. Nancy Rosenblum (Cambridge, Mass.: Harvard University Press, 1989), pp. 21–38. See also Bernard Williams, *In the Beginning Was the Deed* (Princeton, N.J.: Princeton University Press, 2005).

15. Machiavelli, *The Prince*, Chapter 7.

16. Jan Werner Mueller, *A Dangerous Mind: Carl Schmitt in Post-War European Thought* (New Haven, Conn.: Yale University Pres, 2003), p. 37.

17. The conception of a practice and that of thick ethical concepts, drawn from MacIntyre and Williams's work, ties together what the practice is with the ends it serves. Similarly, Bernard Crick's immensely stimulating and insightful *In De-fense of Politics,* 4th ed. (Chicago: University of Chicago Press, 1993), chapter 1, also runs together facts and values and descriptive and normative statements

for the types of reasons discussed here. Nonetheless, it is a discomfiting aspect of ordinary language that it tolerates a split between what counts as political activity and the question of what might make it valuable, to the extent that "a good politician" can be used pejoratively.

18. Although I recognize that there is much evidence of wide complicity with the regime and an acceptance of certain aspects of its brutality, one must consider the real problem of how people could register their dissent. See Detlev Peukert, *Inside Nazi Germany* (London: Penguin, 1993), and Robert Gellately, *Backing Hitler* (Oxford: Oxford University Press, 2001).

19. J. Noakes and G. Pridham, *Nazism 1919–1945*, vol. 3: *Foreign Policy, War and Racial Extermination* (Exeter: University of Exeter Press, 1995), pp. 1199–1200; Gitta Sereny, *Albert Speer: His Battle with Truth* (London: Picador, 1996), p. 384.

20. See, for example, the case for the political orchestration of genocidal violence in Alison Des Forges, *"Leave None to Tell the Story": Genocide in Rwanda* (New York: Human Rights Watch, 1999). Also consider the cases of Cambodia under Pol Pot—see Someth May, *Cambodian Witness* (London: Faber and Faber, 1986), the Kurds in Iraq under Saddam Hussein, and the Bosnians and Kosovans in the wake of the collapse of Yugoslavia (and this is hardly an exhaustive list). Politically orchestrated violence that is not exclusively ethnically directed was also a central feature of the period of Soviet rule and rule under Communist China. In many more cases, political leaderships ignore the potential and actual human costs that their policies impose with equally devastating consequences.

4. Resolved to Rule

1. Pierre Bourdieu, *Outline of a Theory of Practice* (Cambridge: Cambridge University Press, 1977), p. 190. Bourdieu contrasts this activity with its opposite, "a system of mechanisms . . . capable of ensuring the reproduction of the existing order by its own motion . . . the dominant class have only to *let the system they dominate take its own course* in order to exercise their domination" (emphasis in original).

2. See my "Republicanism and Liberalism: On Leadership and Political Order—A Review," *Democratization* 3, no. 4 (Winter 1996): 383–419. The situation has not greatly changed with more recent works on republicanism, for example Philip Pettit, *Republicanism: A Theory of Freedom and Government* (Oxford: Oxford University Press, 1997); John Maynor, *Republicanism in the Modern World* (Oxford: Blackwell, 2003); Maurizio Viroli, *Republicanism* (New York: Hill and Wang, 2002); and Isuelt Honohan, *Civic Republicanism* (London: Routledge, 2002).

3. There is, however, an extensive leadership literature in management studies, and there is some interesting literature in political science. For example, see James MacGregor Burns, *Leadership* (New York: Harper, 1978). For an informative study of more recent institutional approaches see R. Elgie, *Political Leadership in Liberal Democracies* (Basingstoke: Macmillan, 1995). For those wanting more sense of the often vicious character of political leadership within institu-

tional constraints it is difficult to fault Robert Caro's study of Johnson's time in the Senate, or his work on Robert Moses. Indeed, they underline the fact that institutional constraints ought to be understood as defining a much more complex and sophisticated game in which leadership can have a key role—much as the rules of chess make possible a level of sophistication and strategy that sweeping them aside would eliminate. R. A. Caro, *Master of the Senate* (New York: Knopf, 2002) and *The Power Broker: Robert Moses and the Fall of New York* (New York: Random House, 1975).

4. Burns, *Leadership*, pp. 19, 27 (emphasis in original).

5. Max Weber, "Politics as a Vocation," in *From Max Weber*, ed. H. H. Gerth and C. Wright Mills (London: Routledge and Kegan Paul, 1948), p. 78.

6. Ibid., pp. 115, 84–85 (emphasis in original).

7. Ibid., p. 95.

8. Ibid., pp. 116–117.

9. Ibid., pp. 119–123.

10. Ibid., p. 121.

11. Ibid., pp. 126, 128.

12. Those prepared to press beyond Weber's position and endorse egoism include B. De Jouvenal, *On Power* (Indianapolis: Liberty Fund, 1993), p. 133: "In the order of nature everything dies which is not sustained by an intense and brutal love of self. Power, in the same way, can only maintain the ascendancy necessary to it by the intense and brutal love which rulers have for their authority." Nietzsche's position is often characterized as similar, but see Robert C. Solomon, "The Virtues of the Passionate Life: Erotic Love and the 'Will to Power,'" *Social Philosophy and Policy* 15, no. 1 (Winter 1998): 110–116; Nietzsche, *Beyond Good and Evil*, section 274; cf. *Will to Power*, section 972.

13. Weber, "politics as a Vocation," p. 116.

14. Ibid., pp. 115–116.

15. On which see Bernard Williams, *Shame and Necessity* (Berkeley: University of California Press, 1993), pp. 219–223; Robert A. Kaster, *Emotion, Restraint, and Community in Ancient Rome* (Princeton, N.J.: Princeton University Press, 2005), chapter 2.

16. Alvin Gouldner, *The Coming Crisis in Western Sociology* (London: Heinemann, 1970), pp. 221–222. Although I cannot do justice to the richness of Geoffrey Brennan and Philip Pettit's *The Economy of Esteem* (Oxford: Oxford University Press, 2004), they have difficulty integrating these two dimensions that are associated with a sense of self; nonetheless, their analysis of the motive for esteem is unparalleled.

17. To link compliance with norms to a sense of self-esteem and self-regard helps provide part of the explanation for the power of cultural norms. A strong political culture is one where norms of political conduct and principles of action have a grip on the minds of its participants, so that norm violations are accompanied by anxiety, embarrassment, guilt, and above all, shame. Clearly, not all elite political cultures have this deep grip on its members, but those lacking it

will be dramatically more precarious. See Jon Elster, *Cement of Society* (Cambridge: Cambridge University Press, 1989), p. 100.

18. This is a complex issue. We might see political virtue as having clear implications for sexual continence: as in the view that someone who had real political qualities would not be distracted by sex. It is more plausible to think that being a naturally skilled politician has no necessary connection with being naturally sexually continent and success in politics may dramatically increase the opportunities for sexual indulgence. If we see the demands of political virtue flowing from and with the agent's will, then the issue of how well someone deals with a domain outside politics might appropriately be treated as not strictly relevant in evaluating people's political conduct, even if we might think that the politician should recognize that being exposed through scandal will harm his political career and should desist from risk taking for that reason. This last suggestion is not entirely satisfactory since it assumes that it is appropriate for the public and media to have an interest in the nonpolitical activities of politicians. On the other hand, lauding one's personal integrity as a political ploy does make subsequent exposure seem fair game.

19. Julia Annas, *The Morality of Happiness* (Oxford: Oxford University Press, 1993), p. 51.

20. Bernard Williams, *Ethics and the Limits of Philosophy* (London: Fontana, 1985), p. 10.

21. One that would not have been recognized in Caesar's time but which a degree of moral universalism and the development of a global order have now made more widespread, although certainly not inevitable.

22. Cf. Michael Stocker, *Plural and Conflicting Values* (Oxford: Clarendon Press, 1990), p. 34: "The demand that it must be possible for us to be good and also innocent, and also to retain emotional wholeness, it not a demand for a conceptually or even a morally coherent morality. It is, rather, a demand for something else—a morally good world or at least not an evil or bad world."

23. See Judith Shklar, "The Liberalism of Fear," in *Liberalism and the Moral Life*, ed. Nancy Rosenblum (Cambridge, Mass.: Harvard University Press, 1989), pp. 21–37, and Bernard Williams, "Liberalism of Fear," in *In the Beginning Was the Deed: Realism and Moralism in Political Argument*, ed. Geoffrey Hawthorne (Princeton, N.J.: Princeton University Press, 2005).

24. See especially Michael Walzer, "Political Action: The Problem of Dirty Hands," *Philosophy and Public Affairs* 2, no. 2 (1973): 160–180; Martin Hollis, "Dirty Hands," *British Journal of Political Science* 12, no. 4 (1982): 385–398; the references in Stocker, *Plural and Conflicting Values*, pp. 9–10, 52, 85; and Sartre's *Dirty Hands* in *No Exit and Three Other Plays* (New York: Vintage, 1955).

25. This is certainly one way to read Machiavelli's claim that "a ruler who wishes to maintain his power must be prepared to act immorally when this becomes necessary." *The Prince*, ed. Q. Skinner and R. Price (Cambridge: Cambridge University Press, 1988), p. 55.

26. See Terry L. Price, *Understanding Ethical Failures in Leadership* (Cambridge: Cam-

bridge University Press, 2006), who emphasizes the things that lead politicians cognitively astray and takes the view that this should predispose us to require that leadership should conform to general moral requirements (see p. 121)—the politics of fear strategy. But this does not really address real cases, such as Churchill's dilemma as to whether to warn the people of Coventry that they would be bombed, or to remain silent to prevent Germany from learning that the Enigma cypher had been broken. See Hollis, "Dirty Hands," p. 391. Even if we think Churchill's decision was understandable and, in the situation, the right one to make, we (and he) might nonetheless feel that he is tarnished by it. Price is right to ask how frequent such cases are, and to think that they are not as common as politicians themselves like to think, but doing so does not amount to disproving that these types of cases may be a structural feature of the nature of politics and political morality.

27. Bernard Williams, "Politics and Moral Character," in *Public and Private Morality,* ed. Stuart Hampshire (Cambridge: Cambridge University Press, 1978), p. 63.

28. But see also Stocker, *Plural Values,* pp. 29–32, who concludes that individual emotional characters might reasonably respond differently and that not all good people necessarily show shame or guilt over dirty hands.

29. See the concluding thoughts of "The Golden Ass" in *Machiavelli: The Chief Works and Others,* vol. 2, trans. A. Gilbert (Durham, N.C.: Duke University Press, 1989), p. 772.

30. Not, that is, as involving the calculative resolution of quandaries. See Edmund Pincoffs, "Quandary Ethics," in *Ethnical Theory,* ed. James Rachels (Oxford: Oxford University Press, 1998), pp. 435–453.

31. Williams argues that political decisions concern not right and wrong so much as "who lost" (after Weber, "Politics as a Vocation," p. 118), see *In the Beginning,* p. 13. This is certainly one dimension of political struggle, although politics is not always zero sum, but that "take" also focuses more on the gaining and retaining of power than with the question of the legitimate ends pursued by those in power.

32. Williams, "Politics and Moral Character," p. 70. The following concerns draw in part on Williams's discussion on pp. 69–70.

33. Ibid., p. 69.

34. Although see the account of the "morning after" retrospective judgment that democracies enable in S. L. Sutherland, "The Problem of Dirty Hands in Politics: Peace in the Vegetable Trade," *Canadian Journal of Political Science* 28, no. 3 (1995): 490, and Williams's comment on the impact of the requirements for instant publicity in "Politics and Moral Character," p. 69.

35. Williams, "Politics and Moral Character," p. 64.

5. Must Power Corrupt?

1. This claim might take two forms: we might regard the distribution curve for behavior in politics as severely lopsided, with the bulk of cases falling in the poor

half of the range; or we might think of the distribution curve as bell shaped, and in that sense normal, but see the peak of the curve as falling into the poor conduct half of the range. On the latter interpretation, it is the claim that there are objective standards for conduct that allows us to say that behavior is largely poor; on the former, it is the existence of a few good cases that justifies the description of the average case as substandard (that is, such cases are average in terms of numbers, but substandard in terms of the median for the range).

2. Although doing so would itself be a political process, calling on qualities of leadership and integrity!

3. *Beowulf*, trans. Seamus Heaney (London: Faber and Faber, 1999), p. 3.

4. Herodotus, *The Histories*, trans. Robin Waterfield (Oxford: Oxford University Press, 1998), book III, section 80, p. 204.

5. Juvenal, *The Satires*, ed. Niall Rudd (Oxford: Oxford University Press, 1992), satire 10, line 112, note 6. In the Italian tradition, Ceres is the name for Demeter, mother of Persephone.

6. William Godwin, *An Enquiry Concerning Political Justice* (London: G.G.J. and J. Robinson, 1793), book V, chapter 3, p. 399. See also J. S. Mill: "The power of compelling others into it [freedom] is not only inconsistent with the freedom and development of all the rest, but corrupting to the strong man himself." *On Liberty and Other Essays*, ed. J. Gray (Oxford: World's Classics, 1991), p. 74.

7. Michel E. de Montaigne, "On High Rank as a Disadvantage," in *Essays*, ed. M. A. Screech (London: Allen Lane, 1992), book III, essay 7, pp. 1040–1041.

8. Lord Acton, *Historical Essays and Studies*, ed. John Neville Figgis and Reginald Vere Laurence (London: Macmillan, 1907), p. 504.

9. It is often thought that it must be collective capacities to attain collective ends, but the pressure to accept that description arises from a desire to ensure that "power to" does not become confused with "power over"—and if "power to" is about collective capacity and ends, then it is not being exercised over anyone. There seems no reason to deny that individuals may have the power to x or y, without that necessarily involving power over other agents.

10. Thus recognizing that power needs to be understood as a capacity or resource, not simply as existing in its exercise, as Peter Morriss has rightly emphasized in his *Power: A Philosophical Analysis* (Manchester: Manchester University Press, 2002).

11. "The whole point of an autocracy . . . is that the accounts will not come right unless the ruler is their only auditor." Tacitus, *Annals of Imperial Rome*, rev. ed., trans. M. Grant (Harmondsworth: Penguin, 1996), p. 35.

12. For example, in European democracies in the inter-war period and in ancient Greek critiques of democracy. See Josiah Ober, *Political Dissent in Democratic Athens* (Princeton, N.J.: Princeton University Press, 2001).

13. Acton's position is a good deal looser: it is corrupt if it violates "the inflexible integrity of the moral code." This effectively subordinates the assessment of politics to morality and treats all forms of dereliction involving power as corrupt.

14. However, see Thomas Pogge's astute discussion of the opportunities that office

offers to those who assume power in less economically developed states—they are suddenly given the opportunity to raise loans and incur debts, to buy arms, to sell national resources, and to make treaties. That combination of temptations does seem acutely destabilizing, especially when accompanied by demands for patronage from those on whose support one must rely to stay in power. See Thomas Pogge, "Achieving Democracy," in *World Poverty and Human Rights* (Cambridge: Polity Press, 2002), chapter 6. See also "Recognized and Violated by International Law: The Human Rights of the Global Poor," *Leiden International Law Journal* 18, no. 4 (2005): 717–745.

15. That is, we recognize with Montaigne that "unless we draw the rules of right conduct from within ourselves . . . how many wicked deeds must we daily abandon ourselves to!" "On Glory," in *Essays,* book II, essay 16, pp. 705–706.

16. Although this is similar terrain to Terry Price's *Understanding Ethical Failures in Leadership* (Cambridge: Cambridge University Press, 2006), Price's focus on leadership in all its forms means that the particular problems that arise in politics, discussed here and throughout, are displaced by concerns with cognitive failure that apply to all those in positions of leadership.

17. Consider the apparent lack of embarrassment on the part of Sir William Armstrong in admitting that he had been "economical with the truth" in relation to his 1987 performance at the court hearing in Australia to prevent the publication of Peter Wright's memoir *Spycatcher*, and the consequent press outcry.

18. Which is not to say that muckraking journalists are only interested in their reputations, so much that they have less interest in sustaining authority than in questioning it, and have correspondingly less concern for the office-related outcomes of that questioning. But the line between this behavior and the genuine and conscientious pursuit of the facts of the matter is not easily drawn.

19. Rather than in the more complex, classical Greek sense of the self-indulgent misuse of energy or power. See Douglas M. MacDowell, *"Hybris in Athens,"* *Greece and Rome* 23 (1976): 14–31.

20. See Christopher Bobonich, *Plato's Utopia Recast: His Later Ethics and Politics* (Oxford: Oxford University Press, 2003) and the opening discussion of the role of philosophic virtue and nonphilosophic virtue in relation to the goods of honor.

21. Montaigne, "On Glory," book 2, essay 16, p. 706.

22. Leo Strauss, *On Tyranny*, ed. V. Gourevitch and M. S. Roth (New York: Free Press, 1991).

23. See note 1 above.

6. Loyalty in Politics

1. N. I. Bukharin's speech at the Central Committee plenum of January 7–12, 1933, in J. Arch Getty and Oleg V. Naumov, *The Road to Terror: Stalin and the Self-Destruction of the Bolsheviks, 1932–1939* (New Haven, Conn.: Yale University Press, 1999), p. 96.

2. Bukharin, letter to Stalin, December 10, 1937, in Getty and Naumov, *The Road to Terror,* pp. 556–558.

3. Michel de Montaigne, *The Complete Essays,* trans. and ed. M. A. Screech (London: Allen Lane, 1993), p. 212.

4. A. O. Hirschman, *Exit, Voice, and Loyalty* (Cambridge, Mass.: Harvard University Press, 1970), p. 79.

5. Ibid., p. 98.

6. George P. Fletcher, *Loyalty: An Essay on the Morality of Relationships* (Oxford: Oxford University Press, 1993), p. 8.

7. J. Royce, *The Social Philosophy of Josiah Royce,* ed. Stuart Gerry Brown (Syracuse, N.Y.: Syracuse University Press, 1950), pp. 75–76 (emphasis in original).

8. Ibid., p. 77.

9. Following, again, Bernard Williams, *Ethics and the Limits of Philosophy* (London: Fontana, 1985), p. 10. See also Chapter 4.

10. Thomas Nagel, *The View from Nowhere* (New York: Oxford University Press, 1986), pp. 152–163.

11. Philip Pettit, "The Paradox of Loyalty," *American Philosophical Quarterly* 25, no. 2 (1988): 163.

12. Andrew Oldenquist, "Loyalties," *Journal of Philosophy* 79, no. 4 (1982): 175. Here Fletcher's suggestion that loyalty requires a triadic relationship can be helpful—I am loyal to my country, in contrast to other countries; I am loyal to my ideals, in contrast to other ideals. Loyalty to an ideal may, on the one hand, preclude loyalty to any particular instantiation of it relative to other particular instantiations of it. On the other hand, I may certainly have ideals without my relationship to those ideals being understood in terms of loyalty. For someone to be loyal to an ideal we must see their attachment to the ideal in ways that are not simply agent-neutral reasons for action.

13. See Nick Hornby's novel *Fever Pitch* (London: Gollancz, 1992) for an instance of a very low level of judgment sensitivity.

14. Royce, *Social Philosophy,* p. 115 (emphasis in original).

15. "[A]ll those duties which we have learned to recognize as the fundamental duties of the civilised man, the duties that every man owes to every other man, are to be rightly interpreted as special instances of loyalty to loyalty . . . when rightly understood, loyalty is the whole duty of man." Ibid., p. 122 (emphasis in original).

16. Ibid., 140.

17. "When I have loyalty to something I have somehow come to view it as mine." Oldenquist, "Loyalties," p. 175.

18. See J. Raz, "Reasons for Action, Decisions and Norms," in *Practical Reasoning,* ed. J. Raz (Oxford: Oxford University Press, 1978), pp. 132–133. Although Raz's account is helpful in looking at types of conflict between reasons, there are grounds for thinking that loyalties do not act on the will in the same way that reasons do. A loyalty to one's family may exclude that person from acting on certain kinds of reason under certain circumstances, but the exclusion looks

less like a higher order reason and more like a set of feelings, attitudes, and dispositions that form an emotional bedrock from which people act. This rules out certain types of conflicting interests or desires, but it is not clear that it can be identified as a higher order reason unless we follow Royce.

19. The comments on Montaigne later in the chapter pick up his sense that real friendship must have some cognitive component. The point remains that loyalties are not instrumentally rational, but there is some room for a cognitive dimension in that being loyal to something involves treating it as being of value.

20. This ambiguous position with respect to rationality influences how we make the case for loyalty having a moral content. Although the limited judgment-sensitivity of loyalties weakens the basis for claiming loyalty as a moral virtue (since the considerations which move me do not move others), Pettit, "The Paradox of Loyalty," offers a solution to the paradox that loyalty poses for moral philosophy by asking that we see loyalty as a moral value or virtue which is particular rather than universal in form. For example, my loyalty to X is a loyalty to X, not to all those who have the same general properties as X. Or, I am loyal to my friend John. I am moved to help John, not because he is the most deserving person, nor because he in some other way meets some universalizable criterion, but because he is my friend John. My reason and motive for helping is context-bound to this particular person (rather than being context free) since, absent this friend, I have no reason to act—and my reasons are agent-relative, applying to me, as John's particular friend. I am moved by *this* friend's need, not by the fact that there is a friend in need. However, my action does not lack moral content in the way that we assume particularized agent-relative reasons do, because the reason for acting is universalizable—not in the sense that what moves me will move others similarly placed, but in the sense that although each of us acts on distinct considerations which particularize our friends, our reasons motivate us to act on the basis of shared universal properties; namely, that he is a friend, that he is in need, and that he is there needing me now. What gives our recognition of our friend's need a potential moral status is (1) that it involves a judgment that the principal or object has a value that, while specific to me, is of a type that is generalizable in that others will recognize similar claims arising from their commitments; and (2) that it involves a constraint on self-interest in the name of some higher claim.

21. Hirschman, *Exit, Voice, and Loyalty,* pp. 76–105; see also Fletcher, *Loyalty,* pp. 4–6.

22. Hirschman, *Exit, Voice, and Loyalty,* p. 79.

23. Along with Royce, we should insist that loyalty may, but need not, attach to these relationships. I may have feelings of love, friendship, or comradeship with another, but I am not thereby necessarily loyal to them. Loyalty objectifies those feelings so that they are seen as instantiations of values which I accept as normative for me in this particular case.

24. *Oxford Dictionary of Political Quotations.*

25. *King Lear,* act 1, scene 1, lines 154–156.

26. Robert Caro's claim throughout his biography is that Johnson assiduously

sought loyalty on a personal, not positional basis, and that he sought out individuals whom he could wholly bend to his will. See R. Caro, *The Years of Lyndon Johnson*, vol. 1, *The Path to Power* (London: Pimlico, 1982); vol. 2, *Means of Ascent* (New York: Vintage, 1990); vol. 3, *Master of the Senate* (New York: Knopf, 2002).

27. In this context it is interesting to look at the types of arguments used to keep people to their loyalties, such as "jeopardy." See A. O. Hirschman, *The Rhetoric of Reaction: Perversity, Jeopardy and Futility* (Cambridge, Mass.: Harvard University Press, 1991). Bukharin's comments at the beginning of this chapter exemplify this.

28. In his term as the British Prime Minister, Tony Blair faced a series of cases in which a senior minister whom he wished to stand by and retain in office (for example, Mandelson, Blunkett, Byers, and Morris) proved too costly a political liability and had to be asked to resign. With respect to Fletcher's triadic view of loyalty, binary relationships can be extremely intense because there are no sources of information about the other except what A or B observe for themselves, and those observations are colored by the existing relationship. The wider the range of competing sources of information, and the range of contexts in which each sees the other acting, the more the judgment sensitivity of the attitudes of each are invoked. This does not necessarily lead to a decline in loyalty, not least since more reasons to be loyal may accrue, but it can test loyalty to a greater extent than when the relationship is insulated, and it can result in a more nuanced and precise character to the loyalties that are felt.

29. David Hume, "Of Parties in General," in *Essays: Moral, Political and Literary*, ed. Eugene F. Miller (Indianapolis: Liberty Fund, 1987), pp. 60–62. Hume's position might be that parties of principle do not involve loyalty but fanaticism—based on the distinction drawn above between a loyalty that is particular, as against commitments which are agent-neutral. But Hume was smart enough to see that really clean abstract commitments are probably few and far between, whereas the tendency to turn one's personal beliefs and commitments into abstract principles against which one finds others wanting is a much more common phenomenon.

30. As Hirschman recognizes (*Exit, Voice, and Loyalty*, p. 93), and as Erlichman, Halderman, Dean, and others were graphically to illustrate shortly after Hirschman's book appeared.

31. Although we might also find that such costs generate a higher level of protest (or what Hirschman calls voice), this is a complex issue. Voice implies some form of basic equality (in making a demand to be heard), and it is also plausible that higher entry costs will be associated with greater equality, since the difference between insiders and outsiders is greater than those between insiders. In fact, these are contingent relationships. For example, a gang with high entry costs may also have a steep hierarchy based on the willingness of members to engage in certain types of behavior; see Clifford Geertz, *Interpretation of Cultures* (New York: Basic Books, 1973), chapter 15.

262 **Notes to Pages 133–142**

262. Hume's essay follows a similar line, suggesting that priests need to be understood as parties of interest, and those they lead act as parties of principle. Hume, "Of Parties in General," p. 62.

33. Indeed, these tensions are still greater in political systems that eschew the adversarial, Westminster-style of politics (which legitimates very strong forms of partisanship and thus loyalty), and place still greater emphasis on the neutrality and impartiality of the political process (as in the United States).

34. The categorization is from Mark Bovens, *The Quest for Responsibility* (Cambridge: Cambridge University Press, 1998), pp. 148–168.

35. Max Weber, "Politics as a Vocation," in *From Max Weber*, ed. H. H. Gerth and C. Wright Mills (London: Routledge and Kegan Paul, 1948), pp. 125–128.

36. McCarthyism is a suitable Western example.

37. Hard, but not impossible. Love can do terrible things to our other relationships, but in the modern world, marked by atomism and pluralism, absolute personal devotion is less likely than in hierarchical and relatively static orders—simply on the grounds that the possibility of exit means that those to whom we are loyal can make fewer and less extreme demands.

38. See V. M. Molotov's comment: "It is interesting that before the events of the thirties, we lived all the time with oppositionists, with opposition groups. After the war, there were no opposition groups; it was such a relief that it made it easier to give a correct, better direction, but if a majority of these people had remained alive, I don't know if we would be standing solidly on our feet." In Getty and Naumov, *The Road to Terror*, p. 551.

39. This needs to be considered in the light of the arguments in chapters 2 and 4 about the way that having political virtues involves being open to certain ranges of fact, and recognizing in the political domain a set of demands and concerns that one understands sufficiently and which has normative weight. Not everyone will respond to these demands in the same way, on the contrary, only those who identify with the political realm in certain ways will feel the force of such loyalties.

40. Of course "we" means those who take a detached view of the political process. It is doubtful that politicians and political leaders actively want less than exclusionary loyalty, nor that they always value the cognitive judgments of their followers.

7. Officials and Public Servants

1. Fergus Millar, *The Emperor in the Roman World: 31 BC–AD 337* (London: Duckworth, 1977), chapter 3.
2. Max Weber, *Economy and Society*, ed. Guenther Roth and Claus Wittich (Berkeley: University of California Press, 1978), pp. 1006–1069.
3. Millar, *Emperor*, p. 82; on the late empire, see Keith Hopkins, *Conquerors and Slaves* (Cambridge: Cambridge University Press, 1978), chapter 4; Shaun Tougher, "Ammianus and the Eunuchs," in *The Late Roman World and Its Histo-*

rian: Interpreting Ammianus Marcellinus, ed. Jan Willem Drijvers and David Hunt (London: Routledge, 1999), pp. 64–73; John Matthews, *The Roman Empire of Ammianus* (London: Duckworth, 1989), pp. 274–278.

4. For example, Jonathan Spence, *The Search for Modern China,* 2nd ed. (New York: Norton, 1999), pp. 16–17. Earlier examples exist in China, in the Persian Court under Alexander (see, e.g., Herodotus, *The Historians,* trans. Robin Waterfield [Oxford: Oxford University Press, 1998], book 8, sections 104–106, pp. 523–524), and in the first-century Egyptian court.

5. Hopkins, *Conquerors and Slaves,* p. 190.

6. Matthews, *The Roman Empire,* p. 276. Although physiologically this seems applicable only to those castrated before puberty; and, as Montesquieu's *Persian Letters* makes clear, eunuchs are not completely neutralized sexually. (Montesquieu, *Persian Letters,* trans. C. J. Betts [Harmondsworth: Penguin, 1973].)

7. On "blocked exchange" see Michael Walzer, *Spheres of Justice* (Oxford: Blackwell, 1983), pp. 100–103; and Judith Andre, "Blocked Exchanges: A Taxonomy," in *Pluralism, Justice and Equality,* ed. David Miller and Michael Walzer (Oxford: Oxford University Press, 1995), pp. 171–196.

8. For Greek conceptions of this subordination see Lynette G. Mitchell, *Greeks Bearing Gifts: The Public Use of Private Relationships in the Greek World 435–323 BC* (Cambridge: Cambridge University Press, 1997), chapter 3; and W. Robert Connor, *The New Politicians of Fifth Century Athens* (Princeton; N.J.: Princeton University Press, 1971), pp. 121–122, 127–128.

9. *Ammianus Marcellinus,* vol. 1, trans. John C. Rolfe (Cambridge, Mass.: Harvard University Press, 1935), book XIV, section 11, paragraphs 1–5, pp. 89–93.

10. For example, Malcolm Vale, *The Princely Court: Medieval Courts and Culture in North West Europe* (Oxford: Oxford University Press, 2001), p. 45; and J. Horace Round, *The King's Serjeants and Officers of State* (London: J. Nisbet and Co. Ltd., 1911), pp. 1–52.

11. For a more subtle discussion of some of the pressures on the master servant relationship in England in the eighteenth century, see Paul Langford, *Public Life and the Propertied Englishman 1689–1798* (Oxford: Oxford University Press, 1991), pp. 503–506; and J. Jean Hecht, *The Domestic Servant Class in Eighteenth Century England* (London: Routledge and Kegan Paul, 1956), esp. chapter 3. And for an example of the anxieties about servants, raised to high ironic form, see Jonathan Swift's *Directions to Servants* (London: R. Dodsley, 1745).

12. Weber, *Economy and Society,* p. 988.

13. See Dennis Thompson's appropriate reservations about the hierarchical model in *Political Ethics and Public Office* (Cambridge, Mass.: Harvard University Press, 1987), especially chapter 2; and those of Douglas T. Yates, "Hard Choices: Justifying Bureaucratic Decisions," in *Public Duties: The Moral Obligations of Government Officials,* ed. Joel Fleishman, Lance Liebman, and Mark H. Moore (Cambridge, Mass.: Harvard University Press, 1981), pp. 32–51.

14. Jeremy Bentham, "Supreme Operative," in *First Principles Preparatory to Constitutional Code* (Oxford: Oxford University Press, 1989), p. 154: "It is in a word his

interest that in all points in which any contrariety has place between his particular interest and the universal interest, a sacrifice of the universal interest to his particular interest shall have place. This sacrifice may be termed a sinister sacrifice—in the present instance, the Monarch's sinister sacrifice."

15. For example, *Ninth Report of the Committee on Standards in Public Life, April 2003: Defining the Boundaries within the Executive: Ministers, Special Advisers and the Permanent Civil Service* (London: HMSO, 2003, Cm 5775). For a comparative history of bureaucratic orders that examines the United States, United Kingdom, France, and Japan, see Bernard S. Silberman, *Cages of Reason: The Rise of the Rational State in France, Japan, the United States and Great Britain* (Chicago: Chicago University Press, 1993).

16. Bernard Williams, "Utilitarianism and Moral Self-Indulgence," in *Moral Luck* (Cambridge: Cambridge University Press, 1981), p. 49: "one who displays integrity acts from those dispositions and motives which are most deeply his, and has the virtues that enable him to do that." Along with Williams, we should resist the idea that it is the desire to stick to one's principles, rather than the sheer commitment to one's principles that matters, since the former leads down the road to what Williams has called "moral self-indulgence." Integrity is concerned with character and its virtues rather than with particular attitudes or desires.

17. Frank Anechiarico and James B. Jacobs, *The Pursuit of Absolute Integrity: How Corruption Control Makes Government Ineffective* (Chicago: University of Chicago Press, 1996), p. 202. Although see Christopher Hood's "The Politics of Fasting and Feasting," in *Sleaze*, ed. F. F. Ridley and Alan Doig (Oxford: Oxford University Press, 1995) for a recognition of the force of Tocqueville's caveat that democracies are resistant to paying their public servants more.

18. For example, Susan Pharr and Robert Putnam, *Disaffected Democracies: What's Troubling the Trilateral Countries* (Princeton, N.J.: Princeton University Press, 2000). In fact, we need much more sensitive and discriminating work on levels of trust that look at different types of public officeholders and assess the impact of respondents' knowledge of officeholders on their attitudes. There is some good work on this, such as William F. Miller et al.'s study of political corruption in former communist countries, *A Culture of Corruption* (Budapest: Central European University Press, 2001).

19. That is, the system of moving between public service, political office, and the private sector, which is characteristic of the French administrative elite.

20. I am conscious here, and above in Chapter 4, of the difficulty of doing justice to the sophisticated analysis of esteem by Geoffrey Brennan and Philip Petit in *The Economy of Esteem* (Oxford: Oxford University Press, 2004).

21. Karl Marx, *The Communist Manifesto*, ed. Gareth Stedman Jones (London: Penguin, 2002), p. 223.

22. A. J. Simmons, *Moral Principles and Political Obligations* (Princeton, N.J.: Princeton University Press, 1979), pp. 16–23.

23. A. Shleifer and R. W. Vishny, "Corruption," *Quarterly Journal of Economics* 108 (1993): 599–600.

24. A. MacIntyre on "practices" in *After Virtue* (London: Duckworth, 1984), chapter 14, and the discussion in Chapter 2.

25. See G.W.F. Hegel on the bureaucracy in sections of 289–297 of *Elements of the Philosophy of Right*, ed. Allen W. Wood (Cambridge: Cambridge University Press, 1991), pp. 329–336; and Karl Marx's "Critique of Hegel's Doctrine of the State," in *Karl Marx: Early Writings*, ed. Lucio Colletti (Harmondsworth: Penguin, 1975), pp. 105–116.

26. For example, the *UK Civil Service Code 1995* (rev. 1999), sections 10–13; and the draft *New Civil Service Code 2006*, sections 15–18—neither of which legitimates such actions.

27. See, e.g., the case of Serpico in Myron P. Glazer and Penina M. Glazer, *The Whistleblowers: Exposing Corruption in Government and Industry* (New York: Basic Books, 1989), pp. 53–58.

28. As Sisela Bok makes clear, whistleblowing must be distinguished from dissent on the grounds of policy, even if the two tend to shade into each other: S. Bok, "Blowing the Whistle," in Fleishman et al., *Public Duties*, p. 207. See also Arthur Isak Applebaum, *Ethics for Adversaries: The Morality of Roles in Public and Professional Life* (Princeton, N.J.: Princeton University Press, 1999), chapter 4, who argues for a short-circuit of such distinctions by treating the principle of moral legitimacy as among the first of the principles of political morality, versus Michael Qunlan, "Ethics in the Public Service," *Governance* 6 (1993): 538–544, who takes a view closer to that advocated here in which the role and its ends are the appropriate reference point for those who act in their official rather than their personal capacity.

29. See the distinction drawn by Michael Walzer, *Obligations* (Princeton, N.J.: Princeton University Press, 1970), especially chapter 7.

30. Christopher Browning, "One Day in Józefów," in *The Path to Genocide* (Cambridge: Cambridge University Press, 1992). There is little sense that those who resisted did so from a belief that the order was incompatible with their positional duties, so much as with their sense of moral responsibility, although there is evidence that there was a strong feeling among many that their orders were deeply distasteful and for many distressing. See also Browning's "Ordinary Men or Ordinary Germans," in *Unwilling Germans: The Goldhagen Debate*, ed. R. Shandley (Minneapolis: University of Minnesota Press, 1998), pp. 55–57. In Browning's *The Origins of the Final Solution* (Lincoln: University of Nebraska Press, 2004), p. 20, he makes the point that the senior German generals who reached an accommodation with Heydrich made the fatal mistake of not sharing their knowledge more widely within the officer corps, which could have formed a basis for resistance—suggesting that whistle-blowing was a possibility.

31. On positional duties see A. J. Simmons, *Moral Principles;* also John Dunn, *Political Obligation in Its Historical Context* (Cambridge: Cambridge University Press, 1980), chapter 10. For an early instance, see the heliastic oath sworn by members of the people's court in Athens: "I will cast my vote in consonance with

the laws and the decrees passed by the Assembly and by the Council, but, if there is no law, in consonance with my sense of what is most just, without favour or enmity." Mogens Herman Hansen, *The Athenian Democracy in the Age of Demosthenes* (Bristol: Classical Press, 1999), p. 182.

32. For example, the "Nolan Principles," that is, "The Seven Principles of Public Life" in the United Kingdom; *Sixth Report of the Committee on Standards in Public Life* (London: HMSO, 2000, Cm 4557-1); or the "Code of Conduct for Members of the UK Parliament," cited in Appendix G of the *Eighth Report of the Committee on Standards in Public Life: Standards of Conduct in the House of Commons* (London: HMSO, 2002, Cm 5663), which states: "Members have a duty to uphold the law and to act on all occasions in accordance with the public trust placed in them"; "Members have a general duty to act in the interests of the nation as a whole; and a special duty to their constituents"; and "Members shall base their conduct on a consideration of the public interest." See more widely *Trust in Government: Ethics Measures in OECD Countries* (Paris: OECD, 2000) for a comprehensive account of the various codes and expectations of public servants in OECD countries.

33. Glazer and Glazer, *The Whistleblowers*, pp. 5–6.

34. For example, Gerald Vinten, ed., *Whistleblowing: Subversion or Corporate Citizenship* (New York: St Martin's Press, 1994); Glazer and Glazer, *The Whistleblowers*; Nicholas Lampert, *Whistleblowing in the Soviet Union: Complaints and Abuses under State Socialism* (London: Macmillan, 1985); Marcia P. Miceli and Janet P. Near, *Blowing the Whistle: The Organizational and Legal Implications for Companies and Employees* (New York: Macmillan, 1992). In July 2003, in the United Kingdom, Dr. David Kelly, an advisor in the Ministry of Defence who had stated in an interview with a BBC reporter that Downing Street had "sexed-up" the dossier on Iraq's weapons of mass destruction, committed suicide after being hugely cross-pressured by the government, parliament, and media.

35. Switzerland, an otherwise largely liberal society, proved wholly unsympathetic toward whistle-blowing in the case of Stanley Adams, a former executive with the La Roche drugs company, who exposed illegal price fixing to the European Community and was imprisoned for his pains. Vinten, *Whistleblowing*, p. 11.

36. See Peter Drucker's piece in A. P. Iannone, *Contemporary Controversies in Business* (Oxford: Oxford University Press, 1989).

37. Vinten, "Whistleblowing—Fact or Fiction," in *Whistleblowing*, pp. 7–8.

38. The cases become closer insofar as "artistic integrity" is accorded independent ethical weight.

39. Herman R. van Gunsteren, *A Theory of Citizenship: Organizing Plurality in Contemporary Democracies* (Boulder, Colo.: Westview Press, 1998), chapter 6.

8. Resistance and Protest

1. Taylor Branch, *Parting the Waters: America in the King Years 1954–63* (New York: Simon and Schuster, 1988), p. 689.

2. Henry Hampton and Steve Fayer, *Voices of Freedom: An Oral History of the Civil Rights Movement from the 1950s through the 1980s* (New York: Vintage, 1995), pp. 134–135.

3. Moreover, the restraint owes much to the supporters themselves as is evidenced in their response to John Doar's Gary Cooper-like performance in Jackson following Medgar Evers's funeral, when he calmed a riotous mob by walking between it and the police lines and assuring them of Washington's commitment to justice. See Branch, *Parting the Waters*, pp. 826–827.

4. Hampton and Fayer, *Voices of Freedom*, p. 347, attributed to Martin Luther King Jr. by Kwame Ture (Stokely Carmichael).

5. Ibid., p. 173.

6. Ibid., p. 276, Kwame Ture (Stokely Carmichael).

7. Dennis Chong, *Collective Action and the Civil Rights Movement* (Chicago: University of Chicago Press, 1991), p. 128.

8. Sidney Tarrow, *Power in Movement: Social Movements and Contentious Politics*, 2nd ed. (Cambridge: Cambridge University Press, 1998), pp. 4–7.

9. Unfortunately, their historical grasp is not always good. Green movements go back at least to the 1930s, women's suffrage groups to the nineteenth century, and confrontational forms of resistance and opposition are a central part of popular politics from the eighteenth century, if not before. Moreover, the so-called old social movements, such as trade unions, have used, and on some issues are willing still to resort to, such tactics.

10. New social movements are often also referred to as "post-materialist." In fact, the major division in labor movements should be drawn between those who see the struggle as a zero-sum one, and those who see it as having positive-sum potential. For anti-capitalists in the former group, their confrontation has the features of a value conflict.

11. David Hume, "Of Parties in General," in *Essays: Moral, Political and Literary*, ed. Eugene F. Miller (Indianapolis: Liberty Fund, 1987); Edmund Burke, *Reflections on the Revolution in France*, ed. Conor Cruise O'Brien (Harmondsworth: Penguin, 1968), p. 172.

12. Or between what the state takes its duty to be and what we believe its duty to be.

13. J. Rawls, *A Theory of Justice* (Oxford: Oxford University Press, 1971), p. 366.

14. David Lyons, "Moral Judgment, Historical Reality, and Civil Disobedience," *Philosophy and Public Affairs* (1998): 31–49.

15. Rawls, *A Theory of Justice*, sections 56 and 58, pp. 368–371 and 377–382.

16. For example, ethnic identities and long-standing cultural memories are rarely the major driving force for internecine political struggle even in, for example, regions such as the Balkans. On the contrary, such memories may weaken trust, but it is when a strong political system, which has been able to guarantee its citizens a relatively equal baseline of welfare, begins to move toward a liberal democratic form which dramatically increases uncertainty and destroys the economic basis for its welfarism, and when those involved lack the assuredness

of their security, that they organize themselves into groups and press for the state to act in ways which further weaken its capacity to deliver constitutional protections and general security. If it is not unreasonable for one group to act in such ways, it is not unreasonable for others to respond in similar ways.

17. Branch, *Parting the Waters,* p. 692.

18. Cited in Herbert J. Storing, "The Case against Civil Disobedience," in *Civil Disobedience in Focus,* ed. Hugo Adam Bedau (London: Routledge, 1991), p. 93.

19. E. P. Thompson, *Customs in Common* (London: Penguin, 1993), chapter 4. See also J. Bohstedt, *Riot and Community Politics in England and Wales 1790–1810* (Cambridge, Mass.: Harvard University Press, 1983).

20. Hampton and Fayer, *Voices of Freedom,* p. 138; Branch, *Parting the Waters,* p. 893.

21. J. Rawls, *Political Liberalism* (New York: Columbia University Press, 1993), pp. 36–37, 58–66.

22. Thomas Nagel, *Equality and Partiality* (Oxford: Oxford University Press, 1991), p. 172.

9. Democratic Citizenship

1. The classical statement of the rise of citizenship rights is by T. H. Marshall, *Citizenship and Social Class* (Cambridge: Cambridge University Press, 1950); but see also the extensive discussion of theories of citizenship by Desmond King and Jeremy Waldron, "Citizenship, Social Citizenship and the Defence of Welfare Provision," *British Journal of Political Science* 18 (1988): 415–443; David Miller, "Citizenship and Pluralism," *Political Studies* 43, no. 3 (1995): 432–450; and Will Kymlicka and Wayne Norman, "Return of the Citizen: A Survey of Recent Work on Citizenship Theory," *Ethics* 104, no. 2 (January 1994): 352–381. See also the collection of essays, which includes Kymlicka and Norman, in *Theorizing Citizenship,* ed. Ronald Beiner (Albany: State University of New York Press, 1995). See also Michael Sandel, "The Procedural Republic and the Unencumbered Self," *Political Theory* 12 (1984): 81–96; and Benjamin Barber, *Strong Democracy: Participatory Politics for a New Age* (Berkeley: University of California Press, 1984).

2. There is no straightforward answer to the question of what renders democratic rule stable. My concern here is mainly to indicate what type of citizenship seems to be required at a minimum, and to argue that we should be wary of arguments that rest responsibility for stability on the civic virtue of their citizens. See, for example, Adam Przeworski et al., *Sustainable Democracy* (Cambridge: Cambridge University Press, 1995), especially part I, chapters 3 and 4, and the striking comment made about the Brazilian voter who, having waited two hours to cast his vote in the presidential election, said: " 'Now I have done my share. The rest is theirs." The requirement that the account of democratic citizenship should be compatible with the preservation of political stability and individual liberty does affect how far the political order can be at variance with people's conceptions of justice. At the same time, the demands of citizenship

may constrain how far individuals or groups can insist on their particular conceptions of the good in the face of the disagreement of others. So the theory of citizenship should contribute to a theory of the political principles that must regulate citizens' actions in the public domain. The connection between these issues is discussed in T. Nagel, "Moral Conflict and Political Legitimacy," in *Authority*, ed. J. Raz (Oxford: Blackwell, 1990), pp. 300–324. See especially, p. 302: "arguments that justify may fail to persuade, if addressed to an unreasonable audience; and arguments that persuade may fail to justify. Nevertheless, justifications hope to persuade the reasonable, so these attempts have a practical point: political stability is helped by wide agreement to the principles underlying the political order."

3. On the list of virtues see Andrew Sabl's commendably comprehensive "Virtues for Pluralists," *Journal of Moral Philosophy* 2, no. 2 (2005): 207–235.

4. An early sketch of the argument in this section can be found in my "Motivating Liberal Citizenship," in *The Demands of Citizenship*, ed. Catriona McKinnon and Iain Hampsher-Monk (London: Continuum, 2000), pp. 165–189.

5. Groups, such as children, may lack rights to full civic voice, but they are the recipients of political concern, and their interests can be represented in the political domain and in the various institutions of the state.

6. Clearly, there are issues about what proportion of a population must be ruled in this way, but there remains a clear distinction between a democratic state seeking wide public legitimation and an autocratic state seeking at best a very narrow legitimation sufficient to maintain its control over the means of coercion.

7. Thus Constant's and Tocqueville's belief that a system may fail because, despite procedural compliance, the lack of participation results in despotism. Modern theorists who take this line have generally been identified as participatory democrats. Benjamin Constant, "The Liberty of the Ancients Compared with that of the Moderns," in *Political Writings*, ed. B. Fontana (Cambridge: Cambridge University Press, 1988), pp. 309–328; Alexis de Tocqueville, *Democracy in America*, vol. 1, trans. H. Reeve, rev. F. Bowen and P. Bradley (New York: Knopf, 1945), pp. 281–342.

8. Formally, of course, free-riding is costless. The free-rider problem is one in which "it is possible for an individual to . . . benefit from whatever amount of the good is provided without contributing to its production costs." A problem arises because if every member is a free-rider then no public good will be provided, and where only some free-ride, their activity violates a broader sense of fairness within the political system, and the "game" can deteriorate into a form of chicken, with potentially disastrous effects. See, for example, Michael Taylor and Hugh Ward, "Chickens, Whales and Lumpy Public Goods: Alternative Models of Public Goods Provision," *Political Studies* 30, no. 3 (1982): 350–370; and Philip Pettit, "Free-Riding and Foul Dealing," *Journal of Philosophy* 83 (1986): 361–379.

9. Cf. James S. Coleman, *Foundations of Social Theory* (Cambridge, Mass.: Harvard

University Press, 1990), pp. 300–321, although this has since been extensively popularized by Robert Putnam, not least in his *Bowling Alone: The Collapse and Revival of American Community* (New York: Simon & Schuster, 2000).

10. Tocqueville, *Democracy in America,* vol. 1, chapter 5 and vol. 2, book 2, chapter 2.

11. In this tradition see, for example, the litany of community participation reeled off by Robert Putman in his eulogy to the civic spirit of the Northern Italians: "neighbourhood associations, choral societies, cooperatives, sports clubs, mass based parties." In Putman, *Making Democracy Work* (Princeton, N.J.: Princeton University Press, 1993), p. 173.

12. Which, James Madison argues, is the virtue of republican (that is, representative) government with a large and diverse citizenry, see *The Federalist Papers* no. 10, ed. C. Rossiter (New York: New American Library, 1961).

13. Adam Smith, *The Wealth of Nations* (Oxford: Clarendon Press, 1976), p. 145. In a similar vein, Mancur Olson argues, in his *The Rise and Decline of Nations* (New Haven, Conn.: Yale University Press, 1982) that special interest groups, subcommunities, and organizations with limited *civitas* (i.e., limited engagement or commonality of interest with the broader community of citizens) that play a major participatory role in the institutions of the state can have extremely destructive effects on the political system.

14. Sandel, "The Procedural Republic." See also Will Kymlicka, *Multicultural Citizenship: A Liberal Theory of Minority Rights* (Oxford: Clarendon Press, 1995) and his edited collection *The Rights of Minority Cultures* (Oxford: Oxford University Press, 1995), and, more generally, Iris Marion Young, *Justice and the Politics of Difference* (Princeton, N.J.: Princeton University Press, 1990); Anne Phillips, *The Politics of Presence* (Oxford: Clarendon Press, 1995); and John Rawls, *Political Liberalism* (New York: Columbia University Press, 1993).

15. Drawing on Rawls, *Political Liberalism*, p. 147.

16. For example, when compliance is conditional on the solution maximizing my community's security or welfare, or when it is conditional on minimizing global ecological damage. The ends may be worthy; what modus vivendi indicates is that we treat the pursuit of our ends as of prime importance, and we stick to political rules and norms only because and insofar as doing so serves those ends.

17. Cf. Mark Granovetter, "Threshold Models of Collective Behavior," *American Journal of Sociology* 83 (1978): 1420–1443. Granovetter points out that, because a person's threshold is "simply that point where the perceived benefits to an individual of doing the thing in question exceed the perceived costs," two people with different beliefs, preferences, and intensity of preferences may none the less end up with the same threshold. This underlines that we cannot assume that just because collective action takes place there must be a single, widely shared norm prescribing that action.

18. I understand atomism as a situation in which there is a breakdown of collective or communal norms and value systems and where each individual's identification and pursuit of his or her ends takes place without reference to the norms and values of some larger social unit.

19. This does not mean punishing every offender—just doing enough to ensure that the vast majority of the people perceive the costs of noncompliance to outweigh its benefits.

20. Cf. Michael Taylor, "Rationality and Revolutionary Collective Action," in *Rationality and Revolution,* ed. M. Taylor (Cambridge: Cambridge University Press, 1988).

21. See, for example, the unravelling of an honor system of time-keeping in A. Gouldner, *Patterns of Industrial Bureaucracy* (New York: Free Press, 1954), and the associated discussion in Gary J. Miller, *Managerial Dilemmas* (Cambridge: Cambridge University Press, 1992), pp. 207–210.

22. Richard Dagger's suggestion that "someone expresses civic virtue when he or she does what a citizen is supposed to do" (*Civic Virtues: Rights, Citizenship, and Republican Liberalism* [Oxford: Oxford University Press, 1997], p. 13) fails to distinguish behavioral conformity and types of agency. As we have seen, doing what a citizen is supposed to do may be variously motivated. The crucial point for republicans is that the citizen is committed to serving the public good, and to putting his or her duties as a citizen before all other concerns. In Nagel's lucid formulation this position is a "common standpoint" theory of legitimacy, which asks us to evaluate institutions on the basis of a common moral motive that makes no reference to our own interests. Nagel, "Moral Conflict," pp. 303–304.

23. Goodin's argument, that there may be no need to distinguish between motives when there are many possible motives that could have led to an act, runs very much contrary to the republican project. It does so because republicans do not see the compatibility of motives that Goodin hypothesizes as a naturally occurring phenomenon. If we find Goodin's hypothesis more plausible than, say, Machiavelli's, then we will not see the need for civic virtue. Cf. R. Goodin, "Do Motives Matter?" in *Utilitarianism as a Public Philosophy* (Cambridge: Cambridge University Press, 1995), chapter 3.

24. This is why Machiavelli talks about civic virtue only within the already constituted republic. The *virtù* of the legislator is of a different order, and is more like virtue in the international arena where, clearly, heroism in the service of the state vis-à-vis other states may indicate internal strength rather than weakness—but it is still not easy to motivate.

25. Hence, for all his love for ancient republics, Montesquieu clearly believed that they could not be created in the modern commercial societies of his day.

26. Karl Marx and Friedrich Engels, *The Holy Family,* cited by Patrice Higonnet, *Goodness Beyond Virtue: Jacobins during the French Revolution* (Cambridge, Mass.: Harvard University Press, 1998), p. 1.

27. Although face-to-face communities *might* have enough solidarity, it is also likely that they will have it at the expense of critical distance.

28. Constant, "The Liberty of the Ancients."

29. See Nagel, "Moral Conflict and Political Legitimacy," pp. 304–305, on a similar attempt to mix "convergence" and "common standpoint" theories.

30. Rawls, *Political Liberalism,* pp. 158–168.

31. Ibid., pp. 163–164.

32. Ibid., p. 165.

33. David Hume, *Enquiries Concerning Human Understanding and Concerning the Principles of Morals,* 3rd ed., ed. L. A. Selby-Bigge (Oxford: Clarendon Press, 1975), section IX, part II, p. 283.

34. For example, Blaise Pascal's famous argument for how one develops a belief in God once one has determined that it is in one's interest to have such a belief. See Jon Elster's discussion in *Ulysses and the Sirens,* rev. ed. (Cambridge: Cambridge University Press, 1984), pp. 47–54; and Joshua Cohen, "A More Democratic Liberalism," *Michigan Law Review* 92 (1994): 1503–1546.

35. Both trust and transparency can legitimate the outcome of procedures either through their intrinsic authority or through the fact that the participants can themselves assess the fairness of the outcomes. In either case, groups that defect from the agreements they have negotiated find it difficult publicly to legitimate their action, and there is correspondingly more chance of others supporting the enforcement of agreements by the state. Of course, we then face the problem of explaining where this trust comes from. See, for example, Martin Hollis, *Trust within Reason* (Cambridge: Cambridge University Press, 1998).

36. For example, nationalist political parties in a multinational state may, while acknowledging the legitimacy of the national constitution and its political procedures, act in ways which serve to consolidate their popular support while eroding their supporters' identification with the broader political system.

37. If we try to reduce the costs of participation we risk rendering it so empty that it could not plausibly serve as a bulwark against political oppression; if we attach differential rewards to it we threaten to turn the political arena into a struggle for access to and control over the distribution of such rewards.

38. See John Rawls, *A Theory of Justice* (Oxford: Oxford University Press, 1972), pp. 84–86.

39. Rawls thinks that cake-dividing is a perfect procedure because the desired outcome is equal shares and if one person cuts and must take the piece remaining after others have chosen this will ensure that the pieces will be equal in size. Anyone, other than an only child, will know that this describes the incentive for the cutter, but not necessarily the result of his actions! In this view, cake-cutting tends to be an imperfect procedure. Ibid., p. 85.

40. Although the value of the outcome may be outweighed by other values: If questioning by torture were a perfect procedure for ascertaining guilt, we might still reject it because we value a society without torture more than we value the perfect ascertaining of guilt or innocence.

41. See, for example, William Riker, *Liberalism against Populism* (San Francisco: W. H. Freeman & Co., 1982).

42. John Dunn, *Western Political Theory in the Face of the Future* (Cambridge: Cambridge University Press, 1979), p. 17; Mogens Herman Hansen, *The Athenian Democracy in the Age of Demosthenes* (Bristol: Bristol Classical Press, 1999).

43. Consider Michael Sandel's case that modern states simply cannot meet the conditions required for the maintenance of a self-reproducing, procedural, democratic order. Sandel, "The Procedural Republic and the Unencumbered Self."

44. J. Cohen, "Deliberation and Democratic Legitimacy," in *The Good Polity,* ed. A. Hamlin and P. Pettit (Oxford: B. H. Blackwell, 1989), pp. 17–34; and J. Habermas, *Moral Consciousness and Communicative Action* (Cambridge: Polity Press, 1990). For a more practical and engaging account that meshes with the concerns of this book, see Amy Gutmann and Dennis Thompson, *Democracy and Disagreement* (Cambridge, Mass.: Harvard University Press, 1996); the commentary on that book in Stephen Macedo, *Deliberative Politics* (Oxford: Oxford University Pres, 1999); and the further development of their position in Gutmann and Thompson, *Why Deliberative Democracy* (Princeton, N.J.: Princeton University Press, 2004).

45. Again, the implicit reference is to the account of practices given by Alasdair MacIntyre in chapter 14 of *After Virtue* (London: Duckworth, 1981).

10. Institutions and Integrity

1. As Brian Barry says in his *Political Argument* (London: Routledge and Kegan Paul, 1965, p. 190), Sir George Cornewall Lewis's definition of *public* is hard to improve upon: "*Public,* as opposed to *private,* is that which has no immediate relation to any specified person or persons, but may directly concern any member or members of the community, without distinction. . . . So a theatre, or a place of amusement, is said to be public, not because it is actually visited by every member of the community, but because it is open to all indifferently."

2. *Standards in Public Life: First Report of the Committee on Standards in Public Life,* vol. 1, chaired by Lord Nolan (London: HMSO, 1995, Cm 2850-1), p. 14. At the time of writing the committee is in the process of reviewing these principles in the light of research on what the public see as relevant to those in public office.

3. See the still more stringent developments in the concept of conflict of interests as discussed in Andrew Stark's *Conflict of Interest in American Public Life* (Cambridge, Mass.: Harvard University Press, 2000).

4. For example, with respect to friendships and gifts and public office, Lynette G. Mitchell, *Greeks Bearing Gifts: The Public Use of Private Relationships in the Greek World, 435–323 BC* (Cambridge: Cambridge University Press, 1997).

5. We can define such autonomy, following Adam Przeworski, as combining the capacity of those who manage the state to formulate policy, with the capacity to implement it (and in neither case to be hostage to groups or factions either in or outside the state in the process—although that clearly will be a matter of degree). Adam Przeworski, *The State and the Economy under Capitalism* (Chur, Switzerland: Harwood Academic, 1990), pp. 31–33.

6. See J. Elster, C. Offe, and U. Preuss, *Institutional Design in Post-Communist Societies* (Cambridge: Cambridge University Press, 1998), pp. 30–31.

7. On liberal neutrality see John Rawls, *Political Liberalism* (New York: Columbia University Press, 1993), lectures 4 and 6; and *Collected Papers,* ed. Samuel

Freeman (Cambridge, Mass.: Harvard University Press, 1999), esp. chapters 20, 22, and 26; Thomas Nagel, "Moral Conflict and Political Legitimacy," in *Authority,* ed. Joseph Raz (Oxford: Blackwell, 1990), pp. 300–324; Ronald Dworkin, "Foundations of Liberal Equality," in *The Tanner Lectures on Human Values,* Series II, ed. G. Peterson (Salt Lake City: University of Utah Press, 1990); and Matthew Clayton, "Educating Liberals: An Argument about Political Neutrality, Equality of Opportunity, and Parental Autonomy" (Ph.D. diss., Oxford University, 1997).

8. For example, Jeremy Pope, *Source Book 2000: Confronting Corruption: The Elements of a National Integrity System* (Berlin: Transparency International, 2000), combines a range of extremely sensible recommendations (that assume a high degree of potential convergence on a liberal democratic state) with an almost entirely unquestioned assumption that big government is itself the prime cause of corruption and the source of disequilibria in the state, and that those introducing the changes can somehow withstand the pressures that affect normal politicians.

9. For example, G. Bingham Powell Jr., *Elections as Instruments of Democracy* (New Haven, Conn.: Yale University Press, 2000), chapter 3.

10. A. Przeworski, S. C. Stokes, and Bernard Manin, eds., *Democracy, Accountability and Representation* (Cambridge: Cambridge University Press, 1999), p. 10.

11. James Fearon, "Electoral Accountability and the Control of Politicians," in Przeworski et al., *Democracy, Accountability and Representation,* p. 55.

12. That is, "political accountability" is where the conduct of officeholders is judged in terms of whether it meets the demands and expectations of the public, as against "formal accountability," which concerns how far the officeholder acts within his rights and responsibilities as laid down in defining his office. In the latter case we are asking whether those in office act in accordance with its norms, rules, and principles; in the former case, we are asking whether the public approve of the decisions and policies that issue from those in office. The two are easily muddled, and the politicization of public officials can have a major impact on their capacity to act impartially. A well regulated and integrated or consolidated political system will instance both forms of accountability and will draw the lines between them clearly; in weakly integrated systems, accountability may be almost wholly political in character—with formal mechanisms collapsing into political ones and with an absence of any form of trust in the political system. See Ezra Sulieman, *Dismantling Democratic States* (Princeton, N.J.: Princeton University Press, 2003), for an eloquent discussion of the trend toward politicization in Western bureaucratic systems.

13. Fearon's paper, "Electoral Accountability," begins, in fact, with an extremely lucid account of the ways in which elections may function as something other than an accountability mechanism, and offers a range of examples that demonstrate that a number of features of contemporary U.S. elections simply do not make sense if they are understood as accountability mechanisms.

14. See the work on the way that certain institutional mechanisms that imply distrust of politicians (and citizens) produce perverse effects, leading to them being

less trustworthy, and crowding out the very virtues they want to encourage: Bruno S. Frey, "A Constitution for Knaves Crowds Out Civic Virtues," *The Economic Journal* 107, no. 443 (1997): 1043–1053; and B. S. Frey and R. Jegen, "Motivation Crowding Theory: A Survey," *Journal of Economic Surveys* 15 (2001): 589–611.

15. See Joel Aberbach, *Keeping a Watchful Eye: The Politics of Congressional Oversight* (Washington, D.C.: Brookings, 1990).

16. A. Przeworski, *Democracy and the Market* (Cambridge: Cambridge University Press, 1991), pp. 25–26.

17. See Polybius, *The Rise of the Roman Empire* 6.3–18; Machiavelli then repeats the analysis in *The Discourses* 1.2, but takes a much more strongly interest-based line. See the review of the classical and seventeenth-century literature by Wilfried Nippel, "Ancient and Modern Republicanism: 'Mixed Constitution' and 'Ephors,'" in *The Invention of the Modern Republic,* ed. Biancamaria Fontana (Cambridge: Cambridge University Press, 1994), pp. 6–26.

18. See Benjamin Constant, "The Liberty of the Ancients Compared with that of the Moderns," in *Political Writings,* ed. B. Fontana (Cambridge: Cambridge University Press, 1988), pp. 309–328; or, indeed, Tocqueville's suggestion that democratic society tends toward a stark opposition between the mass and a very small elite, in *Democracy in America,* vol. 1, trans. H. Reeve, rev. F. Bowen and P. Bradley (New York: Knopf, 1945), book 2, chapter 2, pp. 104–106.

19. Although it must also be said, such face-to-face communities also make vicious conduct easier to sustain, once it is established. The crucial question becomes one of how far the community is open to influence and scrutiny by other groups, and what standards of conduct these other groups sustain. Thus a corrupt police force will be difficult to break open if all the control institutions are corrupt, but substantially easier if they are clean.

20. See Tocqueville's similar argument for the role of the judiciary and lawyers— even if, with hindsight, one should avoid overdoing one's confidence in any one professional body.

21. On the press see Robert M. Entman's salutary *Democracy without Citizens: Media and the Decay of American Politics* (Oxford: Oxford University Press, 1989) and John Lloyd, *What the Media Are Doing to Our Politics* (London: Faber, 2005).

22. Robert A. Dahl, *Polyarchy: Participation and Opposition* (New Haven, Conn.: Yale University Press, 1971).

23. Frank Anechiarico and James B. Jacobs's insight in *The Pursuit of Absolute Integrity* (Chicago: University of Chicago Press, 1996), is worth emphasizing: "there is no substitute for a professional civil service populated by competent, committed, enthusiastic public servants who like their work and feel adequately compensated and appreciated. In short, if public officials are treated like second- or third-class citizens, they will act accordingly, and no amount of laws and controls will remedy the situation. . . . Poorly paid, poorly treated public employees will be alienated and demoralized. Under such circumstances corruption is easily rationalized" (p. 202).

24. Hume's account of the basic idea of integrity is still plausible. "[I]n all ingen-uous natures, the antipathy to treachery and roguery is too strong to be counter-balanced by any views of profit or pecuniary advantage. Inward peace of mind, consciousness of integrity, a satisfactory review of our own conduct; these are circumstances, very requisite to happiness, and will be cherished and cultivated by every honest man, who feels the importance of them." Hume, *En-quiries Concerning Human Understanding and Concerning the Principles of Morals*, 3rd ed., ed. L. A. Selby-Bigge (Oxford: Clarendon Press, 1975), section IX, part II, p. 283. Note the apparent circularity—"they will be cherished by those who feel the importance of them." The circularity *is* only apparent if "the feeling of their importance" is a story of the cultivation of the passions, and the cherishing a story about our reflective endorsement of our conduct. More broadly, see G. Brennan and P. Pettit, *The Economy of Esteem* (Oxford: Oxford University Press, 2004).

25. See, e.g., Open Society Institute, *Monitoring the EU Accession Process: Corruption and Anti-Corruption Policy* (Budapest: OSI, 2002); David Stark and Lazlo Bruszt, *Post-Socialist Pathways: Transforming Politics and Property in Eastern Europe* (Cam-bridge: Cambridge University Press, 1998); and my "Access, Accountability and Authority: Corruption and the Democratic Process," *Crime, Law and Social Change* 36 (2001): 357–377.

26. For example, see Dennis Thomson's crucial *Political Ethics and Public Office* (Cam-bridge, Mass.: Harvard University Press, 1987) and his *Ethics in Congress* (Wash-ington, D.C.: Brookings, 1995); the essays in Joel L. Fleishman, Lance Liebman, and Mark H. Moore, eds., *Public Duties: The Moral Obligations of Government Offi-cials* (Cambridge, Mass.: Harvard University Press, 1981); and Andrew Sabl, *Ruling Passions: Political Offices and Democratic Ethics* (Princeton, N.J.: Princeton University Press, 2002).

27. Colin Turnbull, *The Mountain People* (New York: Simon & Schuster, 1972).

Index